Bolc
Natural Language
Based Computer
Systems

Natural Communication with Computers

Edited by Leonard Bolc

Carl Hanser Verlag
München Wien

M

Natural Language Based Computer Systems

Edited by Leonard Bolc

Carl Hanser Verlag
München Wien 1980

M

Editor:
Leonard Bolc, Institute of Informatics, Warsaw University, PKiN, pok. 850,
00-901 Warszawa, Poland

CIP-Kurztitelaufnahme der Deutschen Bibliothek

Natural language based computer systems / ed. by
Leonard Bolc. - München, Wien : Hanser; London,
Basingstoke : Macmillan, 1980.
(Natural communication with computers)
ISBN 3-446-13059-4 (Hanser)
ISBN 0-333-29527-7 (Macmillan)

NE: Bolc, Leonard (Hrsg.)

First published 1980 in Europe
Carl Hanser Verlag München Wien

and

The Macmillan Press Ltd., London and Basingstoke
Associated companies in Delhi Dublin
Hongkong Johannesburg Lagos Melbourne
New York Singapore Tokyo

ISBN 0-333-29527-7 (paper cover - United Kingdom)

ISBN 3-446-13059-4 (German Federal Republic)

Printed in German Federal Republic

PREFACE

For a few years in nearly every country in the world scientists have been working on Natural Language Based Computer Systems.

This collection of papers deals with each system as a complex unity and presents in detail its particular components. The systems presented were worked out in well-known American and European scientific centres.

Jack Minker and Patricia B.Powell, from University of Maryland, USA present the output component of a deductive relational data base. The data base in the system consists of the π-clauses which make it possible to pack similar relations into a single relation but with multiple values.

Christopher V.Habel, Claus-Rainer Rollinger, Arno Schmidt and Hans-Jochen Schneider, from the Technical University of Berlin, West Berlin outline the BEAS-System (Berlin Automatic Semantic-Oriented Translation) which is used for mapping the natural language expressions into a semantic representation. In other words, the BEAS-System is used to assign the meaning, or, to translate from the natural language into a logical representation language. The paper discusses not only the general ideas of the system but also subcomponents and its underlying principles.

The scientific team of Walther von Hahn, Wolfgang Hoeppner, Anthony Jameson and Wolfgang Wahlster, from the University of Hamburg, FDR give a detailed examination of an interesting dialogue system. This is the HAM-RPM (Hamburger Redepartner-modell) system which can converse with a human being about interchangeable scenes. The work presents descriptions of ideas, methods which were used and the computer implementation of the system.

Larry R.Harris, from the Dartmouth College, USA devotes his presentation to descriptions of the ROBOT system. This system was developed with the aim of enabling users who are not specialists in data processing to obtain necessary information from a data base. This is performed by using a translation from the natural language into the formal retrieval language of the data base management system.

Nikolaus Ott and Magdalena Zoeppritz, from the Heidelberg Scientific Centre, IBM Germany, FDR give a brief survey of the USL (User Specialty Language) which is an experimental information system. This paper presents some important modules and methods which were used in the system as a revised version of Kay's parser or relational model of the data base. As in ROBOT, each natural language query is translated into expressions of ISBL (Information System Base Language) which is also presented in the paper.

Günther Görz, from the University of Erlangen-Nürnberg, FDR presents the conversational HEX system which enables human users to play the "HEX" game with the computer. The author describes the strategy and particular modules of the system, including, smong others, the parser and the interpreter. At present, some modules of the HEX system have not yet been implemented, but those programs already prepared like the parser are included in the paper.

The papers presented outline the current state of scientific research and the future trends in Nautral Language Based Computer Systems.

Warsaw, Spring 1980 Leonard B o l c

TABLE OF CONTENTS

ANSWER AND REASON EXTRACTION, NATURAL LANGUAGE AND VOICE OUTPUT* FOR DEDUCTIVE RELATIONAL DATA BASES

by

Jack Minker and Patricia B. Powell

Department of Computer Science
University of Maryland
College Park, MD 20742
USA

* The authors gratefully acknowledge the support that has been provided to them by the National Aeronautics and Space Administration under Grant No. NGR 21-002-270.

Abstract

The output component of a deductive relational data base system which consists of an answer reason extractor, a natural language output translator, and a text translator to voice output is described. A new method is developed for keeping track of both the answers and the reasons leading to the deduction. The method obviates the need to retain the proof path as it is effectively built into each deduction. The rational data base is represented in Π-clause format. It condenses similar relations into a single relation with multiple values.

The natural language translator accepts a relation or a general axiom consisting of a conjunction of atomic formulae (the antecedent) that imply a single atomic formula (the consequent), and outputs an English sentence. The voice output mechanism synthesizes a natural language sentence to produce voice output. Algorithms are presented for the answer/reason extractor and the natural language output translator. The production rules used to transform strings of characters into the International Phonetic Alphabet are listed.

1. Introduction

The subject of relational data bases has generated considerable interest starting from the work of Codd [1970,1972]. This is concerned with relational data bases of a particular kind - those on which deduction is performed to extract information implicit within the data base. The subject of deduction and data bases is described extensively in the articles of the book edited by Gallaire and Minker [1978]. The focal point in this paper is to describe the output component of a deductive relational data base system. A deductive relational data base system, described more fully later consists of a relational data base augmented by general axioms. The deductive component is not developed in detail here, but merely outlined. The interested reader can see the articles by Reiter [1978], and Kellogg [1978], for details on how deductive search may be performed. Emphasis is given to the answer and reason extraction process and the mechanisms required to translate output from a relational representation to natural language and voice output.

It is assumed that the reader is familiar with relational data bases. The basic ideas in relational data base work are reviewed, emphasis is given to the differences between a relational data base system and a deductive relational data base system. Although a particular deductive relational data base system termed the Maryland Refutation Proof Procedure System 3.0 (MRPPS, which rhymes with TERPS), is described, the techniques described here are general and not restricted to MRPPS 3.0.

The differences between a relational and a deductive relational data base system are described in Section two. A particular representation for relational data, useful both for deduction and natural language and voice follows. A brief description of how deduction is performed is presented in Section three. A method is developed to keep track of how deduction is being performed so that when a query is answered, one can output directly both the answers and the reasons leading to the deduction. In Section four the natural language output component is discussed and the translation of an answer or a reason sentence into natural language is outlined. Section five discusses the translation from natural language to voice output. A summary of the main developments is presented in Section six. Three appendixes are included. Appendix A provides an algorithm to extract the answer and reason. Appendix B provides an algorithm to transform an answer or reason statement into a natural language sentence. Finally, Appendix C contains the productions used to transform words into voice output.

2. Deductive Relational Data Base

A relational data base can be thought of as being defined by a set of tables. The set of entries in a particular table comprise a relation. The set of explicit facts in the tables constitute what is termed the extensional data base (EDB).

A deductive relational data base consists of an EDB and a set of general statements. A statement of the type, "all computer science courses are given in the computer science building", is an instance of a general statement. It avoids the necessity of listing explicitly in a table the name of each computer science course and that it is given in the computer science building. General statements, also termed axioms, are retained in an intensional data base (IDB). Such statements may be viewed as virtual relations. They are virtual relations in that a relational represented by a general axiom is not explicitly listed, but may be made explicit in response to a query.

A relation may be defined exclusively as an extensional relation specified completely in the EDB, exclusively as a virtual relation, specified completely in the IDB or partially as an extensional and a virtual relation. An example of a relation that might be defined both in the EDB and the IDB is the CLASSLOCATION relation. For example, in the EDB one might have a table with two entries specifying that Computer Science 100 is given in the Mathematics Building and Computer Science 200 is given in the Electrical Engineering Building. In the IDB one might have that, "all computer science courses except for 100 and 200 are given in the Computer Science Building".

In a deductive relational data base system the user need not be aware which relations are virtual, and which are explicit. It is the function of the system to accept queries from the user and to make virtual relations explicit. A deductive search component is required to work with virtual and explicit relations, to make a virtual relation explicit.

2.1 Syntax of EDB and IDB Entries

A deductive relational data base system as discussed in this paper is defined in terms of first-order predicate calculus. A subset of the predicate calculus is used in the paper. The MRPPS 3.0 System, as described by Minker [1978] and McSkimin and Minker [1977,1979], is not so restricted. In the predicate calculus sentences are expressed in clausal form. A sentence in clausal form is a set of clauses. A clause is a set of atomic formulas written

$$A_1 \wedge A_2 \wedge \cdots \wedge A_n \rightarrow B_1 \vee B_2 \vee \cdots \vee B_m .$$

An atomic formula, $A_i(i=1,\ldots,n)$, $B_j(j=1,\ldots,m)$, has the form $P(t_1,\cdots,t_k)$, where P is a k-ary predicate symbol and the t_i are terms. A term is either a variable x, y, z, $\cdots$, or an expression $f(t_1,\cdots,t_k)$, where f is a k-ary function symbol and the t_i are terms. Constants are 0-ary function symbols. The sets of all predicate, function, and variable symbols are mutually disjoint.

The above definition of a clause gives the full power of the predicate calculus. However, in the following m is restricted to m=1. The set of such clauses is termed Horn clauses in honor of the individual who studied them (Horn [1951]). Restricting m to 1 allows only definite data (Reiter [1978]). Such data is typically handled by relational data base systems. However, it is not possible to handle indefinite data (Reiter [1978]). Data in a conventional relational data base is definite. Data is indefinite when it is a disjunction. That is, data which states "A is located either at B or C," and we do not know which of these locations is the actual one. Relational data base systems are presently unable to handle indefinite data. Although not described here MRPPS 3.0 can handle indefinite data.

The atomic formulae $P(t_1,\cdots,t_k)$, where each t_i is a constant, form the entries in the "P" relation in a conventional relational data base system. The atomic formulae where the t_i is a ground term are stored in the EDB. A ground term contains no variable symbols. The EDB generalizes the concept of a conventional relational data base as functions are permitted in relational tables. However, except for the natural language component, we will not be concerned with anything other than constant or variable symbols in the EDB. This is so for two reasons: first, conventional relational data base systems do not consider functions and, second, functions symbols introduce problems with respect to equality (see Reiter [1977]). The EDB corresponds to the clause where n=0 and m=1 , and the terms are all ground, or contain no variables.

The IDB corresponds to the set of Horn clauses where n>0 and m=1.

2.2 Semantics of EDB and IDB Entries

The semantics of sentences in clausal form is easily interpreted. A clause $A_1 \wedge \cdots \wedge A_n$ is read as

$$A_1 \text{ and } A_2 \text{ and } \cdots A_n .$$

For example,

MANUFACTURE(ABC,pencils) ∧ DISTRIBUTE(ABC,pencils,KLM).

The clause $A_1 \wedge A_2 \wedge \cdots \wedge A_n \rightarrow B_1 \vee B_2 \vee \cdots \vee B_m$ containing variables $x_1,\cdots,x_k$ is a universally quantified implication and read as

for all $x_1,\cdots,x_k$, A_1 and A_2 and $\cdots$ and A_n

imply B_1 or B_2 or $\cdots$ or B_m .

For example,

for all x, y, z

LOCATION(x,y) ∧ WORKS AT(z,x) → LIVES z,y),

states that if x is located at y and z works at x , then x lives in y. In the cases where m=0 or n=0 special interpretation are provided.

If n=0 , read

for all $x_1,\cdots,x_k$ B_1 or B_2 or $\cdots$ or B_m .

Since m is restricted to 1 or 0 , read for m=1 ,

for all $x_1,\cdots,x_k$ B_1 .

for all x LOCATION(x,New York) ,

states that all individuals in the particular application are located in New York.

When B_1 is free of variables it denotes an assertion of a fact which corresponds to an entry in the relation whose name is the predicate name of B_1.

MANUFACTURE(ABC,pencils)

If m=0 , read

for no $x_1,\cdots,x_k$ A_1 and A_2 and $\cdots$ and A_n .

This type of sentence will be considered a <u>query clause</u>. It can be read equivalently

for all $x_1,\cdots,x_k$ not A_1 or not A_2 or $\cdots$ or not A_n .

If n=0 and m=0, write the null <u>clause</u>.

$\Box$,

interpreted as denoting that an answer to a query has been found.

2.3 Many-Sorted Logic

The MRPPS 3.0 System deviates from the above in that a many-sorted logic is used. Instead of permitting variables to range over the entire universe, they are restricted to range over subsets of the universe. Since the universe is a subset of the universe, some variables can range over the entire universe. These subsets of the universe are termed sorts and correspond to domains or attributes in a conventional relational data base.

The clause

$$A_1 \wedge A_2 \wedge \cdots \wedge A_n \rightarrow B_1 \vee B_2 \vee \cdots \vee B_m ,$$

containing variables $x_1^{s_1}$, $x_2^{s_2}$,$\cdots$, $x_k^{s_k}$, where $x_i^{s_i}$ is a variable that can range over the domain defined by sort s_i may now be interpreted as,

for all $x_1^{s_1},\cdots,x_k^{s_k}$ A_1 and A_2 and $\cdots$ and A_n

implies B_1 or B_2 or $\cdots$ or B_m .

Let s_1 denote the sort "company", s_2 the sort "city", and s_3 the sort "individual". Then

for all $x^{s_1} y^{s_2} z^{s_3}$ LOCATION$(x^{s_1},y^{s_2}) \wedge$ WORKS$(z^{s_3},x^{s_1}) \rightarrow$ LIVES(z^{s_3},y^{s_2})

states that if company x^{s_1} is located in city y^{s_2} and individual z^{s_3} works at company x^{s_1} then the individual z^{s_3} lives in city y^{s_2} . A many-sorted logic is equivalent to a first-order logic in that it has no more power than first-order logic, and first-order logic has no more power than a many-sorted logic. For details of this equivalence, see Zanon and Minker [1979].

2.4 Relational Data Base

A relational data base is a convenient representation for both expressing natural language statements, and for performing deductive searches. Externally, the user may consider the data base to be stored in tables. The name of the table is the relation or predicate name. Each row of the table is a data base entry that represents the elements contained in a relation.

For example, the two relations "Company x manufacutres product y" and "Company x distributes product y to store z" are depicted in the following two tables, MANUFACTURE and DISTRIBUTE.

It is easy for the user to peruse a table entry and reconstruct the sentence expressing the information. The above explanation of a relational data base is very cursory. Codd [1970,1972] gives a full tutorial of relational data bases. Chamberlin [1976] contrasts relational models with other models.

Table 1. MANUFACTURE Relation

COMPANY	PRODUCT
ABC	pencils
ABC	paper
ABC	notebooks
XYZ	notebooks
ABC	paper clips
XYZ	erasers
XYZ	paper
XYZ	paper clips
ABC	erasers
XYZ	pencils

Table 2. DISTRIBUTE Relation

COMPANY	PRODUCT	STORE
ABC	pencils	KLM
ABC	paper	PQR
ABC	notebooks	PQR
XYZ	notebooks	KLM
ABC	paper clips	KLM
XYZ	erasers	KLM
XYZ	paper	KLM
XYZ	paper clips	PQR
ABC	erasers	PQR
XYZ	pencils	PQR

2.5 π-Representation and Relational Data Bases

For realistic applications, a data base has many entries in each table. Fishman and Minker [1975] developed a notation to compact relational tables. The amount of compactness depends on the similarity of entries in a relation. For example, in Table 1, pencils, paper, notebooks, paper clips and erasers are manufactured by companies ABC and XYZ. It is easier to write and to gather information if Table 1 is reduced to:

Table 3. Compace MANUFACTURE Relation

COMPANY	PRODUCT
ABC	pencils, paper, notebooks, paper clips, erasers
XYZ	pencils, paper, notebooks, paper clips, erasers

Table 3 may be reduced further to:

Table 4. Minimal MANUFACTURE Relation

COMPANY	PRODUCT
ABC, XYZ	pencils, paper, notebooks, paper clips, erasers

In the notation of Fishman and Minker, Table 3 becomes:

$((\alpha,x,y),\{\{[M]/\alpha,[ABC]/x,[\text{pencils},\text{paper},\text{notebooks},\text{paper clips},\text{erasers}]/y\}$
$\{[M]/\alpha,[XYZ]/x,[\text{pencils},\text{paper},\text{notebooks},\text{paper clips},\text{erasers}]/y\}\})$,

and Table 4 is:

$((\beta,z,y)\ \{\{[M]/\beta,[ABC,XYZ]/z,[\text{pencils},\text{paper},\text{notebooks},\text{paper clips},\text{erasers}]/y\}\})$.

The set notation of relations is termed Π-clause notation. It was designed to consolidate the expression of similar first-order predicate calculus clauses. Formally, the syntax of a Π-clause consists of an ordered pair, (T,Φ), where T is a template and Φ is a set of substitution sets. A template is a clause,

$$A_1 \wedge A_2 \wedge \cdots \wedge A_n \rightarrow B_1$$

where each A_i, $i=1,\cdots,n$, and B_1 is free of constants. The predicate names have been replaced by variables. Therefore the template contains either variables or functions of arity >0. A substitution set φ is given the form

$$\varphi = \{[S_{0_1}]/v_{0_1},\ [S_{0_2}]/v_{0_2},\cdots,[S_{0_{n+1}}]/v_{0_{n+1}},[S_1]/v_1,\cdots,[S_k]/v_k\},$$

where the v_i are variables that appear in the template. The variables v_{0_j} are those that replace the predicate names. Each S_i, $i \geq 1$ is a set of either a finite number of elements with cardinality $|S_i|$, or is the name of a potentially infinite number of elements. If it is the name of a potentially infinite set of elements it represents the sort (or domain) over which the variable might range, and the item is underlined. The sets S_{0_k}, $1 \leq k \leq n+1$ must be finite sets of elements and represent predicate names. Every variable that appears in a template must have a corresponding variable in every substitution set.

The semantics of Π-clauses are easy to interpret. Consider the case where each S_{0_j}, $1 \leq j \leq n+1$ consists of exactly one element (the name of each distinct predicate), and the sets S_i, $1 \leq i \leq k$ are all infinite. The Π-clause represents $|S_1| \cdot |S_2| \cdots |S_k|$ clauses

$$A_1 \wedge A_2 \wedge \cdots \wedge A_n \rightarrow B_1$$

The names of the predicates have been entered for the variable, and one entry from each set S_i is used to replace the variable v_i wherever it appears in the template. If any of the S_i represent the names of sets, the variable is not changed in the template, but is restricted to the sort designated by S_i.

The following examples illustrate Π-clauses. If $n=0$ and $m=1$, the Π-clause,

$((\alpha,x,y),\ \{[MANUFACTURE]/\alpha,[ABC,XYZ]/x,$
$[\text{pencils},\text{paper},\text{notebooks},\text{paper clips},\text{erasers}]/y\})$,

represent the ten entries in the MANUFACTURE relation shown in Table 1 in relational form and the one entry in Table 4.

If $n=m=1$, the Π-clause,

$((\alpha,x,y) \rightarrow (\beta,x,y),\ \{[MANUFACTURE]/\alpha,\ [DISTRIBUTE]/\beta,\ [\underline{company}]/x,$
$[\underline{product}]/y\})$,

represents a single clause

$$MANUFACTURE(x,y) \rightarrow DISTRIBUTE(x,y),$$

where x is restricted to sort company, and y to sort product.

If n=2, m=1, the Π-clause,

$$((\alpha,x,y) \wedge (\beta,x,z) \rightarrow (\gamma,x,z), \{[PRODUCES]/\alpha, [LOCATION]/\beta, [MANUFACTURE]/\gamma, [company]/x, [state]/z, [wrenches,saws]/y\}),$$

represents two clauses,

PRODUCES(x,wrenches) $\wedge$ LOCATION(x,z) $\rightarrow$ MANUFACTURES(x,z)

PRODUCES(x,saws) $\wedge$ LOCATION(x,z) $\rightarrow$ MANUFACTURES(x,z) ,

where x is of sort company and z of sort state.

The Π-notation was devised primarily for a deductive search opeartion. However, it has certain advantages over a relational data base for providing natural language output. Consider Table 1. If one wants to output the table in natural language, then each line must appear as, for example,

"The (company name) manufactures (product name)".

The table is not sorted by company name. If one wants all products by company name listed together, a sort on company name could be performed first. Were this done, then it would be possible to provide one statement for all products. When there are k-ary relations, it becomes more complicated to manipulate the relational table to provide natural language output that combines like-relational statements.

Consider Table 3, all products manufactured by a particular company are co-located. Hence, it is a simple matter using Π-notation to output like entries. Indeed, using Table 4, one can output a statement of the form:

"The ABC and XYZ companies manufacture pencils and paper and notebooks and paper clips and erasers."

We do not claim that more can be done with Π-notation, but that at the time of output the relational table need not be manipulated to achieve a combined output that represents a single natural language statement for many entries in a relational table.

3. Deduction and Answer/Reason Extraction

3.1 Deduction and Relational Data Bases

To understand how answers and reasons are extracted from a deductive relational data base, one approach to deduction is outlined as exemplified in the work by Minker [1978]. The reader is referred to papers by Chang [1978], Kellogg et al. [1978], and Reiter [1978] for other approaches. The work described may be considered an interpretive approach. In this mode, the EDB and IDB operations are intermixed. This is in contrast to a compiled approach in which the query is first operated upon by entries in a conventional relational data base system for look-up in the EDB.

The discussion is motivated by providing a procedural interpretation of Horn clauses as developed by Kowalski [1974]. There are four kinds of Horn clauses.

(1) $A_1 \wedge A_2 \wedge \cdots \wedge A_n \rightarrow B$ (when $n \neq 0$) is interpreted as a procedure definition. Hence, an entry in the IDB may be interpreted as a procedure where the consequent B is interpreted as the procedure name.

The antecedent $A_1 \wedge \cdots \wedge A_n$ is interpreted as the procedure body. The entries A_i can be considered as procedure calls.

(2) $\rightarrow B$, or simply B (when n=0) is interpreted as an assertion of fact. It can be considered a procedure with an empty body, or as a known fact with the procedure B solved.

(3) $A_1 \wedge \cdots \wedge A_n \rightarrow$ (when m=0) or simply $A_1 \wedge \cdots \wedge A_n$, is interpreted as a goal statement, or a conjunction of problems to be solved.

(4) $\square$ (when n=0 and m=0), the null clause, is interpreted as a halt statement, or as a solved goal statement.

In the following a particular method for invoking procedures is discussed. Although the discussion is in terms of clauses, everything that is stated applies equally to Π-clauses. LUSH resolution (Hill [1974]) is used to describe how a particular procedure is invoked. In the following goal clauses are used. For simplicity, and bookkeeping purposes, all conjunction signs are eliminated. Parentheses and the * symbol are introduced. The revised clause will be referred to as a T-clause. Thus, the goal clause

$$A_1 \wedge A_2 \wedge \cdots \wedge A_n$$

is written as the T-clause,

$$A_1\ A_2\ \cdots\ A_n\ .$$

A T-clause such as $A_1\ A_2\ {*}(A_3 A_4 A_5)\ A_6{*}$ is permitted. A T-clause may be interpreted to be a clause where the * and parentheses symbol in the T-clause are eliminated and conjunctions placed between atomic formulae. Thus, the T-clause corresponds to the clause $A_1 \wedge A_3 \wedge A_4 \wedge A_5$.

LUSH resolution is explained as modified into T-clauses to incorporate the simplification and bookkeeping operation. LUSH resolution is used in deducing data. The objective is to start with a T-goal clause, and to derive a T-halt statement. A T-halt statement is a T-goal clause, all of whose atomic formulae are followed immediately by an *. Procedures are invoked on T-goal statements to derive new T-goal statements. A procedure can be invoked on an T-goal statement only on a distinguished atomic formula. A distinguished atomic formula in a T-goal clause is underlined. An atomic formula is selected as a problem to be solved. One and only one atomic formula that is not followed immediately by an asterisk (*) can be distinguished in any T-clause.

Assuming that a mechanism exists to distinguish an atomic formula, two operations of extension are permitted which derive a new T-clause from a T-goal clause and either an EDB T-clause or an IDB T-clause. The distinguished, or selected, atomic formula is underlined in a T-clause.

3.1.1 Extension of an L-Goal Clause with an EDB Clause

Let α be a T-goal clause with selected atomic formula $\underline{G_i}$, where G_i is not followed immediately by an * , and let G^1 be an EDB clause. Let $\underline{G_i}$ and G^1 match in that they share the same predicate name, and a substitution Θ can be found to make the two atomic formulae match in every position. Then, a new T-goal statement α^1 may be derived by following $\underline{G_i}$ by an * , and removing the distinguishing mark. All other atomic formulae in the given T-clause remain unchanged. The derived T-clause is the given T-clause with $\underline{G_i}$ replaced by $G_i{*}$, and the substitution Θ applied to the resultant.

Thus, if

$$\alpha = G_1 \cdots G_{i-1}, \underline{G_i} \; G_{i+1} \cdots G_n ,$$

then the derived T-clause α^1 is,

$$\alpha^1 = (G_1 \cdots G_{i-1} \; G_i * G_{i+1} \cdots G_n)\Theta$$

For example, if

$$\alpha = G_1(x,y) \; \underline{G_2(x,a)} \; G_3(y,z) ,$$

and

$$G^1 = G_2(b,a) ,$$

then

$$\Theta = \{b/x\} \quad \text{and}$$

$$\alpha^1 = (G_1(x,y) \; G_2(x,a) * G_3(y,z)) \; \{b/x\} .$$

The notation $\{b/x\}$ denotes that b is to be substituted for x, and hence,

$$\alpha^1 = G_1(b,y) \; G_2(b,a) * G_3(y,z)$$

is the derived T-clause.

In the procedural interpretation, the procedure $G_2(b,a)$ effectively solves the atomic formula $G_2(x,a)$ in the T-goal clause, . Now, solutions must be found for $G_1(b,y)$ and $G_3(y,z)$ for the original T-goal clause to be solved. Notice that by retaining $G_2(b,a)*$, an answer (or a reason) for $G_2(x,a)$ has been found.

3.1.2 Extension on a T-Goal Clause with an IDB T-Clause

Let α be a T-goal clause with selected literal $\underline{G_i}$ where G_i is not followed immediately by *, and let

$$A_1 \; A_2 \cdots A_n \rightarrow G^1$$

be a T-clause in the IDB. In the procedural interpretation, the T-clause represents a procedure whose procedure name is G^1. If the procedure name G^1 matches the atomic formula G_i in that they share the same predicate name, and a substitution Θ can be found to make the two atomic formulae match in every position, then, a new T-goal clause, α^1, can be derived. In the original T-clause, the atomic formula (problem to be solved) G_i is replaced by $G_i * (A_1 \; A_2 \cdots A_n)$, and the distinguishing mark is removed. All other atomic formulae in the given T-clause remain unchanged. The derived T-clause is the given T-clause with $\underline{G_i}$ replaced by the new form, and the substitution Θ applied to the resultant. If

$$\alpha = G_1 \cdots G_{i-1} \; \underline{G_i} \; G_{i+1} \cdots G_n , \text{ then}$$

$$\alpha^1 = (G_1 \cdots G_{i-1} \; G_i * (A_1 \cdots A_n) \; G_{i+1} \cdots G_n)\Theta$$

is the derived T-goal clause. Each atomic formula in a T-goal clause represents a problem to be solved. In replacing an atomic formula with an * and a non-null procedure body, an interpretation may be that to solve the asterished atomic formula it is necessary to solve each of the atomic formulae in the procedure body that follows.

For example, if

$$\alpha = G_1(x,y)\ \underline{G_2(x,a)}\ G_3(y,z) ,$$

and

$$G_4(u,v)\ G_5(v,w) \rightarrow G_2(u,w) ,$$

then

$$G^1 = G_2(u,w), \quad \Theta = \{x/y, a/w\} ,$$

and

$$\alpha^1 = (G_1(x,y)\ G_2(x,a) * (G_4(u,v)\ G_5(v,w))\ G_3(y,z)) \quad \{x/u, a/w\} .$$

Since the substitution specifies that u is to be replaced by x and w by a,

$$\alpha^1 = G_1(x,y)\ G_2(x,a) * (G_4(x,v)\ G_5(v,a))\ G_3(y,z) .$$

To solve the original T-goal clause, it is now necessary to solve each of the unasterisked atomic formulae in α^1. The asterisked atomic formula, $G_2(x,a)*$, is solved when $G_4(x,v)$ <u>and</u> $G_5(v,a)$ are solved.

Starting with a T-goal clause, procedures are applied as described above until a T-halt statement is found, or time and space are exhausted. The above is illustrated with a simple example. Consider the following EDB which consists of a subset of Table 1:

EDB: MANUFACTURE(ABC,pencils)

IDB: MANUFACTURE(x,y) → DISTRIBUTE(x,y)

GOAL CLAUSE: DISTRIBUTE(x,pencils).

That is, an answer to the question "Who distributes pencils?" is the goal. The T-goal clause may be solved as follows:

(1) <u>DISTRIBUTE(x,pencils)</u>

In the starting T-goal clause, DISTRIBUTE(x,pencils) is selected (and hence underlined) to be solved.

(2) DISTRIBUTE(x,pencils)*(MANUFACTURE(x,pencils))

The only T-clause on which the T-clause in (1) can be extended is the IDB clause. The right hand atomic formula in the IDB T-clause can match (1) if {pencils/y} is the substitution. Hence, (2) is the new T-goal clause to be solved.

(2^1) DISTRIBUTE(x,pencils)*<u>(MANUFACTURE(x,pencils))</u>

The only atomic formula in (2) that is not followed by an asterisk is MANUFACTURE(x,pencils). Hence, it is selected for extension and underlined. The only T-clause that can be used to extend (2^1) is the EDB T-clause. The selected atomic formula in (2^1) can be matched with the EDB T-clause by performing the substitution {ABC/x}.

(3) DISTRIBUTE(ABC,pencils)*(MANUFACTURE(ABC,pencils)*).

The derived T-clause has no atomic formulae not followed by an * . Hence, it is a T-halt statement.

As will be seen subsequently, statement (3) alone can be used to provide the answer and reasons as follows:

DISTRIBUTE(ABC,pencils)	- answers
MANUFACTURE(ABC,pencils)⟶ DISTRIBUTES(ABC,pencils)	- implication
MANUFACTURE(ABC,pencils)	- assertion

The bookkeeping, as outlined above, can be used with the interpretive approach as exemplified by Minker [1978]. The same bookkeeping mechanism can be incorporated into other approaches to performing deduction as exemplified by Chang [1978], Kellogg et al. [1978] and Reiter [1978]. Hence, the reasons and the answer can be extracted readily in alternative approaches to deduction.

3.2 Answer and Reason Extraction

The use of extended form of LUSH resolution and bookkeeping to achieve a halt statement that contains the answer and reasons embedded in it differs from previous approaches (Green [1969], Luckham and Nilsson [1971], Minker and Wilson [1977], Powell [1977]). The answer/reason extraction algorithm is outlined here and details are provided in Appendix A.

Assume the following T-halt statement:

$$G_1 *(A_1 *(A_2 *A_3 *) A_4 *) G_2 *(A_5 * A_6 *)$$

The T-halt statement is scanned from left to right. Begin scanning with level set to zero. All atomic formulae at level zero constitute the answer. The scanner recognizes G_1 as part of the answer and outputs G_1 on the first line of Figure 1. Next a left parenthesis is encountered, and the level is increased by one and G_1 is recognized as the consequent of an implicant statement since it is followed by an * and a left parenthesis. The scanner picks up on A_1*. Hence, on the second line A_1 is entered as part of the antecedent of G_1. The following left parenthesis indicates that A_1 is itself a consequent, and the level is increased by one. On line three the implicant with A_1 as consequent is begun. Now, A_2* is found and is an antecedent of A_1 and placed on line three. Furthermore, since A_2* is not followed by a left parenthesis, it is an assertion and is specified as such on line four. Similarly, A_3* is recognized as part of the antecedent at level two, and conjoined with A_2 on line three, and specified as an assertion

1.	$G_1 \wedge G_2$	answer
2.	$A_1 \wedge A_4 \rightarrow G_1$	implicant
3.	$A_2 \wedge A_3 \rightarrow A_1$	implicant
4.	A_2	assertion
5.	A_3	assertion
6.	A_4	assertion
7.	$A_5 \wedge A_6 \rightarrow G_2$	implicant
8.	A_5	assertion
9.	A_6	assertion

Figure 1. Answer-Extraction for $G_1 *(A_1 *(A_2 * A_3 *) A_4 *) G_2 *(A_5 * A_6 *)$

on line five. The right parenthesis decrements the level by one. Now A_4 is part of the antecedent at level one and is specified as such on line two and is listed as an assertion on line two. The following right parenthesis decrements the level to zero. G_2 is scanned next and is conjoined with G_1 on line one. Since G_2 is followed by a left parenthesis, it is a consequent of an implicant. As before, A_5 and A_6 are found to be the antecedents. They are specified as such on line seven and are listed as assertions on lines eight and nine respectively.

A more precise algorithm for answer and reason extraction is given in Appendix A.

4. Natural Language Output

Following answer/reason extraction, the information must be given to the user in an easily interpreted form. Three choices are available: relational format, natural language or voice. Relational format is valuable to a user who works mainly with data bases and is accustomed to seeing data as relations or to a computer scientist who works closely to machine representation. Natural language output is important to a casual user to whom language is the natural means of communication. A way to attain natural language output from relational output is described in Section five. Voice output is important to another class of users. These include the blind, systems where volumes of paper are undersirable, computerized telephone systems plus any type of system where vocal communication is the preferred mode.

The method of communication whether between man and man, man and animal, or man and computer, is almost as important as the act of communicating. It is useless to show a blind man a picture. Instead, the communicator needs to have the vocabulary and the ability to utilize the vocabulary to convey the content of the picture. So it is between man and computer. The computer needs a means to output the result of its computations in a form readily understandable by the user. For many years the computer scientist has had the means to format output both for debugging purposes and final output. With increasing non-scientific computer applications and non-computer oriented users, computer communication has become a necessary area for research. The MRPPS 3.0 System gives the user the option of Π-clause, natural language and/or voice output. Section two describes Π-clause format. Section five describes voice output.

When the user wants natural language output, he must input a pattern for each predicate or function in the relational data base. A pattern consists of a string of characters representing English characters and special symbols which are interpreted by the natural language translator. The English characters represent the skeleton of the sentence to be output. The special symbols indicate where to insert the arguments of the predicate of the relation, how to treat singular and plural arguments and how to treat negated relations. For example, given the following Π-clause:

$$((\alpha,x,y), \{[S]/\alpha, [XEROX]/x, [COPIERS]/y\})$$

and the following pattern:

%@1 SELLS @2% ,

the sentence

XEROX SELLS COPIERS

is output. The % symbols enclose the pattern. The @1 symbol means to substitute the value(s) or the substitution set(s) for the first argument of the relation. The characters SELLS are not special symbols and therefore are output directly. The @2 symbol means to substitute the value(s) or the substitution set(s) for the second argument of the relation.

The special symbols reserved by the pattern parser are %, <, > , [,], /, @, and #. All the symbols except @ and # are reserved because they appear in the Π-clause sent to the natural language translator. The @ and # symbols give directions to the translator. The symbol @ followed by a number, n, means insert the value(s) represented by the nth argument into the pattern. Multiple values are separated by AND. The symbol @ followed by a S and a number, n, means to include the characters up to the next @ if the nth argument has only one (singular) value. Similarly, an @Pn means include the characters up to the next @ if the nth argument has more than one (plural) value. Characters surrounded by the # symbol are included in the output if the relation is negated.

The following is an example illustrating multiple values in the substitution set. The Π-clause is,

$((\alpha,x,y),\ \{[M]/\alpha,\ [A,B,C]/x,\ [VITAMINS,ASPIRIN]/y\})$.

The pattern associated with M as given by the user is,

%THE PHARMACEUTICAL COMPAN@S1Y@S1@P1IES@P1
@1 DO@S1ES@S1 #NOT# MARKET@S1S@S1 @2%.

The sentence output is:

THE PHARMACEUTICAL COMPANIES A AND B AND C DO MARKET VITAMINS AND ASPIRIN.

If the template had been negated in the previous example, the sentence would be:

THE PHARMACEUTICAL COMPANYIES A AND B AND C DO NOT MARKET VITAMINS AND ASPIRIN.

An advantage to Π-clause notation is brought out in the above example. If a conventional relational format is used either three almost identical sentences are output or a pre-pass of the entire output is required to combine A, B and C as a compound subject. Additionally, when Π-clauses are used in the proof procedure a single T-halt clause is derived that contains A, B, and C. If conventional relations are used, three separate T-halt statements are generated.

A pattern for a function is specified in the same manner as a pattern for a predicate. If the nth argument of the predicate is a function, @n is specified in the predicate pattern at the place in the sentence where the function appears. Within the function pattern, @n refers to the nth argument of the function. An example of a relation with a function as an argument is:

$((\alpha,f(x),y)\ \{[L]/\alpha,\ [ZENN]/x,\ [AMERICAN]/y\})$.

The pattern for the predicate might be:

%@1 @S1IS@S1@P1ARE@P1 LISTED ON THE @2 STOCK EXCHANGE% .

The pattern for the function might be:

%THE PARENT COMPAN@S1Y@S1@P1IES@P1 of @1%

The sentence output based upon these patterns is:

THE PARENT COMPANY OF ZENN IS LISTED ON THE AMERICAN STOCK EXCHANGE.

A relation with multiple values for a predicate in a substitution set causes one sentence to be printed for each predicate value. For example,

$((\alpha,x,y), \{[D,B]/\alpha, [ZENN]/x, [SHIPS]/y\})$,

the pattern for D ,

% @1 DESIGN@S1S@S1 @2 % ,

the pattern for B,

% @1 BUILD@S1S@S1 @2 %,

the sentences output are:

ZENN DESIGNS SHIPS.

ZENN BUILDS SHIPS.

Two sentences are output because on input a pattern is required for each predicate. If it is known that all companies which design ships also build ships then the two predicates can be combined as illustrated in the following example. Given

$((\alpha,x,y), \{[DB]/\alpha, [ZENN]/x, [SHIPS]/y\})$,

the pattern for DB ,

%@1 DESIGN@S1S@S1 AND BUILD@S1S@S1 @2 % ,

the sentence output is,

ZENN DESIGNS AND BUILDS SHIPS.

If the template of a Π-clause contains multiple relations, an AND is inserted between the pattern translation for each literal. If any of the predicates have multiple values, a new sentence is generated for each combination of predicate values. For example, consider the Π-clause,

$((\alpha,x,y)(\beta,z,x), \{[D,B]/\alpha, [ZENN]/x, [SHIPS]/y, [P]/\beta, [BENN]/z\})$.

The patterns for D and B are the same as in the above example. The pattern for P is

% @1 IS THE PARENT COMPANY OF @2 % .

The output is:

ZENN DESIGNS SHIPS AND BENN IS THE PARENT COMPANY OF ZENN.

ZENN BUILDS SHIPS AND BEEN IS THE PARENT COMPANY OF ZENN.

In the MRPPS 3.0 System, the answer and reasons for deriving the answer are output. The answer is output as described above. Reasons containing one relation (assertion) are output as described above. Reasons containing more than one relation are axioms. They contain two parts - an antecedent and a consequent. Each relation in the antecedent is separated by ALSO and the consequent is preceded by IMPLIES. In addition, each relation in the antecedent has a number in brackets following the pattern translation which indicates forward line reference to the reasons this relation is solved. This number is provided by the answer/reason extraction algorithm given in Appendix A.

To illustrate the natural language output of the answer and reasons extracted from a proof graph, consider the following relations:

answer: S(BIP,WRENCHES)

reasons: P(ZIP,WRENCHES) $\wedge$ D(ZIP,WRENCHES,BIP) $\rightarrow$ S(BIP,WRENCHES)

P(ZIP,WRENCHES)

D(ZIP,WRENCHES,BIP)

where the letters S, P, and D, respectively, stand for the predicates "sells", "produces", and "distributes". The associated patterns for S, P, and D are:

% @1 SELL@S1S@S1 @2 %,

% @1 PRODUCE@S1S@S1 @2 %,

% @1 DISTRIBUTE@S1S@S1 @2 TO @3 % .

The natural language output is:

ANSWER

BIP SELLS WRENCHES

REASONS

1. ZIP PRODUCES WRENCHES [2] ALSO ZIP DISTRIBUTES WRENCHES TO BIP[3] IMPLIES BIP SELLS WRENCHES.

2. ZIP PRODUCES WRENCHES.

3. ZIP DISTRIBUTES WRENCHES TO BIP.

Pattern translation as described above is operational in the MRPPS 3.0 System and was implemented by Klein [1976]. The algorithm that translates patterns is described in Appendix B.

Pattern variations are not currently permitted in MRPPS 3.0 Once a pattern is input for a predicate or function, it cannot be changed. Including active and passive pattern variations would produce more varied output. A simple change might be to allow more than one pattern for a predicate or function. Each time a predicate or function is output, the next pattern for it would be selected in cyclic mode. For example, if a predicate has three patterns then every third time that predicate is output the same pattern is output. More complicated to implement but perhaps a better mode of cycling is to select the next pattern each time an implication and the substantiating reasons are encountered.

Another passive variation could be to permit several patterns which are associated with an implication by a user specified number. A number, n, could be input as part of a relation in the data base. The number would mean to select the nth pattern for the implication and wherever the same predicate appears in the substantiating reasons of the implication. Any assertion not associated with an implication could have a standard pattern or some method of cycling could be employed.

Active pattern variation could be accomplished by the system asking the user which pattern he wants for a particular predicate or function. Again, a predicate or function pattern should remain the same for an implication and its substantiating reasons.

A further minor refinement could be to replace multiple ANDs by commas. For example, A AND B AND C would be A, B, and C.

5. Voice Output

Vocal expression is an important means of communication. Spoken thought is often remembered more easily than a thought read. Also, many people prefer to listen to information vocally conveyed rather than to scan printed output. As an experimental tool, voice output is included in MRPPS 3.0.

The design objectives are to produce quality output using a small amount of memory, being able to accommodate a large vocabulary without including an exceptions dictionary, keeping programming efforts to a minimum and being able to output using different voice synthesizers. To accomplish the objectives, the MRPPS 3.0 voice output is based on the NRL (Naval Research Laboratory) text translator to speech output (Elovitz [1975]).

The NRL text translator scans the natural language text left-to-right without any back-tracking looking up a character or group of characters in the translation rules, outputting the IPA (International Phonetic Alphabet) translation, and passes to the next untranslated character. There are about three hundred and fifty translation rules - productions. They are grouped alphabetically and ordered so that during a sequential scan of an alphabetic grouping the most appropriate production is encountered and therefore selected first. The last production is a default production which guarantees that a translation for each letter is found. A few of the productions translate entire common words such as ARE or NOW or parts of words such as UN or ALLY.

The productions are context-sensitive. This means that included in each production are characters which may precede or follow the character being scanned. A production is in the following form:

$$\alpha[\beta]\gamma = \delta$$

Alpha and gamma may be a character, a special symbol or null. Beta is the character being scanned or may be a sequence of characters the first of which is the character being scanned. Delta is the IPA translation of beta in the context of alpha and gamma. The special symbols for alpha and gamma represent such entities as any consonant, specific vowels or suffixes. They form patterns for common characters which may precede or follow a given letter. For example, the production $:[A]\Delta + = EY$ where $:$ represents zero or more consonants , Δ represents one consonant and $+$ represents the vowels e, i or y. A word that matches this production is BARE. The production $[A]\Delta + : \# = AE$ where $\#$ represents one or more vowels matches the word ABIDE. The $[A]\Delta + : \#$ production precedes the $: [A]\Delta +$ production in the A group so the AE phoneme is chosen to translate the A in ABIDE rather than the EY phoneme whose production also matches A in the context of ABIDE. Conversely, the A in BARE is translated by the phoneme EY since the $[A]\Delta + : \#$ production is rejected in the sequential scan.

A great deal of time was spent by NRL listening to the voice output and rearranging productions to attain the best pronunciation possible. The NRL translator demonstrates that a simple algorithm with a relatively small set of translated productions can produce viable IPA phonemes for a large majority of English words. On the average, less than one word per sentence in normal conversation is mispronounced. Most of the mispronunciations are single-phoneme errors and can be corrected by the user from the context. Presumably, additions and refinements to the productions could further reduce errors (Elovitz [1975]).

The same algorithm used to translate natural language characters to IPA can be used to translate the IPA phonemes to the symbols acceptable to a commercial voice synthesizer.

As an example, the translation of CHURCH to IPA is as follows:

input: CHURCH
↑

the C productions are:

_ [CH] △ = K

△ [CH] = K

[CH] = CH

⋮

[C] = K

where

_ means a space

△ means a single consonant

the first matching production is [CH] = CH

output phoneme: CH

input: CHURCH
  ↑

the U productions are:

␣ [UN] I = Y1UW1N

␣ [UN] = AH1N

␣ [UPON] = AX1P1AO1N

@[UR]# = UH1R

[UR]# = Y1UH1R

[UR] = ER

[U] △ = AN

⋮

[U] = Y1UW

where

␣ means a space

@ means (T,S,R,D,L,Z,N,J), TH, CH or SH

means 1 or more vowels

Δ means a single consonant

the first matching production is [UR] = ER

output phonemes: CH ER

input: CHURCH
↑

The [CH] = CH production is again chosen.

output phonemes: CH ER CH

The MRPPS 3.0 text translator (Thompson [1976]) is based on the NRL translator. The principal difference is that in the first pass translating English to IPA phonemes, the productions within each letter group are clustered such that the first production in a cluster is the least context-sensitive production for that cluster. If the character or characters pointed to by the parser match the left side of the first production in a cluster then the production which translates the designated character is contained within the cluster. Conversely, if the designated character(s) does not match the first production of a cluster, the remainder of the cluster need not be scanned. The revised MRPPS 3.0 translator yields an efficiency gain of about one-third over the NRL translator.

A cluster is a recursive grouping of rules. The first rule in a cluster is the header rule. All rules within the cluster are a subset of the header rule. A rule within a cluster may itself be a header rule for a sub-cluster. The sub-clusters form the recursive nature of the production grammar. Within a cluster, although rules are a subset of its header rule, there is no defined relationship between the other rules in the cluster. For example, the P cluster is

```
[P] = P1 → [PH] = F1
             ↓
           [PEOP] = P1IYP1
             ↓
           [POW] = P1AW
             ↓
           [PUT] = P1UHT1
```

P is the header rule. The other four rules are a subset of P but are not themselves related. The original NRL ordering is retained in the manner in which the clusters are scanned. The first rule is the default translation for a character. It is also the main header rule for all clusters for that character. The clustered rules may be found in Appendix C.

The algorithm which finds the correct cluster and then the best sounding rule for the character(s) pointed to by the parser follows. Briefly, the algorithm selects the first rule which is the default case. The brother link is taken to the first sub-cluster. As long as brother link rules match, the brother link is taken until there are no more links. The last matching rule is the translation. If a brother link does not match, the son link is taken. The process of recursively taking a brother link on match and a son link on a no-match continues until a chain is exhausted. The last matching rule is the translation. The algorithm always terminates because the left hand side of the first rule contains only a single character matching the character pointed to by the parser.

Algorithm 5.1 Character to IPA Translation - MRPPS 3.0

```
P: = pointer to 1st character
C: = character pointed to by P
while text exists do
    get production group for C
    while productions exist do
        N: = Length of β
        if β = C + N - 1 characters in context α and γ
            then OUTPUT:= δ
            take brother link
            if brother is null
                then exit inner while
            end
            else take son link
              if son is null
                  then exit inner while
              end
        end
    end

    move P over N characters
    while P points to a space do
        move P over 1 character
    end
    C: = character pointed to by P
end
```

If changes to rules are made or rules are added or deleted, a pre-pass is made of the rules to re-cluster them.

The following example illustrates how the proper rule is chosen.

G RULES

(1) [GIV] = G1IHV1

(2) ␣ [G] I Δ = G1

(3) [GE]T = G1EH

(4) SU[GGES] = G1JHEHS1

(5) [GG] = G1

(6) B#[G] = G1

(7) [G]+ = JH

(8) [GREAT] = G1R1EYT1

(9) #[GH] = φ

(10) [G] = G1

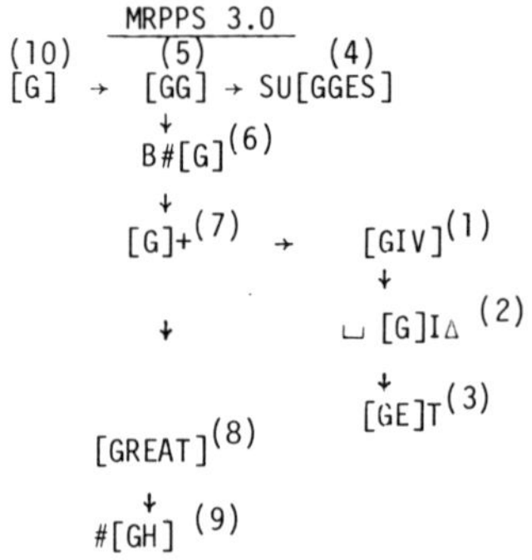

The meanings of the special symbols are:

- ␣ means a space
- # means a sequence of one or more vowels
- + E, I or Y
- Δ one consonant
- φ denotes that no translation is required since we have silent letters

The number in parenthesis in the cluster refer to the NRL ordering of the rules. The words GREAT, FOREIGN, HEIGHT and GIFT produce the following sequences:

	NRL	MRPPS 3.0
GREAT :	1, 2, ..., 8	10, 5, 6, 7, 8
FOREIGN :	1, 2, ..., 10	10, 5, 6, 7, 8, 9
HEIGHT :	1, 2, ..., 9	10, 5, 6, 7, 8, 9
GIFT :	1, 2	10, 5, 6, 7, 1, 2, 3

The numbers underlined are those which are chosen by the MRPPS 3.0 translator.

In summary, the MRPPS 3.0 text translator points to a letter, ℓ . The productions for ℓ are referenced, If a production matches ℓ in its context, the brother link is taken. If a production does not match ℓ , the son link is taken. Either a brother or son link is taken until a chain is exhausted. The last production which matches is selected for output. Punctuation marks are converted to pauses. The second pass converts IPA phonemes to symbols acceptable by the Votrax voice synthesizer.

Although additional time could be spent reordering the pronunciation rules (Elovitz [1976]), the time would be better spent on inflection-pitch stress and timing - rather than pronunciation errors which are in a tolerable range. The monotone quality of a synthesizer is boring and loses the listener's interest. Two simple additions using limited look ahead are falling inflection before a period and rising inflection before a question mark. Some of the output phonemes can be said to always have a particular stress irregardless of surrounding output. The inflection symbols can be inserted directly into the output phoneme. Common endings such as ES or ED have universal inflection. It would not be difficult to add the tonal symbols when the common endings are identified. The tendency for stress to fall on alternating syllables in English is another simple means of removing the monotone quality of the output.

6. Summary

The output components of a deductive relational data system are discussed. A new answer/reason extraction algorithm is presented. A new method is developed that utilizes the bookkeeping functions of LUSH resolution (Hill [1974]), and permits the answers and the reasons incorporated in each derived clause. The final clause in the proof contains all the information required by the answer/reason algorithm to output the answers and the reasons.

Utilizing Π-notation combines like relational entries so that multiple entries in a relation may be output in a single sentence. To achieve the same results in relational data base using one of the normal forms would require a post processor which would effectively manipulate the output into Π-notation. The natural language translator, although unsophisticated is powerful and provides clear natural language sentences.

The voice output synthesizer does an effective job in obtaining the correct pronunciation of words. Additional work is required to place inflection into sentences so as to avoid monotone output sentences.

References

1. Chamberlin, D. D. [1976] "Relational Data Base Management Systems," Computing Surveys 8 (1976), 43-66.

2. Chang, C. L. [1978] "DEDUCE 2: Further Investigations of Deduction in Relational Data Bases," In Logic and Data Bases (H. Gallaire and J. Minker, Eds.), Plenum Press, New York, 1978, 201-236.

3. Codd, E. F. [1970] "A Relational Model of Data for Large Shared Data Banks," CACM 13, 6(June 1970), 377-387.

4. Codd, E. F. [1972] "Relational Completeness of Data Base Sublanguages," In Data Base Systems (R. Rustin, Ed.), Prentice Hall, Englewood Cliffs, NJ, 1972, 65-98.

5. Elovitz, H. S. [1975] "Automatic Text Translations to Speech Via Letter-To-Sound Rules," Scholarly Paper, Department of Computer Science, University of Maryland, College Park, MD, 20742, 1975.

6. Fishman, D. H. and Minker, J. [1975] "Π-Representation. A Clause Representation for Parallel Search," Artificial Intelligence 6, 2(1975), 103-127.

7. Gallaire, H. and Minker, J. [1978] Logic and Data Bases, Plenum Press, New York, NY, 1978.

8. Green, C. C. [1969] "Theorem Proving by Resolution as a Basis for Question-Answering Systems," In Machine Intelligence 4 (B. Meltzer and D. Michie, Eds.), American Elsevier, New York, 1969, 193-205.

9. Hill, R. [1974] "LUSH Resolution and Its Completeness," DCL Memo No. 78, University of Edinburgh, School of Artificial Intelligence, August 1974.

10. Horn, A. [1951] "On Sentences which are True of Direct Unions of Algebra," J. Symbolic Logic 16, 14-21.

11. Kellogg, C., Klahr, P. and Travis, L. [1978] "Deductive Planning and Pathfinding for Relational Data Bases," In Logic and Data Bases (H. Gallaire and J. Minker, Eds.), Plenum Press, New York, NY, 1978, 179-200.

12. Klein, M. [1976] "Translating Π-Clauses into English," Scholarly Paper, Department of Computer Science, University of Maryland, College Park, MD, 1976.

13. Kowalski, R. A. [1974] "Predicate Logic as Programming Language," IFIP-74, North Holland, 1947, 569-574.

14. Luckham, D. and Nilsson, N. [1971] "Extracting Information from Resolution Proof Trees," Artificial Intelligence, 1971.

15. McSkimin, J. R. and Minker, J. [1977] "The Use of a Semantic Network in a Deductive Question-Answering System," Proc. IJCAI-77, Cambridge, MA, 1977, 50-58.

16. McSkimin, J. R. and Minker, J. [1979] "A Predicate Calculus Based Semantic Network for Question-Answering Systems," In Associative Networks - The Representation and Use of Knowledge in Computers (N. Findler, Ed.), Academic Press, New York, 1979.

17. Minker, J. and Wilson, G. [1977] "A Note on Answer Extraction in Resolution Based Theorem Proving," International Journal of Computers and Information Sciences, Vol. 6, No. 3, 1977.

18. Minker, J. [1978] "Search Strategy and Selection Function for an Inferential Relational System," ACM Trans. on Database Systems 3, 1(March 1978), 1-31.

19. Minker, J. [1978] "An Experimental Relational Data Base System Based on Logic," In Logic and Data Bases (H. Gallaire and J. Minker, Eds.), Plenum Press, New York, 1978, 107-147.

20. Powell, P. [1977] "Answer-Reason Extraction in a Parallel Relational Data Base System," Master's Thesis, Department of Computer Science, University of Maryland, College Park, MD, 20742, 1977.

21. Reiter, R. [1977] "An Approach to Deductive Question-Answering," BBN Report No. 3649, Bolt, Beranek and Newman, Inc., Cambridge, MA, Sept., 1977.

22. Reiter, R. [1978] "Deductive Qeustion-Answering on Relational Data Bases," In Logic and Data Bases (H. Gallaire and J. Minker, Eds.), Plenum Press, New York, 1978, 149-177.

23. Thompson, P. [1976] "Rule Precedence within Context-Sensitive Grammars: An Extension of the Letter-to-Sound Rules Used in Voice Production," Scholarly Paper, Department of Computer Science, University of Maryland, College Park, MD, 20742, 1976.

APPENDIX A

Answer/Reason Algorithm

Section three describes deduction and answer/reason extraction. This Appendix contains an answer/reason algorithm followed by an example containing atomic formulas without terms and an example containing Π-clauses.

During resolution, the substitution sets of the data base clauses that unified with the template of the selected atomic formula in the proof graph are intersected with the substitution set(s) of the proof graph clause. All combinations of the substitution sets are intersected. Those intersections which are non-null are retained in the resolvent proof graph clause.

Algorithm A: Answer/Reason Extraction

Explanation: The algorithm is passed the terminal clause of the proof graph the T-halt clause. All atomic formulas are solved and marked with an asterisk (*). If an atomic formula is solved by a virtual relation, the relation is enclosed in parenthesis. Nests of parentheses occur when a virtual relation solves an atomic formula with a virtual relation. It is assumed that the clause is pure. That is, there are no syntax errors.

The first atomic formula is always part or all of the answer and is put in an answer table. The reason table consists of two word entries. The first word contains bookkeeping information. The second word contains a pointer to the reason clause. The reason clause is constructed as the input is scanned. The first atomic formula in the reason is the implicant. The antecedents are

```
        end
        if  P ≠ →
            then move P to next character
                FIRST: = 1
        end
    end


Proc BUILD(REASTAB, P, A, PTR, LINE, FIRST)
    REASTAB: = REASTAB +2
    LINE: = LINE + 1
(1) while P ≠ ) do
        if P = *
            then move P to next character
        end
(2)     if P = (
            then move P to next character
                add → A and line number to reason table entry pointed
                        to by REASTAB
                add atomic formula pointed to by P  to current reason
                        table entry
                A: = atomic formula pointed to by P
                move P to next character
                call BUILD(REASTAB, P, A, REASTAB, LINE, FIRST)
                if  P ≠  →
                    then move P to next character
                end
            else if P = atomic formula
              then add atomic formula pointed to by P to reason table
                        entry pointed to by PTR
                if atomic formula pointed to by P not preceded by ( or )
                    then put line number and atomic formula in A in
                            current reason table entry
                        LINE: = LINE + 1
                        REASTAB: = REASTAB + 2
                end
                A: = atomic formula pointed to by P
                Move P to next character
              else move P back one character
             end
(3)          if  P = *)
                then put line number and atomic formula in A in current
                        reason table entry
```

added as they are found. If an atomic formula is solved by a fact in the data base, the fact is a separate entry in the table.

During the scan, an open parenthesis signals the beginning of an implication. The atomic formula preceding the open parenthesis is the implicant. A new entry is started in the reason table. A closed parenthesis signals the end of an implication and reversion to the previous implication.

Two procedures are employed. The first processes the answer atomic formula. The second recursively processes the reasons. The algorithm does not include forward line reference insertion.

Terminology:

REASTAB: A pointer to the next available entry in the reason block.

PTR: A pointer to the implicant entry in the reason block of virtual relation.

P: A pointer to the input string.

LINE: The line number of the reason.

FIRST: A switch variable.

A: Variable which contains an atomic formula.

Assume for simplicity that an atomic formula is a single letter and there are no spaces between characters.

Assume the T-halt clause is terminated by an → .

The parameters REASTAB, LINE, FIRST and P are called by reference. Conversely, the parameters A and PTR are called by value.

The notation ①, ②, and ③ denote the scope of while and if statements.

```
Proc A/R EXTRACTION (T-halt clause)
    P: = first character
    REASTAB: = -1
    PTR: = 1
    LINE: = 0
    FIRST: = 1
    while character ≠ → do
        A: = atomic formula pointed to by P
        make entry for A in answer table
        move P to next character
        if  P+1 = (
            then call BUILD(REASTAB P, A, PTR, LINE, FIRST)
                      PTR: = REASTAB
                      REASTAB: = REASTAB - 2
                      LINE: = LINE - 1
```

```
                    LINE: = LINE + 1
                    REASTAB: = REASTAB + 2
                        if FIRST = 1
                            then FIRST = 2
                                return
                            else move P to next character
                        end
              ③ end
        ② end
   ① 
    end
    return
```

PROOF GRAPH

Query: A

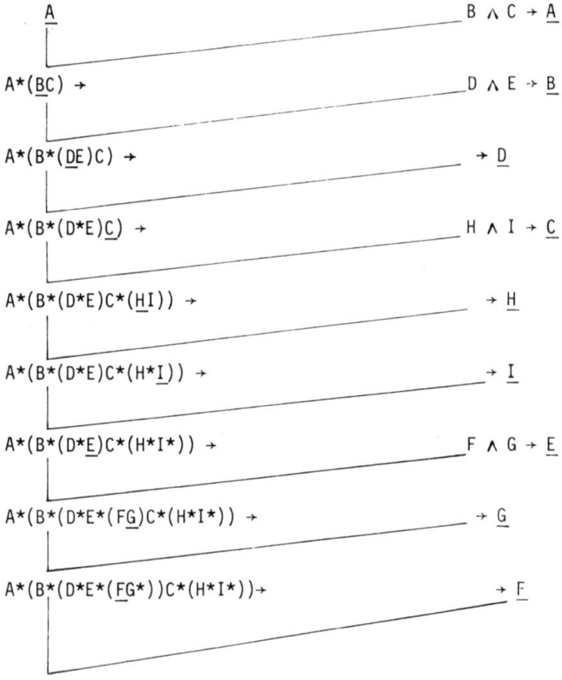

T-halt Statement: A*(B*(D*E*(F*G*))C*(H*I*)) →

Example A1. Typical Proof Graph Using Atomic Formula

Example A2.

The following example correlates the algorithm given with the Π-clauses in MRPPS 3.0. In the algorithm, replace atomic formula by a template. For example, the T-halt clause of example A2 is

$$(\alpha,x,y)*((\beta,x,y)*(\gamma,x,y)*)\rightarrow .$$

It becomes $A*(B*C*)\rightarrow$ when working with atomic formula. Actual implementation becomes a case of writing a routine to identify and scan a template rather than identifying and passing over an atomic formula. Since an entry in the reason block points to a reason clause, the substitution sets can be built as a template is added to a reason clause.

FINAL REASON BLOCK

1	1
→ A, B, C	
2	3
→ B, D, E	
3	5
D	
4	7
→ E, F, G	
5	9
F	
6	11
G	
7	13
→ C, H, I	
8	15
H	
9	17
I	

Figure A1. Reason Block for Atomic Formula

Reasons (Output from Natural Language Output Processor)

1. B ALSO C IMPLIES A
2. D ALSO E IMPLIES B
3. D
4. F ALSO G IMPLIES E
5. F
6. G
7. H ALSO I IMPLIES C
8. H
9. I

Query: ((α,x,y), {[COMPLETE]/α, [human]/x, [CSC 101]/y})

Proof Graph:

((α,x,y) → {[COMPLETE]/α, [human]/x, [CSC 101]/y})

((α,x,y) ∧ (β,x,y) → (γ,x,y) {[ENROLLED]/α, [HAS GRADE]/β, [COMPLETE]/γ, [human]/x, [course]/y})

((α,x,y)*((β,x,y)(γ,x,y)) → {[COMPLETE]/α, [ENROLLED]/β, [HAS GRADE]/γ, [human]/x, [CSC 101]/y})

→((α,x,y) {[ENROLLED]/α, [JIM,JOHN,MARY, PAT,BEV,HARRY]/x, [CSC 101]/y})

((α,x,y)*((β,x,y)*(γ,x,y)) → {[COMPLETE]/α, [ENROLLED]/β, [HAS GRADE]/γ, [JIM,JOHN,MARY,PAT,BEV,HARRY]/x, [CSC 101]/y})

→((α,x,y) {[HAS GRADE]/α, [JIM,JOHN,MARY, PAT,BEV,HARRY]/x, [CSC 101]/y})

((α,x,y)*((β,x,y)*(γ,x,y)*) → {[COMPLETE]/α, [ENROLLED]/β, [HAS GRADE]/γ, [JIM,MARY,PAT,HARRY]/x, [CSC 101]/y})

Figure A2. Proof Graph using Π-Clauses.

Answer: JIM AND MARY AND PAT AND HARRY HAVE COMPLETED CSC 101.

FINAL REASON BLOCK

1
→(α,x,y)(β,x,y)(γ,x,y)
2
(β,x,y)
3
(γ,x,y)

Figure A3 Reason Block Using Π-Clauses.

Reasons:

1. JIM AND MARY AND PAT AND HARRY ARE ENROLLED IN CSC 101 ALSO JIM AND MARY AND PAT AND HARRY HAVE GRADES IN CSC 101 IMPLIES JIM AND MARY AND PAT AND HARRY HAVE COMPLETED CSC 101.
2. JIM AND MARY AND PAT AND HARRY ARE ENROLLED IN CSC 101.
3. JIM AND MARY AND PAT AND HARRY HAVE GRADES IN CSC 101.

APPENDIX B

Natural Language Implementation

Pattern construction for a natural language sentence is described in Section four. The effort described here is the building of a sentence from the pattern and the Π-clause. The data base is input by the user interactively with MRPPS 3.0. If English or voice output is specified, the system asks for a pattern for each new predicate or function in the data base. A parser scans the pattern for syntactic correctness. Minor errors are corrected and a message is sent to the user. A pattern containing errors that cannot be corrected is rejected and the user is asked to input another pattern. Patterns which are accepted are stored and a pointer to the pattern is put in the dictionary entry for the predicate or function with which the pattern is associated.

Following the completion of the answer/reason extraction routine (Appendix A), the answer is printed followed by the reasons. One Π-clause is interpreted at a time. Each Π-clause is converted from the system core representation to the template-substitution set format described in Section two. First the template is scanned for functions. If a function is found, its pattern entry is found in the dictionary and is substituted into the template for the function name.

Each substitution set is scanned for the set associated with the predicate. The pattern for each value in the set - recall a predicate may have a finite number of values in a substitution set - is found in the dictionary and inserted into the set in place of the predicate value.

Next, each set in a substitution set, except the one for the predicate, is examined. If the set contains multiple values, each value is separated by an "AND".

The predicate pattern is scanned for special symbols. In an @n, n is the nth argument of the predicate, if found the substitution set value(s) for the nth argument is inserted in the pattern. If an @Sn is found and there is one value for the nth argument, the characters up to the next @Sn are left in the predicate pattern. An @Pn is analogous to @Sn but for arguments with multiple values. A # means to leave the characters up to the next # if the predicate is negated.

If the nth predicate argument is a function, the function pattern is evaluated the same as a predicate pattern. An n in a function pattern refers to the nth argument of the function. When the function pattern evaluation is complete, it is inserted in the proper argument position of the predicate pattern.

The sentence is now ready to be printed and/or vocalized. All the sentences for a substitution set are processed and output as described above. Succeeding substitution sets for a Π-clause are processed. The natural language translator returns to the system for another answer or reason.

An example in Section four is amplified showing the translation process. The Π-clause is:

$$((\alpha, f(x), y) \quad \{[L]/\alpha,\ [ZENN]/x,\ [AMERICAN]/y\}).$$

The predicate pattern is:

% @1 @S1IS@S1@P1ARE@P1 LISTED ON THE @2 STOCK EXCHANGE %.

The function pattern is:

% THE PARENT COMPAN@S1YS1@P1IES@P1 OF @1 %.

The following translation takes place.

1. Put the function pattern in the template.

   (α, % THE PARENT COMPAN@S1Y@S1@P1IES@P1 OF @1 % (x), y)

2. Put the predicate pattern in the substitution set.

   {[% @1 @S1IS@S1@P1ARE@P1 LISTED ON THE @2 STOCK EXCHANGE %]/α,
   [ZENN]/x, [AMERICAN]/y}

3. Process @1 which is a function.

   Process @1 in the function.

   (α, % THE PARENT COMPAN@S1Y@S1@P1IES@P1 OF ZENN %, y)

   Process @S1 in the function.

   (α, %THE PARENT COMPANY@P1IES@P1 OF ZENN %, y)

   Process @P1 in the function.

   (α, % THE PARENT COMPANY OF ZENN %, y)

   Put the function pattern in predicate pattern.

   {[% THE PARENT COMPANY OF ZENN @S1IS@S1 @P1ARE@P1 LISTED
   ON THE @2 STOCK EXCHANGE%]/α, [ZENN]/x, [AMERICAN]/y}

4. Process @2.

   {[% THE PARENT COMPANY OF ZENN @S1IS@S1 @P1ARE@P1 LISTED ON THE
   AMERICAN STOCK EXCHANGE %]/α, [ZENN]/x, [AMERICAN]/y}

5. Process @S1.

   {[% THE PARENT COMPANY OF ZENN IS @P1ARE@P1 LISTED ON THE
   AMERICAN STOCK EXCHANGE %]/α, [ZENN]/x, [AMERICAN]/y}

6. Process @P1.

   {[% THE PARENT COMPANY OF ZENN IS LISTED ON THE AMERICAN STOCK
   EXCHANGE%]/α, [ZENN]/x, [AMERICAN]/y}

7. Output the sentence.

   THE PARENT COMPANY OF ZENN IS LISTED ON THE AMERICAN STOCK EXCHANGE.

Algorithm B, which follows, formalizes the above description.

Algorithm B: Natural Language Output

Abbreviations used:

s.s. = substitution sets
s.s.(s) = substitution sets
s.s.v. = substitution set values for an argument

Input: Π-clause in system core format

Algorithm: Convert Π-clause into template followed by s.s.(s)

```
while functions exist in template do
    find pattern in dictionary
    put pattern in template in place of function name
end
x = number of s.s.(s)
m = 1
while m ≤ x do
    find s.s.v. for predicate in mth s.s.
    find pattern in dictionary
    put pattern in s.s. in place of s.s.v.
    m = m+1
end
call  SENTINIT (template)
m = 1
while m ≤ x do
    call EVALCL (template, mth s.s.)
    m = m+1
end
return                                      'return to system for next answer/
                                                reason'

Proc SENTINIT (template)                    'sentence  initialization'
x = number of relations in template
m = 1
while m ≤ x do
    if reason
        then if m ≠ 1
                 then reverse sign of relation
             end
        else reverse sign of relation
    end
    m = m+1
end
if reason
    then if x=1
                 then return                          'return template'
                 else append "IMPLIES" to template
                     move 1st relation to end of template
         end
```

```
end
return                                'return altered template which is now a
                                         sentence skeleton'

Proc EVALCL (template, s.s.)          'evaluate clause'
x = number of subsets in a s.s.
m = 1
while m ≤ x do
    if number of s.s.v. in mth subset > 1
        then separate elements by an "AND"
    end
    m = m+1
    call EVALSENT (template s.s.)
    return                                  'all sentences output for a s.s.'

Proc EVALSENT (template s.s.)               'evaluate sentence'
buffer = string of sentences built from number of predicate combinations in s.s.
x = number of sentences in buffer
m = 1
while m ≤ x do
    call EVALPRED (template, s.s., mth sentence)
    if English output specified
        then print mth sentence
    end
    if voice output specified
        then send mth sentence to voice output
    end
    m = m+1
end
return

Proc EVALPRED (template, s.s., sentence)      'evalutate predicate pattern'
x = number patterns in sentence
m = 1
while m ≤ x do
    while mth pattern contains @n do
        delete @n from pattern
        if argument is a function
             then evaluate function pattern
                 insert evaluation in predicate pattern
             else insert s.s.v. for nth argument
```

```
        end
    end
    while mth pattern contains @Sn do
        if nth argument is plural
            then delete @Sn and all info thru next @Sn
            else delete this @Sn and next @Sn
        end
    end
    while mth pattern contains @Pn do
        if nth argument is singular
            then delete @Pn and all info thru next @Pn
            else delete this @Pn and next @Pn
        end
    end
    while mth pattern contains # do
        if mth relation is negative
            then delete this # and next #
            else delete # and all info thru next #
        end
    end
    if m ≠ x
        then if pattern is for a reason
            then insert forward line reference
                if m ≠ x-1
                    then append "ALSO" to pattern
                end
            else append "AND" to pattern
        end
    end
    m = m+1
end
return                                   'sentence is ready for output'
```

APPENDIX C

Voice Productions

The productions, listed alphabetically, on the following pages are those used by the MRPPS 3.0 System to translate English into IPA. The meanings of the special symbols are:

: one or more vowels

: : zero or more consonants

Δ : one consonant

+ : E, I, or Y

% : a suffix (E, ER, ES, ED, ELY, ING)

␣ : space (no symbol)

& : S, C, G, Z, X, J, CH, SH

; : T, R, S, D, L, Z, N, J, TH, SH

* : one or more consonants

$: consonant followed by E or I

· : B, D, V, G, J, L, M, N, R, W, Z

φ : no translation, silent translation

There is an exception to the definition of a cluster as explained in Section five. In the A, I, S, U, and Y productions, some sub-clusters are repeated either by repetition or by having multiple right (brother) entry links. The purpose is to avoid cluster duplication. A repeated cluster is not internally repeated but for writing convenience is repeated in the productions. Multiple references to some productions are required to retain the original NRL ordering in a clustered environment.

The exception to the cluster definition is that all productions in a cluster are not always a subset of the header production. For example, reference the A productions. The ␣[ARE]␣ and ␣[AR]O cluster is referenced by three headers. The ␣[AR]O production is not a subset of either ␣:[A]Δ+␣ or [A]Δ%. It is a subset of the [AR] and [AR]# productions. Including the ␣[AR]O production in a cluster such that it is not a subset of the header does not affect the integrity of the translation. It does mean that an extra production match is performed.

A Productions

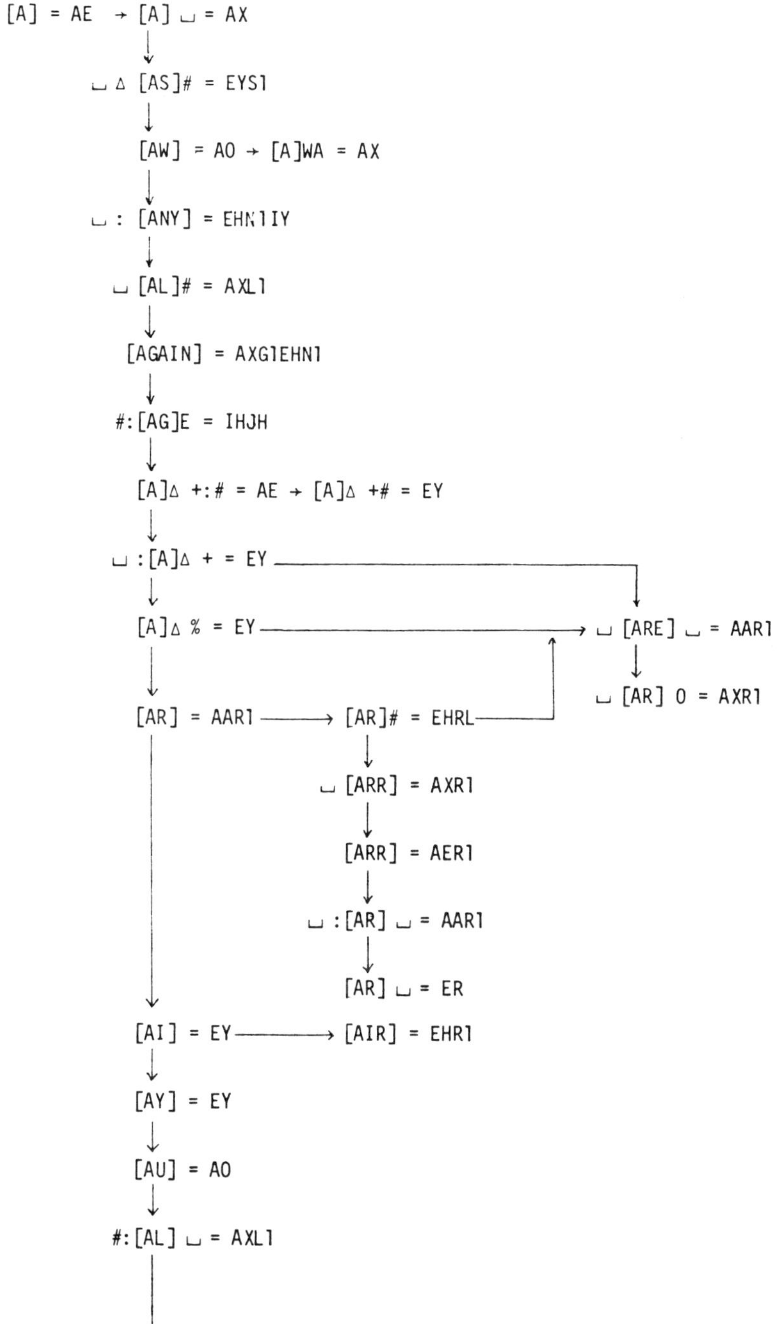

```
  ↓
[AL] Δ  =  AOL1 ——→ #: [ALLY] = AXL1IY
  |                   ↓
  |                 #:[ALS] ⌴ = AXL1Z1
  |                   ↓
  |                  [ALK] = AOK1
  ↓
[ABLE] = AXB1AXL1 → ⌴:[ABLE] = EYB1AXL1
  ↓
[ANG]+ = EYN1JH
```

B Productions

```
[B] = B1 → ⌴ [BE]Δ # = B1IH
              ↓
             [BEING] - B1IYIHNX
              ↓
           ⌴ [BOTH] - B1OWTH
              ↓
           ⌴ [BUS]# = B1IHZ1
              ↓
             [BUIL] - B1IHL1
```

C Productions

```
[C] = K1 → [CH] = CH ——→  ⌴ [CH]   = K1
            |                 ↓
            |            Δ E[CH] = K1
            ↓
           [C]+ = S1 ——→ ⌴ S[CI]# = S1AY
            |                ↓
            |               [CI]A = SH
            |                ↓
            |               [CI]O = SH
            |                ↓
            ↓               [CI]EN = SH
           [CK] = K1
            ↓
           [COM]% = K1AHM1
```

D Productions

[D] = D1 ⟶ # : [DED] ␣ = D1IHD1
↓
·E[D] ␣ = D1
↓
Δ:E[D] ␣ = D1
↓
␣ [DE]Δ # = D1IH
↓
␣ [DO] ␣ = D1UW
↓
␣ [DOES] = D1AHZ1
↓
␣ [DOING] = D1UWIHNX
↓
␣ [DOW] = D1AW
↓
[DU]A = JHUW

E Productions

[E] = EH ⟶ # : [E] ␣ = φ
↓
Δ :[E] ␣ = φ
↓
␣ :[E] ␣ = IY
↓
:[E]D ␣ = φ ⟶ #[ED] ␣ = D1
↓
[EV]ER = EHV1
↓
[E] Δ % = IY
↓
[ER] = ER → [ER]# = EHR1 → [ERI] = EHR1IH → [ERI]# = IYR1IY
(below [ERI] = EHR1IH) ↓ #:[ER]# = ER
↓
␣ [EVEN] = IYV1EHN1
↓
[EW] = Y1UW ⟶ #:[E]W = φ
↓ (below [EW] = Y1UW) ↓ (below #:[E]W = φ)

;[EW] = UW

[E]O = IY

#:[E]S ⊔ = φ ⟶ #:&[ES]= IHZ1

#:[ELY] ⊔ = L1IY

#:[EMENT] = M1EHN1T1

[EFUL] = F1UHL1

[EE] = IY

[EA] = IY ⟶ [EARN] = ERN1

⊔ [EAR] Δ = ER

[EAD] = EHD1

#:[EA] ⊔ = IYAX

[EA]SU = EH

[EI] = IY ⟶ [EIGH] = EY

[EY] = IY ⟶ ⊔ [EYE] = AY

[EY] = Y1UW

F Productions

[F] = FL ⟶ [FUL] = F1UHL1

G Productions

[G] = G1 → [GG] = G1 → SU[GGES] = G1HJGHS1

↓

∟ #B[G] = G1

↓

[G]+ = JH → [GIV] = G1IHV1

↓

∟ [G]IΔ = G1

↓

[GE]T = G1EH

↓

[GREAT] = G1R1EYT1

↓

#[GH] = φ

H Productions

[H] = φ → [H]# = HH → ∟ [HAV] = HHAEV1

↓

∟ [HERE] = HHIYR

↓

∟ [HOUR] = AWER

↓

[HOW] = HHAW

I Productions

[I] = IH → ∟ [IN] = IHN1

↓

∟ [I] ∟ = AY

↓

[IN]D = AYN1

↓

[I]% = IY → [IER] = IYER

↓

[IE] = IY → [IER] = IYER

↓

#:R[IED] ∟ = IYD1

↓

[IED] ␣ = AYD1

[IEN] = IYEHN1

[IE]T = AYEN

␣ :[I]% = AY

[IZ]% = AYZ1

[IS]% = AYZ1

[I]D% = AY

[I]T% = AY

[I] Δ + = AY ⟶ [I] Δ +: # = IH

+Δ [I]Δ+ = IH

#Δ : [I]Δ+ = IH

[IR] = ER

[IGH] = AY

[ILD] = AYL1D1

[IGN] ␣ = AYN1

[IGN] Δ = AYN1

[IGN]% = AYN1

[IQUE] = IYK1

J Productions

[J] = JH

K Productions

[K] = K1 ⟶ [K]N = φ

L Productions

[L] = LL ⟶ [LO]C# = L1OW
↓
L[L] = φ
↓
#Δ:[L]% = AXL1
↓
[LEAD] = L1IYD1

M Productions

[M] = M1 ⟶ [MOV] = M1UWV1

N Productions

[N] = N1 ⟶ [NG] = NX ⟶ [NG]# = NXG1 ⟶ E[NG]+ = N1JH

[NG] = NX ↓ [NK] = NXK1 ↓ ␣[NOW] = N1AW

[NG]# = NXG1 ↓ [NGL]% = NXG1AXL1 ↓ [NG]R = NXG1

O Productions

[O] = AA ⟶ [OF] = AXV1
↓
[OR] = AOR1 ⟶ [OROUGH] = EROW ↓ #:[OR] = ER ↓ #:[ORS] = ERZ1
↓
␣[ONE] = W1AHN1
↓
[OW] = OW
↓

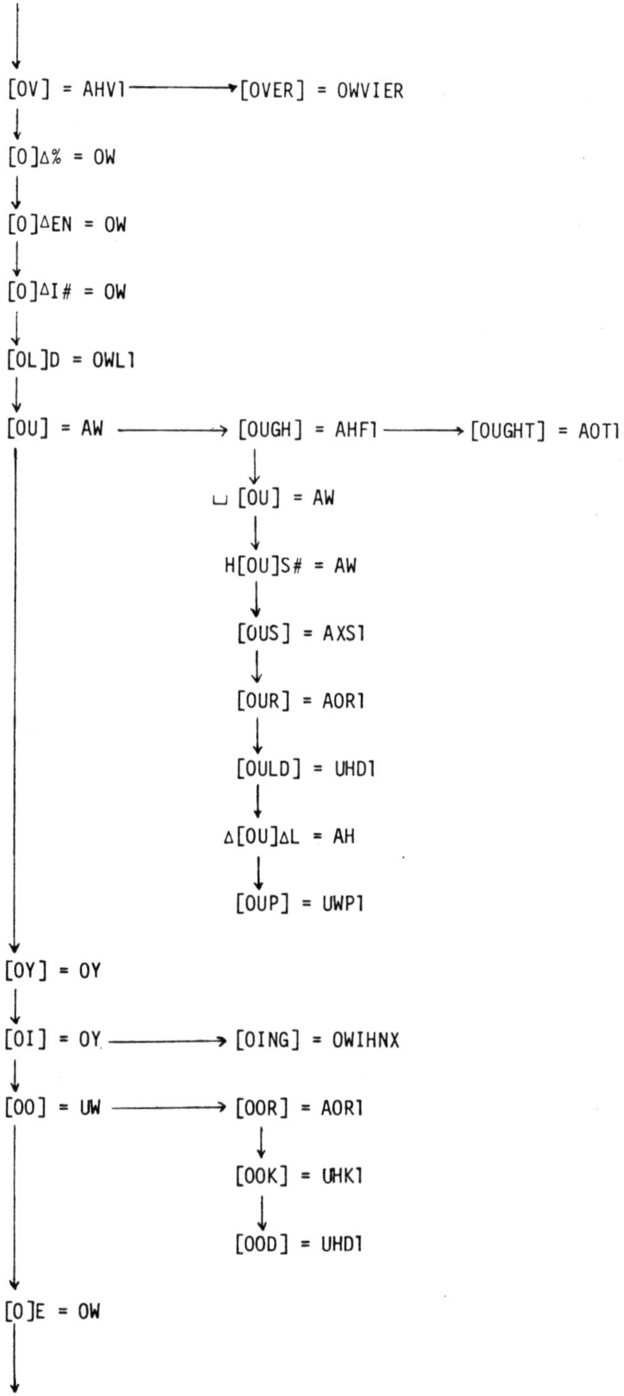
[OV] = AHV1
[OVER] = OWVIER
[O]Δ% = OW
[O]ΔEN = OW
[O]ΔI# = OW
[OL]D = OWL1
[OU] = AW
[OUGH] = AHF1
[OUGHT] = AOT1
␣ [OU] = AW
H[OU]S# = AW
[OUS] = AXS1
[OUR] = AOR1
[OULD] = UHD1
Δ[OU]ΔL = AH
[OUP] = UWP1
[OY] = OY
[OI] = OY
[OING] = OWIHNX
[OO] = UW
[OOR] = AOR1
[OOK] = UHK1
[OOD] = UHD1
[O]E = OW

↓

[O] ␣ = OW

↓

[OA] = OW

↓

␣ [ONLY] = OWN1L1IY

↓

␣ [ONCE] = W1AHN1S1

↓

[ON'T]= OWN1T1

↓

C[O]N = AA

↓

[O]NG = AO

↓

␣ Δ:[O]N = AH

↓

I[ON] = AXN1

↓

#:[ON] ␣ = AXN1

↓

#Δ[ON] = AXN1

↓

[O]ST ␣ = OW

↓

[OF]Δ = AOF1

↓

[OTHER] = AHDHER

↓

[OSS] ␣ = AOS1

↓

#Δ:[OM] = AHM1

P Productions

[P] = P1 → [PH] = F1

→ [PEOP] = P1IYP1

→ [POW] = P1AW

→ [PUT] = P1UHT1

Q Productions

[Q] = K1 → [QU] = K1W1 → [QUAR] = K1W1AOR1

R Productions

[R] = R1 → ⎵ [RE]Δ# = R1IY

S Productions

[S] = S1 → [SH] = SH

→ [SOME] = S1AHM1

→ [SUR]# = SHER → #[SION] = ZHAXN1

→ #[S]# = Z1 → #[SION] = ZHAXN1

→ #[SUR]# = ZHER

→ #[SU]# = ZHUW

→ #[SED] ⎵ = Z1D1

→ [SAID] = S1EHD1

→ Δ[SION] = SHAXN1

→ [S]S = φ → #[SSU]# = SHUW

→ ·[S] = Z1

→

↓

#:·E[S] = Z1

↓

#Δ:##[S] = Z1

↓

#Δ:#[S] = S1

↓

␣ [S] = S1

↓

␣ :#[S] = Z1

↓

␣ [SCH] = S1K1

↓

[S]C+ = φ

↓

#[SM] = Z1M1

↓

#[SN]' = Z1AXN1

T Productions

[T] = T1 → [TO] = T1UW

|

[TH] = TH → ␣ [THE] = DHAX

↓

[THAT] = DHAET1

↓

␣ [THIS] = DHIHS1

↓

␣ [THEY] = DHEY

↓

␣ [THERE] = DHEHR1

↓

[THER] = DHER

↓

[THEIR] = DHEHR1

↓

␣ [THAN] = DHAEN1

↓

␣ [THEM] = DHEHM1

[THESE] = DHIYZ1

␣ [THEN] = DHEHN1

[THROUGH] = THR1UW

[THOSE] = DHOWZ1

[THOUGH] = DHOW

␣ [THUS] = DHAHS1

#:[TED] = T1IHD1

S[TI]#N = CH

[TI]O = SH

[TI]A = SH

[TIEN] = SHAXN1

[TUR]# = CHER

[TU]A = CHUW

␣ [TWO] = T1UW

U Productions

[U] = Y1UW → ⊔ [UN] = AHN1 → ⊔ [UN]I = Y1UWN1

↓

⊔ [UPON] = AXP1AON1

↓

[UR] = ER → [UR]# = Y1UHR1 → ;[UR]# = UHR1

↓ (from ;[UR]# = UHR1)

#N[U] = Y1UW

↓ (from [UR] = ER)

[U] Δ = AH

↓

[U] ΔΔ = AH

↓

[UY] = AY

↓

⊔ G[U]% = φ

↓

G[U]# = W1 → ⊔ G[U]# = φ

↓

;[U] = UW → ;[UR]# = UHR1

↓ (from ;[UR]# = UHR1)

#N[U] = Y1UW

V Productions

[V] = V1 → [VIEW] = V1Y1UW

W Productions

[W] = W1 → ⊔ [WERE] = W1ER

↓

[WA]S = W1AA

↓

[WA]T = W1AA

↓

[WH] = WH → [WHERE] = WHEHR1

↓ (from [WHERE] = WHEHR1)

[WHAT] = WHAAT1

↓

[WHOL] = HHOWL1

↓

[WHO] = HHUW

↓ (from [WH] = WH)

[WAR] = W1AOR1

↓

[WOR]Δ = W1ER

↓

[WR] = R1

X Productions

[X] = K1S1

Y Productions

```
[Y] = IH ——→ [YOUNG] = Y1AHNX
               ↓
             ⊔[Y] = Y1 ————————→ [YOU] = Y1UW
               ↓                   ↓
               ↓                 [YES] = Y1EHS1
               ↓
          #△:[Y] = IY
               ↓
          #△:[Y]I = IY
               ↓
          ⊔ :[Y] □ = AY
               ↓
          ⊔ :[Y]# = AY ————————→ [YOU] = Y1UW
               ↓                   ↓
               ↓                 [YES] = Y1EHS1
               ↓
          ⊔ :[Y]△# = AY ———————→ :[Y]△+:# = IH
```

Z Production

[Z] = Z1

A LOGIC-ORIENTED APPROACH TO AUTOMATIC TEXT UNDERSTANDING

by

Christopher U. Habel, Claus-Rainer Rollinger,
Arno Schmidt, Hans-Jochen Schneider,

Technical University of Berlin

This paper describes research done in the project "Automatische Erstellung semantischer Netze" (Automatic construction of semantic networks) at the "Institut für Angewandte Informatik" of the Technical University of Berlin. The project is supported by the Ministry for Science and Technology (BMFT) of the Federal Republik of Germany under Contract Number PT 131.03.

Abstract
The BEAST-System (Berlin Automatic Semantic-Oriented Translation) is a system for mapping natural language expressions into a semantic representation.
The assignment of meaning, i.e. the translation from natural language (a logical language with operators) is performed step by step through intermediate levels of languages.
In the paper the subcomponents of the BEAST-system and its underlying principles are described. Some applications in the areas of natural language based information systems and computer-aided translation are mentioned.

1. Introduction

During the last two decades many approaches towards natural language understanding systems have been pursued by computer and information scientists using different methods for different task-settings. On the one hand theoretical interests have priority. Especially parts of artificial intelligence as well as computational linguistics are concerned with the principle of human language understanding[1] and simulation of human behaviour[2].

On the other hand parallel to the nearly classical problem of machine translation the interest in understanding natural language texts is steadily rising, especially in the field of user-oriented information systems. In these systems natural language is used as a means for man-machine communication. It is viewed as a tool which diminishes the conceptual distance of the casual user (Codd 1974, Schmidt/Schneider 1978).

Intelligent processing, i.e. "understanding" of natural language texts, causes a semantic representation of the text although this is not always given in an explicit form[3]. It is obvious

[1] Wilks (1974) claimed the algorithmic realization of every linguistic theory by an appropriate system. The algorithmization of a linguistic theory within the scope of natural language processing systems cannot prove this theory, but a successful implementation could be considered as an argument for the related theory.

[2] The research by the group of Norman and Rumelhart could be seen in this context.

[3] See chapter 2.1 in which the problem of the assignment of meaning and the semantic representation is treated in more detail.

that the two directions of the research in this area, the theory and the application-oriented ones, do not necessarily "talk at cross-purposes" because they influence each other in many aspects. The different task-setting should not be considered to define opposite positions. They are far more a spectrum within the application-theory-continuum.

The development from theory to practice - cf. the implementation of the GUS-system (Bobrow et al. 1977) and the history of 'frame-theory' from Minsky (1975) up to Bobrow/Winograd (1977) - can be denoted as a 'change in the objectives'.

Most text understanding systems reduce texts to sentences because of the extreme difficulty and complexity of the problem of understanding natural language.[1] If this idealization has been performed it is necessary to take care of a later extension to real texts so that a new conception of the whole system could be avoided. This problem, however, has to be considered already when sentences are to be treated, because many of the difficulties of text understanding also occur in sentences, e.g. the problem of reference within one sentence (cf. Charniak 1977a,b).

As the term "understanding" of natural language (by machine) has only been used intuitively, we want to give our interpretations of it.[2] For our research it is sufficient to consider a more behaviouristic model of natural language (cf. figure). Here a natural language sentence serves as "stimulus". The system "understands" a natural language input when the system's response

[1]The system presented in this paper also deals with the understanding of natural language sentences.

[2]The scientific terms "understanding", "human intelligence", "artificial intelligence" or "meaning" shall not be extended by a further contribution. We do not want to revive the debate on "artificial intelligence". This has already been done rather exhaustively by Weizenbaum (1976) and Raphael (1976) and can be traced back to Turing (1950). Furthermore, various philosophical considerations shall be disregarded in this paper. (See also 2.1.)

Speaker Hearer

S ⟶ r ⟶ s ⟶ R

Figure 1: Behaviouristic Model of Communication (according to Bloomfield 1939)

S - Stimulus	R - Response
s - linguistic stimulus	r - linguistic response

(The speaker 'reacts' to a stimulus by a linguistic response. This response is a linguistic stimulus for the hearer: "Here r ⟶ s denotes the act of language" (p.15).)

is adequate in a well-defined sense.[1] This means that the language understanding system should react to the stimulus in a reasonable and adequate manner[2] which must be acceptable to the user. This can be the translation of the input into another language as well as the answer to a query or the transport of blocks by a hand-eye machine (cf. Winograd 1972, 1973).

---

[1] i.e. that the criteria for the test whether the system has reacted properly have to be described very precisely.

[2] It is obvious that the problem of clearing up the meaning of "meaning" has been shifted to the problem of clearing up the term "adequate reaction". By this, however, a precise definition of an experiment to show understanding has become possible.

2. Theoretical-methodological remarks

2.1. The assignment of meaning as translation

The language as a tool for the communication between speaker and hearer (i.e. the participants of a simple communication process) makes it necessary that both can assign a meaning to sentences of their (common) language. The discussion about the properties of the term "meaning", i.e. about the meaning of "meaning" is a central point in philosophy and linguistics. So it is not astonishing that "artificial intelligence" joins in the discussion, e.g. the various discussions about different methods for the representation of knowledge. Especially the declarative-procedural controversy (Winograd 1975) is to be considered in this context.

For our purpose a sufficient explanation of the term "meaning" is possible by using a semantic representation language (SRL).

We want to give the following definition[1]: meanings of natural language expressions are well-formed expressions of a semantic representation language.

Hence the assignment of meaning is a mapping from the natural language into the semantic representation language:

$$t : NL \longrightarrow SRL$$

NL = natural language SRL = semantic representation language

Figure 2: The assignment of meaning

---

[1] This definition does not (!) give an exact explanation of the term "meaning" nor does the explanation for the term "understanding" (in 1.). The "equalization" of 'meaning' and 'expression of SRL', however, is sufficient for our further considerations and research.

Figure 2 schematizes - more or less - most of the theories of linguistic semantics: A generative grammar (more precisely: a generative transformational grammar of Chomsky type) can be characterized by the following figure:

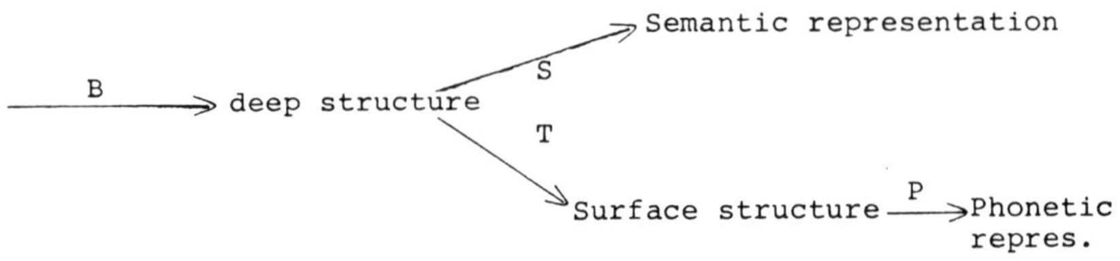

Figure 3: The Chomsky-Model of grammar[1]
(Chomsky 1967)

The mapping (translation) t in figure 2 is also contained in Chomsky's grammatical concept by the following

$$t := T^{-1} \circ S$$ [2].

In the Montague Grammar the explicit relation between sentences of natural language and expressions of the semantic representation language[3] is given by the parallelism of syntactic and semantic rules (cf. Partee 1975).

Both concepts (Chomsky's and Montague's) have in common a generative point of view, the generation resp. the description of

---

[1] B = base, S = semantic interpretation
T = (syntactical) transformational component
P = phonological transformations

[2] T^{-1} is the inverse relation of T. If T is not invertible, then T^{-1} is no (!) mapping and neither is t. The problem of ambiguity, i.e. ambiguity of the assignment of meaning, is treated in chapter 2.2.

[3] Montague uses a language of intensional logic.

a set of sentences by a formal apparatus, the grammar. They do not take into consideration the development of a mechanism creating the relation between a sentence and its meaning. Just this is the main topic of the natural generative grammar (NGG) of Bartsch/Vennemann (1972)[1]. They claim the explicit description of a transformational process transforming the surface strings into a semantic representation.

Let s be a sentence of a natural language NL and t(s) its image in the representation language, then the assignment of meaning t is required to be able to infer the conditions of truth and the mode of application of s from t(s). This is compatible with the most important theories of semantics within linguistics and philosophy.

The above-mentioned demands correspond to those of an adequate translation from one language into another. This concerns natural as well as formal languages. As t is a mapping between two languages, t can be called a translation.

Another problem to be considered concerns the mapping

$$t_2 : SRL \longrightarrow NL .$$

t_2 assigns natural language equivalents to expressions of the semantic representation language. The relation between t and t_2 reflects the relation of the encoding and perception mechanism (resp. process). Up to now it is not clear whether the encoding and perception mechanism are so closely related to each other that $t_2 = t^{-1}$ is valid.

2.2. Ambiguity and precisification

The main problem of the assignment of meaning, i.e. the translation into a semantic representation, is to ensure the mapping

---

[1] A valuation of NGG and a comparison to other concepts of grammar are given in Habel/Kanngießer 1977. The BEAST-system (cf. chapter 3) largely follows the principles of NGG. (cf. Habel/Schmidt/Schweppe 1977a, 1978).

property of t. That is to determine one definite semantic representation t(s) for natural language sentences s.

Hence a partial solution to the problem of ambiguity of natural language has to be found. The most simply one is[1] to perform the mapping t by means of the composition of two relations, where the definite selection (this is the second relation) ensures the mapping-property of t:

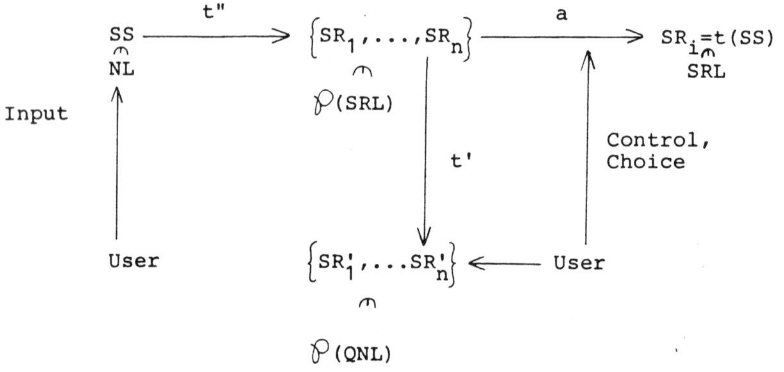

Figure 4: A more precise presentation of the problem of assigning a meaning

For the user's natural language input a set of possible semantic representations SR_1 ... SR_n is generated by an assignment of meaning t" (this relation need not be definite),

$$t" : NL \longrightarrow \wp(SRL)$$

i.e. the set of semantic representations:

---

[1] cf. Habel/Schmidt/Schweppe 1977a, 1978. In these papers a slightly deviant presentation is given.

$\{SR_1, \ldots, SR_n\}$ is assigned to the surface structure SS $\in$ NL.
A mapping (of choice)

$$a: \quad \wp(SRL) \longrightarrow SRL$$

selects <u>exactly one</u> semantic representation a(t"(SS)) from the set $\{SR_1, \ldots, SR_n\}$ = t"(SS).

Hence a definite assignment of meaning is defined by

$$t: = t'' \circ a \quad .$$

Within the BEAST-System the mapping of choice a is performed by the user. In this we consider the user's intention not to be ambiguous. This assumption corresponds to the one which is usually assumed when talking of a normal man-to-man communication.

It is often the case that the other meanings are considered by the speaker to be irrelevant with respect to the situative or textual context. The communication is successful if the assignment of meaning by the hearer has been performed properly. The model of communication (Fig. 1) can be extended in the following way:

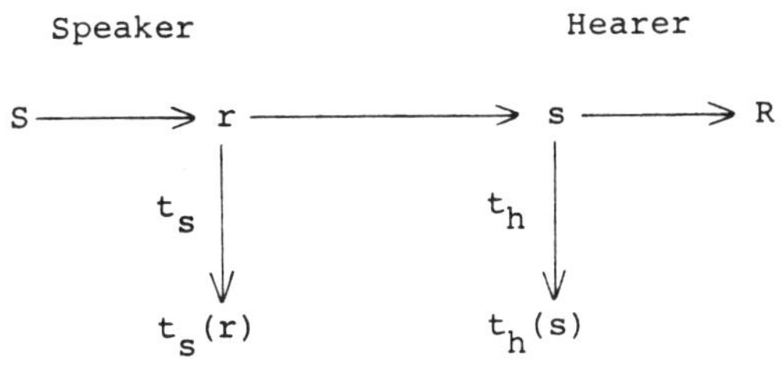

t_s: the assignment of meaning by the speaker
t_h: the assignment of meaning by the hearer

Figure 5: Model of communication with respect to the intentions of the speaker and the hearer.

With his utterance r (cf. chapter 1) the speaker intends to express the meaning of $t_s(r)$. The hearer interprets the same utterance s(=r) by his assignment of meaning $t_h(s)$. Only if $t_s(r)$ and $t_h(s)$ largely correspond to each other (a complete identity can hardly be assumed), then the communication is successful. Especially ambiguous utterances allow different interpretations, i.e. the results of t_s and t_h are different[1].

Analogous to the case of ambiguity this can occur within implicite precisifications. Normally human communication does not need a complete precisification, because of sufficient information gained from the context. Thus, in general, a where-question (cf. the examples of chapter 3) is not to be seen as the question for a directive but for a precise class of objects of directives, e.g. towns, countries etc. Often in this case the assignment of meaning (via intention) t_s and t_h is deviant as well. In our system both cases are handled by the same method. The user is included into the process of disambiguation. He selects one out of several possible alternative interpretations which might be the result of various precisifications. The system performs the representation of the meaning automatically, if necessary with an additional precisification. As the user shall be able to select the intended semantic representation being assigned to his input, he is to interpret and to "understand" it. Of course he will not be able to have a good command of the semantic representation language, so the BEAST-system transforms the definite and precise semantic representations SR_1, ... ,SR_n into a definite and precise form of the natural language (mapping t' of figure 4).

---

[1] In man-man communication the resulting misunderstandings are cleared up by a clarification dialog (cf. chapters 3.1 resp. 3.4.4) too.

[2] This is a subset of the natural language (cf. chapter 2.3.3.). Its expressions consist of a pattern-oriented translation from logical expressions into fixed syntagmas of the natural language. Hence (because of its high degree of unnaturalness) it seems to be better if the target language of the re-translation t' is called a "quasi-natural language" (QNL).

The user selects one of the successively given alternatives, i.e. the one with the intended semantic representation, which will be performed within the further process of the system (cf. 2.4, 3.1 and 4.1).

2.3. The principle of minimal information

Every natural language expression (sentence or text) is redundant at a varying degree. Not all aspects of an utterance are of the same relevance for the assignment of meaning, i.e. not all morphems of a sentence are necessary for the recovery of the semantic (or the pragmatic) information. This can be shown with the German sentence "Ich spreche" (I speak). The information about the grammatical subject of the sentence is encoded twice, explicitly in the pronoun "ich" (I) and implicitly in the inflecting verb by the suffix "-e". The congruence between pronoun and suffix of the verb is not examined by BEAST because this is not necessary for the recovery of the meaning. This attempt allows the processing of deviant utterances, e.g. the incorrect sentence "Du sprechen." and the correct one "Du sprichst." (You speak) are assigned to the same meaning. This is just the meaning being assigned by a native speaker to a deviant utterance of this kind.[1]

---

[1] We cannot discuss this very interesting aspect any more thoroughly. But we want to indicate that BEAST is more effective than the renowned semantic theories in this point, namely the assignment of meaning for "deviant utterances" as claimed by Bar-Hillel as early as in 1967. The possibility to process syntactically incorrect sentences of natural language is not only a very interesting capability of the system from the linguistic point of view. More than this, it allows the communication with the information system on the level of a formatted language (cf. chapter 4.1.).

The above-mentioned kind of processing can be characterized by the "principle of minimal information". The principle means that the process of translation (from natural language into the semantic representation language) is tried out with some basic information[1] (i.e. with minimal information). Only if a further processing is not possible, then the implicitly encoded information has to be recovered or derived.

Such a principle seems to be advantageous because the recovery of syntactic information being done by a native speaker very instantaneously can only be performed by machine with the aid of relatively complex and inefficient algorithms. So we decided only to use some "key-information".

The application and advantages of the principle within the BEAST-system will become clearer in the description of the architecture of the system and its components.

2.4. On the interpretation of semantic representations

The BEAST-system represents an algorithmization of the mapping t (cf. fig. 2). However, the generation of semantic representations is not the sole task of an information system. Semantic representations are only an intermediate level within the entire processing, the interface between the primary and the secondary processing (Petöfi 1977).

In the case of our system BEAST the algorithmization of t, realizes the primary processing of natural language, whereas the retrieval or input of information to the knowledge-base is called the secondary processing.[2]

---

[1]Within the system we have to define what is meant by basic information. We have in mind a hierarchy with respect to the "informational content". In the case of the above-mentioned examples we define the information given by the pronouns as basic information.

[2]cf. the environment of BEAST being described in chapter 3.1. as well as its applications.

The secondary processing corresponds to an interpretation of the semantic representation. We call the interpretation correct or adequate if the system behaves in a manner similar to a human receiver. This means, if it deals with a query it should give the appropriate answer or if it deals with the input of information it should add the semantic information to its knowledge base.

If we consider the knowledge of the system as a description of a part of the real world, then the notation "world of a system" makes sense because this part is just the world of the system.[1]

Considering the simple case of the yes-no question "Reist Hans nach Erlangen?" (Does Hans travel to Erlangen?) it is the task of the system to match the proposition "Hans reist nach Erlangen." (Hans travels to Erlangen) against the knowledge base, i.e. to test if the information is known to the system.[2]

Figure 2 describing the primary processing of natural language can be extended to a diagram which includes the secondary processing as well:

$$NL \xrightarrow{\ t\ } SRL \xrightarrow{\ i\ } \wp(PW)$$

Figure 6: Diagram of model-theoretic semantics

(this diagram has also been used in Habel/Schmidt/Schweppe 1977a, 1978 for the description of "understanding" in the field of language-understanding systems).

The mapping i (= interpretation) corresponds to the interpretation mapping of "possible worlds semantics" (cf. Hintikka 1969, Kripke 1972, Partee 1975). For the field of question answering systems (cf. also Belnap/Steel 1976) the effect of the interpretation i has already been described above. The correspondence to

---

[1] We explain the world of discourse which the examples of this paper refer to in chapter 3.2.

[2] Here we disregard the inferential capabilities of the system. If we consider the proposition to be the input to the system, then it would be added to the knowledge base and the system enlarges its knowledge.

the model-theoretic semantics becomes obvious if we consider the following reflections:

The question "Does Hans travel to Erlangen?" will be answered "Yes" if and only if the corresponding proposition "Hans travels to Erlangen." is true, i.e. if the interpretation mapping assigns the truth value "true" to the proposition in question, or, vice versa, if and only if the world of the system belongs to those worlds where the proposition in question is true. This is the way in which figure 6 should be understood. Mapping i is the mapping specifying the worlds in which the propositions in question are true.

Most information systems are dealing with only one world of discourse (and so do most systems of artificial intelligence). According to this the semantic representation languages in use are able to describe only one world.

The complexity of natural languages is based to a large extent on the possibility of talking about several possible worlds. This is the reason for the application of a sufficiently powerful representation language (e.g. MSRL, cf. 3.3.2).

Expressions of this semantic representation language (SRL) are processed by SIREN (cf. 3.1.3). The possible worlds being referred to within the expressions of SRL are simulated by the one real world of the system.

3. The BEAST-System

3.1. The system's architecture and its environment

3.1.1. BACON

The reflections mentioned in chapter 2 were the basis for the concept of the experimental, intelligent question-answering system BACON (Berlin Automatic Construction of Semantic Networks). The system's architecture corresponds to the schematization of figure 6:

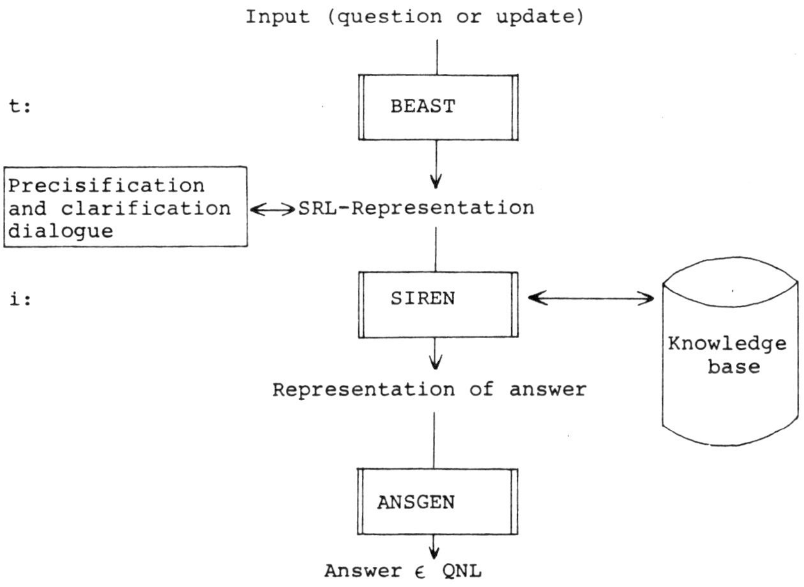

Figure 7a: Architecture of the Question-Answering System BACON

In the center of this paper stands the "language-understanding" component BEAST (cf. 3.1.2, 3.3 and 3.4). The component which performs the interpretation (SIREN) can only be outlined in a rough draft (cf. 3.1.3).

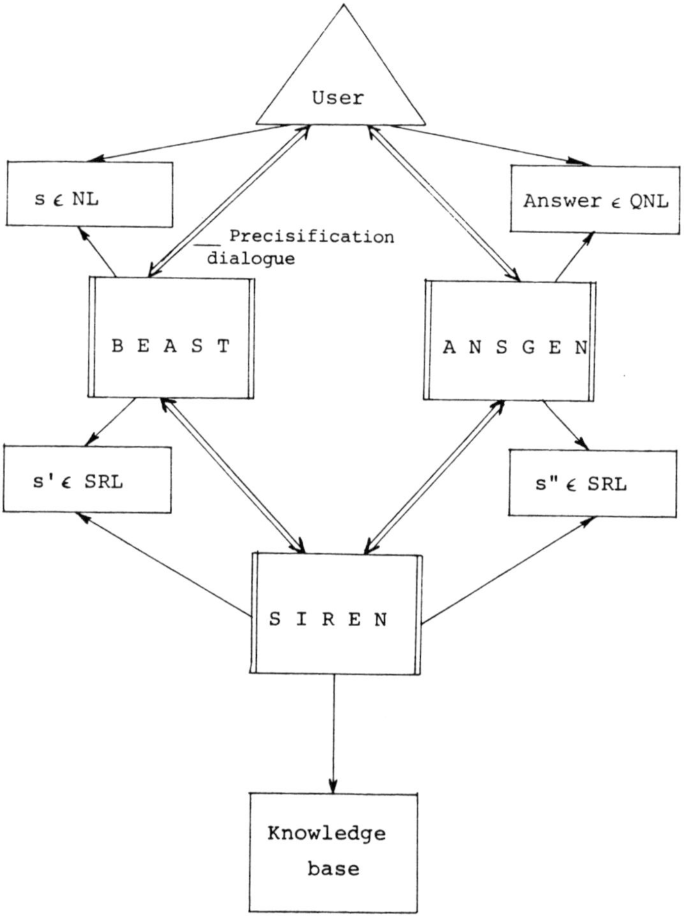

Figure 7b: Architecture of the Question-Answering System BACON

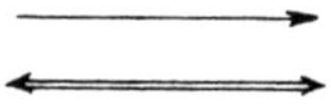

$\hat{=}$ read or write modus

$\hat{=}$ communicates with.

3.1.2. BEAST - an overview

BEAST (Berlin Automatic Semantic-oriented Translation) is the "language-understanding" component of the BACON-System. BEAST performs the translation of expressions of natural language into the semantic representation language. Thus BEAST is an algorithmization of the mapping t (cf. fig. 2). Because of the problems within the scope of precisification and desambiguation (cf. 2.2.) the system first[1] produces a set of alternative, semantic representations offered to the user for the sake of selection (control). This means that the system works as has been stressed in fig. 4.

The mapping t[2] is performed within BEAST by a composition of partial mappings (cf. 3.4) which map the surface string step by step through intermediate strings (cf. 3.3) into its semantic representation.

$$\mathrm{NL} \xrightarrow{\mathrm{lex}} \mathrm{LOL} \xrightarrow{\mathrm{paz}} \mathrm{SOSRL} \xrightarrow{\mathrm{trans}} \mathrm{SRL}$$

Figure 8: The levels of intermediate languages

All mappings in the diagram of figure 8 are partial.

---

[1] The alternatives are not generated in parallel but successively (cf. 3.4.2). This kind of processing has the advantage that certain processes need not be performed when the user has already selected one of the alternatives.

[2] With respect to the diagram of figure 4 it is the mapping t". But it should be mentioned that t" is not very different from t if the image is unique (i.e. the cardinality of the set of semantic representations is one). In this case a selection is not necessary. That is why we talk in either case of the mapping t although there might have been produced several alternatives.

Ambiguities of these mappings which might occur will result in ambiguities of the mapping t. Besides this it cannot be excluded that the algorithms which perform the mappings may work incorrectly. This means that the result of the "attempt to assign a meaning to the surface string" is not an expression of the formally defined semantic representation language SRL. This phenomenon is comparable to the over-capacity of generative grammars. This is why the mapping t has to be defined as the restriction of the composition of mappings on to the origin of SRL under this composition as follows:

$$t: = \text{trans} \circ \text{paz} \circ \text{lex} \Big|_{(\text{trans} \circ \text{paz} \circ \text{lex})^{-1} (\text{SRL})}$$

The translation of a sentence of natural language into an interpretable semantic representation is performed according to the partition of the mapping t into partial mappings. The mappings lex, paz, trans are realized by corresponding partial components of the entire system (cf. 3.4) such that the following architecture of the system emerges.

By means of the components lex, paz and trans a list of alternative expressions of SRL emerges which is controlled by the user in accordance with the schema of figure 4. By means of a clarification dialog the users are successively offered the various attemps of the system to assign a meaning to the surface string in the form of a quasi-natural paraphrase (cf. 3.3.3 and 3.4.4). The user selects the semantic representation which should be interpreted (or translated - cf. 4.1) within the secondary processing of natural language. In our opinion, this method of including the user into the natural language processing offers a way of developing and implementing effective procedures for highly complex and complicated applications.

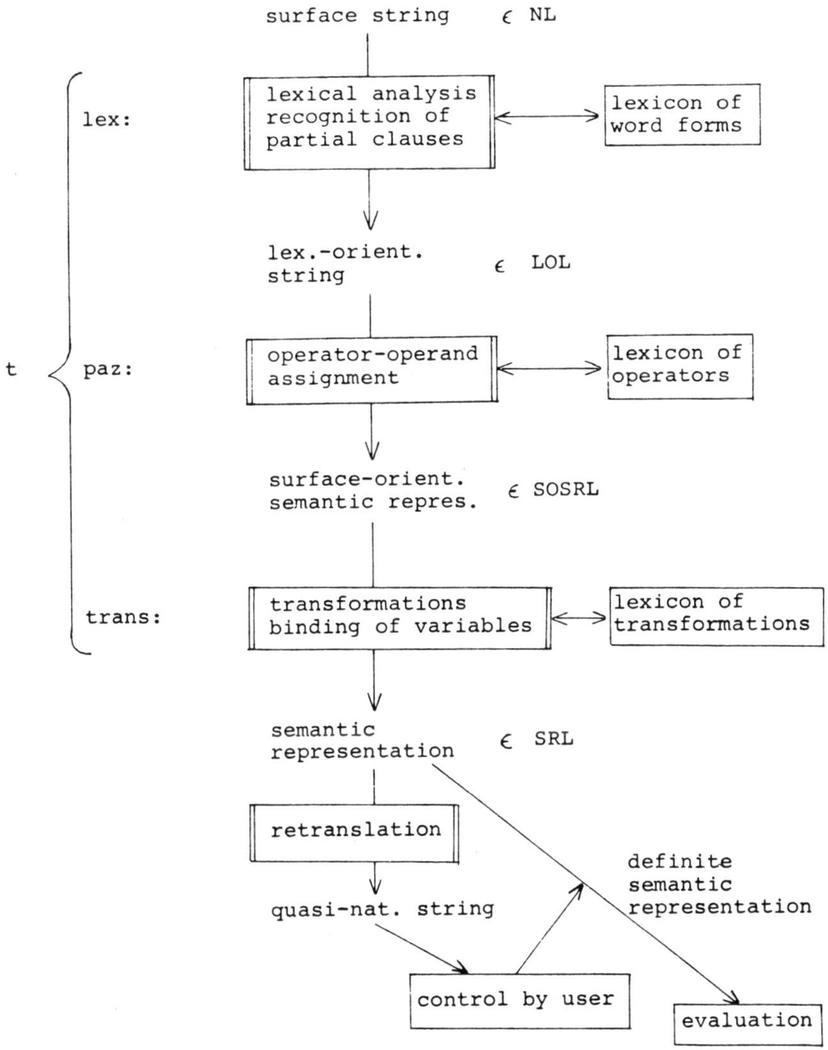

Figure 9a: Architecture of the System BEAST

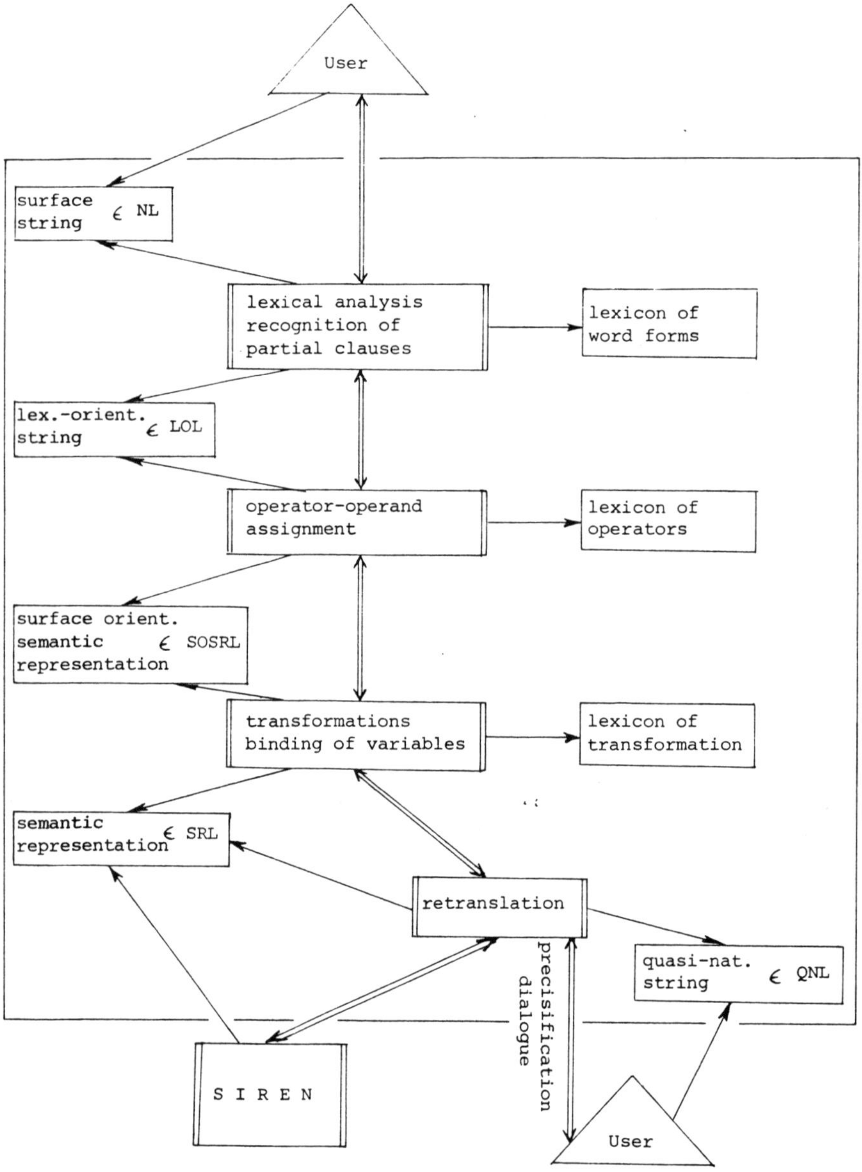

Figure 9b: Architecture of the System BEAST in modified Notation (cf. figure 7b)

3.1.3. SIREN

The secondary processing of natural language within the BACON-system is performed by the component SIREN (Semantic Representation and Net Evaluator)[1]. Starting from semantic representations (those generated from declarative sentences by BEAST) SIREN constructs a semantic network. From the network representing a world - namely the world of the system - questions about this world can be processed. SIREN interprets questions with regard to the network, i.e. the knowledge base of the system. In a subsequent phase of development inferential mechanisms will particularly be used for this.

The semantic representation language described in 3.3.2. has concepts going beyond first order predicate calculus. The SIREN system performs the interpretation of expressions of the semantic representation language and controls the answering processes and the dialog with the user (cf. literature concerning SIREN, see above).

3.2. A world of discourse

During the development of the systems we conceived a "world of travel" as a micro-world. (We plan to explore more complex applications). A short introduction to this shall be given because the examples of the following chapters refer to this world.

The world of travel describes the trips of the members of our project to congresses, workshops etc. Thisworld also includes knowledge about lectures held. Furthermore, relations exist between conferences and places, namely the relation of "a conference being held in a place", as well as the relation "is situated in" between towns and countries.

---

[1] A more detailed description of the system which has only been partially implemented up to now is given in Habel/Rollinger/Schmidt 1978a, Habel/Schmidt 1978 and Rollinger 1978.

Thus the basic structure of the world can be represented as a semantic network[1]:

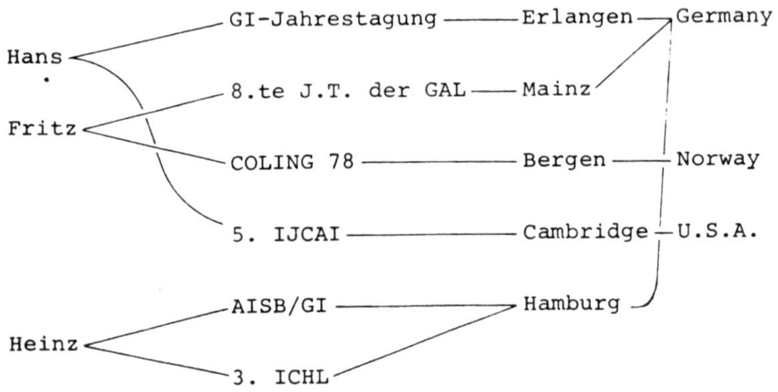

Figure 10: Part of the "World of Travel"

On the base of this structure propositions such as "Hans takes part in the GI Annual Conference" or "Bergen is situated in Norway" are representable. Moreover, the use of a modal logic representation language leads to an essential extension of applications and representation possibilities. Thus, expressions can be formed on the "expressions of the basic structure", e.g.:

---

[1]For the relation between semantic networks and logical representations, see: Simmons/Bruce 1971.
The relations being represented as edges in fig. 10 are marked differently. They have particularly different semantic "values", i.e. the relations "taking part" and "holding a lecture at" between persons and conferences.

"Mary believes that Fritz travels to COLING," or "It would be desirable that a member of our project were to travel to the AISB/GI Meeting in Hamburg," or "Hans travels to Erlangen to take part in the GI Annual Conference."[1]

Analogous to fig. 10 such sentences can be represented as semantic networks (see fig. 11). According to whether the operators 'believe' and 'travel' are represented as nodes and edges we have different forms of representations.

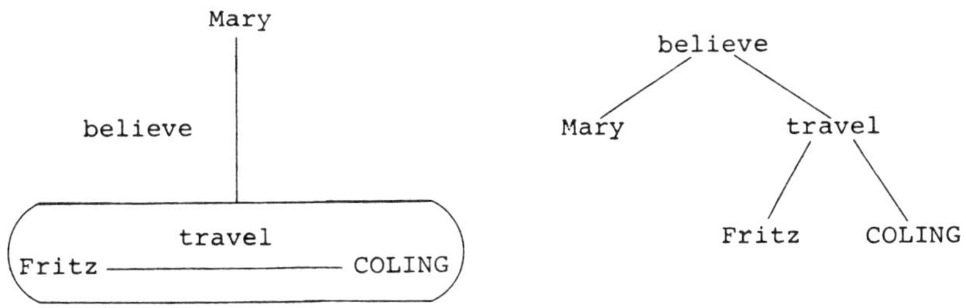

Fig. 11: Semantic Networks for "Mary believes that Fritz travels to COLING."

3.3. The levels of languages

Within the BEAST system different levels of languages occur (cf. fig. 9). The most essential ones shall be treated in more detail in the following:

---

[1]At present not all constructions mentioned here can automatically be processed by BEAST.

3.3.1. The natural language (NL)

NL is a natural language (German) being used for the communication with the system. For the conception of the system it is not necessary to interpret NL as a formal subset of a natural language for example defined by a formal grammar G so that

$$NL = L(G).$$

Our position is that we assume that the user tries to communicate in a "natural" manner not having any knowledge about the formal description of the available subset of natural language.

The user is not given any condition as to which subset of natural language he should use. He is guided by "misunderstandings" or "failures" during his work with the system to learn about the system's scope of language[1] and finally to have a successful communication.

This kind of procedure has the advantage that the scope of language can be extended or changed dynamically. It is not necessary to instruct the user explicitly about every change. The user notices[2] the growing capabilities during the communication. This extends the common scope of language steadily.

Examples for sentences of natural language processable at present[3] (and hence for the scope of language) can be seen in table 12:

---

[1] Cf. the remarks concerning the capacity of mapping t in 3.1.2. This capacity determines the processable set of sentences.

[2] (after having been informed that the scope of language has been extended).

[3] Algorithms which are necessary for the translation have not been completely implemented yet.

a. Hans reist nach Hamburg.
   (Hans travels to Hamburg).

b. Wer reist nach Berlin?
   (Who is travelling to Berlin?)

c. Maria glaubt, daß Hans in Hamburg einen Vortrag hält.
   (Mary believes that Hans is giving a lecture in Hamburg).

d. Jemand weiß, daß Hans in Hamburg keinen Vortrag hält.
   (Someone knows that Hans does not give a lecture in Hamburg).

e. Reist jemand zu einem Kongreß, der in Norwegen stattfindet?
   (Does anyone travel to a conference being held in Norway?)

Table 12: Sentences of NL.[1]

3.2.2. The semantic representation language (SRL)

The semantic representation language (MSRL = Modal Semantic Representation Language)[2] used within BACON has to fulfil two functions[3], at first in the case of input, i.e. declarative sentences, it has to serve as a representation language for knowledge (i.e. a "Knowledge Representation Language" similar to KRL (Bobrow/ Winograd 1977)), secondly in the case of queries, i.e. questions and imperatives it has to serve as query-language.

---

[1]For the processing of the sentences 12c, 12d by SIREN, see the literature mentioned in 3.1.3.

[2]The abbreviation SRL is used for Semantic representation language in general; MSRL for the special case of the modal representation language in BACON.

[3]cf. chapter 3.1., particularly fig. 7.

Each expression of MSRL consists of two components[1], the proposition and the indicator for the illocution.

The term "illocution" has been taken from the theory of speech acts (see also: Searle (1969) or as an overview of the terminology used in this paper: v. Savigny (1974)).

Illocutionary acts had been introduced into analytic philosophy by Austin (1962). The illocution of a speech act is only one partial aspect of the act. It is that one, which refers to the "intention of the effect" of the act. We want to make this clearer by means of examples for types of illocutions: one can ask, warn, propose, order, etc. Within the scope of an information system we can confine ourselves to propositions and questions which are always interpreted as the order for answering the question, while propositions are always interpreted as the request to accept new knowledge, i.e. to extend the knowledge contained in the information system and by doing this to extend the semantic network.

Considering the question "In welche Länder reist Hans" (Which countries does Hans travel to?) the noun phrase "to which countries" is interpreted as the request "Nenne die Namen der Länder...." (Give the names of the countries ..."). By using the name of the class of individuals referred to (corresponding to the one-place sorting-predicate in question) "Land" and the variable "x" ranging over the class of individuals, the indicator for the illocution can be formed as follows:

"Land (x)".

The proposition is built as an open formula with the same free variable "x". The proper names of the world of discourse are added as individual constants to the syntax of MSRL. Thus, with the individual constant "Hans" and the predicate "reisen" (travel)

[1] The components are separated by the symbol "=". The proposition is represented on the right side and the indicator for the illocution on the left.

the following proposition[1] emerges: "reisen ('Hans',x)". From this we can form the following semantic representation of the example:

Land (x) = Reisen('Hans', x) .

The essential task of the indicator for the illocution is similar to the one which in the logic of questions and answers (Belnap/ Steel 1976) is performed by various types of (answering) specifications. The free variables of the components of the illocution and proposition then correspond to the "queriables" of the erotetic logic.[2]

If we are dealing with the input of a declarative sentence (i.e. the semantic representation represents knowledge) then the propositional component of the representation is a closed formula[3]. In this case the indicator for the illocution is represented by "!".

Yes-no questions show a certain parallelism to declarative sentences insofar as the propositional component is also a closed formula. The distinction between yes-no questions and declarations is encoded by the illocutional indicator "?":

---

[1]More general rules for the syntax of propositions in MSRL are given together with the knowledge-representing function of MSRL.

[2]A more detailed description of the indicator for the illocution and a presentation of the connection between MSRL and the question-answering logic of Belnap/Steel (1976) will be found in Habel et al. (forthc.).

[3]This corresponds to the usual methods of representation in logical-linguistic semantics, see below.

a) Hans reist nach Hamburg.
(Hans travels to Hamburg.)
! = Reisen ('Hans','Hamburg')

b) Reist Hans nach Hamburg?
(Does Hans travel to Hamburg?)
? = Reisen ('Hans','Hamburg')

Fig. 13: Declarative Sentence versus Yes-No-Question

The syntax of propositions in MSRL corresponds to the well-known syntax of symbolic (logical) languages with operators like the ones used by Kalish/Montague (1964) for the description of formal theories. The language outlined in this paper[1] allows, among other things, the representation of modal concepts of natural language. That is why we have called it modal (!) semantic representation language. These modal concepts are not only interesting from a philosophical point of view, they also give rise to special problems in the field of question-answering-systems. Moreover, it also concerns phenomena which occur one way or another in non-modal concepts, too, if one considers the syntactic parallelism of the constructions[2] - "Peter sees that ... " and "Mary believes that ... " - or the logic of conjunctions like "because", "although" or others[3].

---

[1]A more detailed description can be found in Habel/Rollinger/Schmidt (1978b). The interrelation between semantic representation and inferential or dialog strategies, i.e. aspects of adequacy with respect to the problems of representation and processing of knowledge is explained in Habel/Schmidt (1978) and Rollinger (1978).

[2]cf. Habel/Rollinger/Schmidt (1978c) where some corresponding translations are described.

[3]Such operators are discussed in detail in Habel/Rollinger/Schmidt (1978b).

We now want to characterize the semantic representations of the sentences from table 12 in more detail:

individual constants[1]:	Hans, Maria, Hamburg, Berlin, Norwegen
predicates:	reisen, Vortrag-halten, teilnehmen, stattfinden (travel, give a lecture, take part in, take place)
operators:	glauben, wissen (believe, know)

and in addition to this the logical operators and the quantifiers of predicate logic.

Fig. 14: Some "lexems" of MSRL.

a. ! = reisen ('Hans','Hamburg')
b. Person(x) = reisen (x,'Berlin')
c. ! = glauben ('Maria',vortrag-halten('Hans','Hamburg'))
d. ! = ex x : wissen (x,not vortrag-halten('Hans','Hamburg'))
e. ? = ex x : ex y:teilnehmen(x,y) $\wedge$ stattfinden(y,'Norwegen')

Fig. 15: Semantic representations in MSRL[2].

[1] The individual domains are sorted by one-place predicates. Similarly, predicates and operators are given a pattern of sorts, i.e. we use a many-sorted logic. A more detailed description is given at the end of this chapter 3.3.2.

[2] The inadequacy of this translation is well-known to the authors, e.g. 'taking part in a conference' and 'travelling to the conference' are regarded as having the same meaning and thus are translated into the same semantic representation. The accuracy and therefore the quality of the translation essentially depends on the relatively small number of applied operators which could easily be extended.

For several reasons it seems favourable to sort the individual domains, i.e. to use a many-sorted logic. The use of a pattern of sorts which is similar (cf. Habel 1977) to case frames in case grammar simplifies the assignment of arguments to the respective positions during the predicate-argument-assignment (cf. 3.4.2.) Moreover it is more efficient to store and retrieve within a "sorted knowledge base" than in an "unsorted" one. For this second reason we decided to "split up" those predicates occurring relatively often in the knowledge base corresponding to the sorts of arguments. This shall be shown by means of an example: If we consider the two-place predicate "reisen" with the pattern of sorts[1] /Person,Reiseziel/, where 'Reiseziel' (destination) is sub-sorted into 'Land', 'Stadt', 'Tagung' (country, town, conference), then we can define a set of three two-place predicates which are more precise:

Predicate	Pattern of sorts
reisenort	/Person,Stadt/
reisenland	/Person,Land/
teilnehmen	/Person,Tagung/

Fig. 16: Precisification of the predicate 'reisen'

This precisification particularly corresponds to the principles of precisification which have been discussed in chapter 2.2.

On the level of the semantic representation language the application of many-sorted logic influences the syntax of this language insofar as for the sorting (whether it concerns basic sorting or sorting generated from set-theoretic operations) one-place predicates and corresponding name functions (e.g. "Person", see below) have to be defined. E.g. the one-place function "person"

[1] A formal definition of the term "Sortencharakteristik", "pattern of sorts" is given in Habel/Schmidt/Schweppe 1977b.

refers to the individuals in question. Beyond the sorting of the individual domains the argument patterns of operators[1] contain information about if and where formulae (in contrast to terms) may occur as arguments. The argument pattern of the operator "glauben" looks as follows: /Person,Formula/.

The informations about argument patterns are used within the levels of the translation (cf. 3.4.2, 3.4.4) as well as within the procedures performing the inferential methods for recovering implicit and hidden knowledge[2].

3.3.3. The quasi-natural language QNL

Within the precisification and during the answering of questions (cf. fig. 7 resp. fig. 9) the expressions of MSRL can be regarded as deep structures (i.e. semantic structures) for natural language sentences used by the system to communicate with the user.

The requirement for a definite meaning to make possible a successful communication between man and machine (cf. 2.2) should lead to the application of disambiguated expressions on that level of language where the precisification-dialog and the answering is performed. That is why we do not intend a really natural language output. Instead of this the casual user is given an easily understandable but desambiguated, almost natural version of the underlying MSRL expressions. Although those expressions could be regarded as belonging to natural language we called them "quasi-natural" since the expressions occurring frequently have a high degree of complexity or imbeddings (cf. the examples of fig. 17). Thus "quasi-natural" seems to fit better than "natural".

---

[1]This corresponds basically to the "type" of an operator in Kalish/Montague (1964); cf. Habel/Rollinger/Schmidt 1978b.

[2]See also Habel/Rollinger/Schmidt 1978a, Habel/Schmidt 1978 and Rollinger 1978.

To represent the structures of embedding of MSRL in QNL we performed this by insertion line by line computed during the translation process.

A satisfactory characterization of the language QNL which is the result of the paraphrasing algorithm will be given by the translations of the examples of fig. 12 and fig. 15.

a. Hans reist nach Hamburg.
(Hans travels to Hamburg)
b. Gib die Namen aller Personen x an, für die gilt:
Die Person x reist nach Berlin.
(Give the names of all those persons x such that:
The person x travels to Berlin.)
c. Maria glaubt, dass gilt:
Hans hält in Hamburg einen Vortrag.
(Maria believes that
Hans gives a lecture in Hamburg.)
d. Es existiert eine Person x, für die gilt:
Die Person x weiss, dass gilt:
Es gilt nicht:
Hans hält in Hamburg einen Vortrag.
(There is a person x such that:
The person x knows that:
It is not the case that:
Hans gives a lecture in Hamburg.
e. Ist die folgende Aussage wahr?
Es existiert eine Person x, für die gilt:
Es existiert eine Tagung y, für die gilt:
Die Person x nimmt an der Tagung y teil
und
Die Tagung y findet in Norwegen statt.
(Is the following proposition true?
There is a person x such that:
There is a conference y such that:
The person x takes part in the conference y
and
The conference y takes place in Norway.

Fig 17: Quasi-natural correspondence of expressions of MSRL

By means of an extension[1] of the related component of the translation (cf. 3.4.4) the naturalness of the expressions of QNL can be considerably improved. This can be done by taking care of the different word order of German in main and subordinate clauses (SVO[2] versus SOV) during the generation. Up to now only SVO-clauses (main clauses) are generated.

3.4. The components of the system

The figures 8 and 9 show that the process of generation of a semantic representation is divided into sub-processes. These constitute the sub-components of the BEAST-system which perform the mapping t. The transition from one sub-component to another is given by additional levels of languages.

3.4.1. The lexical analysis and recognition of partial clauses - lex

The first step of the translation (lex) consists of the recovery of lexical information: The words of the input are searched in a lexicon of word forms. If they have been found, they are substituted by an internal encoding (the base lemma). The lexicon of word forms consists at present only of full forms such that algorithms for the lemmatization are not needed. Especially a small vocabulary occurring in the field of question-answering-systems makes this kind of processing for reasons of efficiency very advantageous.[3]

---

[1] The related algorithms are just now developed and will be implemented in the next phase of development.

[2] SVO or SOV refer to patterns of word order of German (Subject - Verb - Object or Subject - Object - Verb).

[3] We plan to implement algorithms for the lemmatization in a later phase of development. But we also want to base these algorithms on the "principle of minimal information", i.e. they perform essentially reductions onto the base lemma.

```
   4.PAGE:  ERSTER FREIER PLATZ =  10
WELCHES                3 Q002          WELCHEM        3 Q002
WELCHE                 3 Q002          WELCHER        3 Q002
WELCHEN                3 Q002          WER            3 Q003
WEN                    3 Q003          WERDEN         4 HIVB
WERDEN                 4 HIVB
          .
          .
          .
  16.PAGE:  ERSTER FREIER PLATZ =   3
TAGUNG                 3 OT12          TAGUNGEN       3 OT12

  17.PAGE:  ERSTER FREIER PLATZ =   4
KONGRESS               3 OT12          KONGRESSEN     3 OT12
KONGRESSE              3 OT12

  18.PAGE:  ERSTER FREIER PLATZ =   3
PERSON                 3 OT11          PERSONEN       3 OT11

  19.PAGE:  ERSTER FREIER PLATZ =   2
MITARBEITER            3 OT11

  20.PAGE:  ERSTER FREIER PLATZ =   6
STADT                  3 OT13          STAEDTE        3 OT13
STATT                  3 BEIF          STATTFINDET    1 STATTFIND
STATTFINDEN            1 STATTFIND

  21.PAGE:  ERSTER FREIER PLATZ =   5
LAND                   3 OT14          LAENDER        3 OT14
LANDE                  3 OT14          LAENDERN       3 OT14
          .
          .
          .
  30.PAGE:  ERSTER FREIER PLATZ =   3
WO                     3 Q003          WOHIN          3 Q003

  31.PAGE:  ERSTER FREIER PLATZ =   2
JEMAND                 3 OT11

  32.PAGE:  ERSTER FREIER PLATZ =   5
HALTEN                 1 HALT          HAELT          1 HALT
HAMBURG                3 KT13          HANS           3 KT11
          .
          .
          .
  46.PAGE:  ERSTER FREIER PLATZ =   3
REISEN                 1 FAHR          REIST          1 FAHR
```

Figure 18: The Lexicon of Word Forms (Excerpts)

The internal encodings (i.e. the base lemmata) define the vocabulary of the lexicon-oriented language LOL. An overview of a part of the lexicon is given in table 18:

Comments on table 18:

- Table 18 shows an excerpt of the lexicon of word forms with all details of the implementation.
- The first page of the lexicon contains the essential information about the structure of the lexicon: the pointer to the next free page and the assignment of beginnings of a word to the number of the page where all the words are gathered (e.g. WE in page 4).
- Each page of the lexicon contains an entry pointing to the next free place (i.e. "ERSTER FREIER PLATZ"). If the lexicon is to be updated then e.g. in page 20 a word beginning with "ST" can be entered at place 6.
- The other entries shall be discussed according to page 20: The first entry is the word itself, e.g. "STADT", "STATT", etc. Its internal encoding is in the third position, in this case "OT13" and "BEIF". The numbers in the second position give hints to the searching algorithm if a word has been entered twice, e.g. as a possible operator or a category.
- The expressions of LOL are not only operator names like "STATTFIND" or "TEILNEHM" etc. They also hold information about types of words like: "Q001" (marking for one type of interrogative pronoun), "ARTB" and "ARTU" (definite and indefinite article, respectively), "PRAE" (preposition), "BEIF" (verb adjunct), "OT13" (object type with respect to the many-sorted logic, i.e. the type 13, the type of towns)etc.

The access to the lexicon of word forms causes - in many cases - a reduction of the variety of meanings, e.g. when the natural language terms 'person' and 'colleague' are mapped onto the same base lemma (cf. table 18, page 18, 19). i.e. the synonymy of these terms has been assumed inadequately. However, these words are only synonymous with respect to the world of discourse (in the interpretation at hand). That is why it is permitted to process the access to the lexicon non-injectively.

Besides the lexical analysis the component lex performs a recognition and a first processing of partial clauses (i.e. sub-ordinate clauses, embedded clauses). The present version of the system processes two types of sub-clauses, relative clauses (restricted and descriptive) and complementary clauses (cf. 12c). The algorithms are controlled by lexical information, in the case of relative clauses by the recognition of relative pronouns, in the case of complementary clauses by the recognition of the conjunction " dass" (that). (cf. example 19b; see also Habel/Rollinger/Schmidt 1978c).

By using the mapping lex the first intermediate level, the language LOL is defined:

LOL : = lex (NL)

Obviously LOL expressions are expressions over the alphabet of the base lemmata, the syntactic structure of which corresponds to the structure of natural language, in this case German, with the structure being specified by the markings of the procedures processing the partial clauses.

The expressions of LOL consist of strings of such forms being given in the second column of example 19, where constants and verb adjuncts are additionally considered, e.g. by KT11 'Maria' or BEIF 'Vortrag'.

a.	Wohin	Q003	Marking for the interrogative pronoun "wo" (where), "wohin" (where to).
	reist	§FAHR	Base lemma for "fahren", "reisen" (travel).
	Hans	KT11	Denotes a constant of object type OT11 (Person).
	?		Marking for questions.

b. Maria	KT11	Marking for a constant.
glaubt	§GLAUB	Base lemma for "glauben" (believe).
	(2	Marking for the beginning of a complementary clause.
dass	KOKO	Denotes a conjunction for a complementary clause.
Hans	KT11	Marking for a constant.
in	PRAE	denotes a preposition.
Hamburg	KT13	denotes a constant of object type OT13 (towns)
einen	ARTU	denotes indefinite article
Vortrag	BEIF	denotes verb adjunct[1]
hält	§HALT	base lemma for "halten" (hold)
	)2	Marking for the end of a complementary clause.

Example 19: Two expressions of LOL

3.4.2. The predicate argument assignment - paz[2]

The essential problem of the assignment of meaning (cf. also Bartsch/Vennemann, 1972) is to transform the operator-operand-relations of natural language into equivalent predicate-argument-relations of the semantic representation language.

[1] At the next step of translation (paz - see below) a predicate is constructed from the verb adjunct 'Vortrag' and the verb 'halten' which represent the meaning of 'Vortrag halten' (give a lecture).

[2] paz is the acronym for "Prädikat-Argument-Zuweisung" (predicate-argument-assignment).

For this generally syntactic and semantic information is used, e.g. balancing of surface case and numerus, deep case (Fillmore, 1968), word order, common sense knowledge, e.g. representable by frames (Minsky, 1975), or even the intonation[1]. To recover this information from the point of view of efficiency - even though in different degrees - implies a considerable expenditure, such that it is precarious within a system related to practice at today's stage of technology.

The application of the principle of minimal information (cf. 2.3) means that the process of translation is first performed with a small amount of basic information and only in the case of failure additional information will be included. It is obvious that the amount of basic information varies with the setting of the task.

The predicate-argument-assignment paz uses in general argument-type patterns to perform the assignment. This kind of processing being based on the principles of many-sorted logic as well as on Fillmore's case grammar assumes that each predicate (resp. each operator) of the semantic representation language possesses one argument-type pattern. This specifies which sorts (possibly sorts of formulae) are allowed for the argument places in question. For example (cf. fig. 16) for the lemma of "reisen" we find three possible patterns of sorts (i.e. argument-type patterns) and for the lemma of the operator "glauben" we find two possible argument-type patterns:

/Person, Person/	"a glaubt b"
/Person/Formel	"a glaubt, daß p wahr ist"
(/Person, Person/	"a believes b"
/Person, Formula/	"a believes that p is true")

Fig. 20: Argument-pattern of "glauben" (believe)

[1]The application of procedures incorporating intonation within an acoustic system might be possible at some future time.

The assignment is performed by comparing the argument-types occurring in the LOL-string with the argument-type patterns of the verb[1]. For this purpose the lexicon of operators and operands OOL[2] (cf. table 22) is searched within the page of the verb in question for the corresponding predicates of the semantic representation language and the fitting alternatives are generated. In fig. 21 we have three alternatives for the question "Wohin reist Hans?" (Where does Hans travel to? - cf. 19a):

Wohin	QOO2 OT14	"to which country"[3]
	QOO2 OT13	"to which town"
	QOO2 OT12	"to which congress"
reist	§REISENLAND(OT11,OT14)[4]	
	§REISENORT(OT11,OT13)	
	§TEILNEHM(OT11,OT12)	
Hans	KT11	

Figure 21: The Predicate-Argument-Assignment of Example 19a

[1]The requirement that only one lemma representing a verb exists is no restriction because for the operator-operand assignment only one partial clause is considered.

[2]OOL = Operator-Operand Lexicon.

[3]There are natural language expressions for the encodings "QOO2 OT14, QOO2 OT13, QOO2 OT12" having been derived from the semantic context for "wohin".

[4]These are the SRL predicates for the representation of §FAHR with the instantiation of variables with respect to the argument-type pattern.

```
LEXICON OF OPERATORS AND OPERANDS
=================================

NAECHSTER FREIER INDEX:     28
NAECHSTE FREIE PAGE:        30
PRODUZIER       2HERSTELL            3
HERSTELL        3STELL               4
STELL           4LAGER               5
LAGER           5ENTHALT             6
ENTHALT         6LIEFER              7
LIEFER          7BELIEFER            9
BELIEFER        9BEZIEH             10
BEZIEH         10BEKOMM             11
BEKOMM         11BENOETIG           12
BENOETIG       12STATTFIND          13
STATTFIND      13FUEHR              14
FUEHR          14VERANSTALT         15
VERANSTALT     15AUSRICHT           16
AUSRICHT       16RICHT              17
RICHT          17FIND               18
FIND           18TEILNEHM           19
TEILNEHM       19NEHM               20
NEHM           20FAHR               21
FAHR           21REIS               22
REIS           22HALT               23
HALT           23TRAG               24
TRAG           24LIEG               25
LIEG           25BESUCH             26
BESUCH         26DURCHFUEHR         27
DURCHFUEHR     27GLAUB              28
GLAUB          28WISS               29
WISS           29                    0

                 .

                 .

                 .

STATTFIND      13   0   4
      STFINDORT           20T120T13

      STFINDLAND          20T120T14

      STFINDORTLAND       30T120T130T14


FUEHR          14   0   4
DURCH STFINDORT           20T120T13

DURCH STFINDLAND          20T120T14

DURCH STFINDORTLAND       30T120T130T14

                 .

                 .
```

Table 22: (see next page)

```
                  .
                  .
                  .

FIND            18    O    4
STATT STFINDORT                  2OT12OT13

STATT STFINDLAND                 2OT12OT14

STATT STFINDORTLAND              3OT12OT13OT14


TEILNEHM        19    O    4
      TEILNEHMLAND               3OT11OT12OT14

      TEILNEHMORT                3OT11OT12OT13

      TEILNEHM                   2OT11OT12

                  .
FAHR            21    O    7
      TEILNEHMLAND               3OT11OT12OT14

      TEILNEHMORT                3OT11OT12OT13

      TEILNEHM                   2OT11OT12

      REISENLAND                 2OT11OT14

      REISENORT                  2OT11OT13

      REISENORTLAND              3OT11OT13OT14

                  .
HALT            23    O    4
      HALTVORTRAGORT             3OT11OT12OT13

      HALTVORTRAGTG              2OT11OT12

      HALTVORTRAG                1OT11

                  .
LIEG            25    O    2
      LIEGORTLAND                2OT13OT14

                  .
                  .
                  .
```

Table 22: (see next page)

BESUCH	26	0	7	
TEILNEHMLAND				3OT11OT12OT14
TEILNEHMORT				3OT11OT12OT13
TEILNEHM				2OT11OT12
REISENORTLAND				3OT11OT13OT14
REISENORT				2OT11OT13
REISENLAND				2OT11OT14
GLAUB	28	0	3	
GLAUBSACH				2OT11KOSA
GLAUBPERSON				2OT11OT11
WISS	29	0	2	
WISSEN				2OT11KOSA

Table 22: Lexicon of Operators and Operands (OOL) (Excerpt)

Comments on table 22:

- The first page contains - analogously to the lexicon of word forms - the general information about the first free page (for new entries) and the assignment of base lemmata to each page.
- At the head of the page is entered the page number, the name of the lemma and the number of pages to follow (in our example it is zero) and the next free place within the page.
- Each entry consists of an argument type pattern, e.g. "2OT12OT13" (which means two arguments, the first one of type "OT12" and the second one of type "OT13", the possibly occurring verb adjuncts, e.g. "STATT" (if e.g. 'stattfinden' occurs discontinuously ('findet statt')) and the assigned operator (predicate) e.g. 'STFINDORT' of SRL.

As the result of the mapping paz applied to example 19b we have:

§glaubsach('Maria',KOSA)(2 KOKO§haltvortragort('Hans','Hamburg'))2[1]

The operator-operand-assignment leads to a string the syntactic structure of which closely corresponds to the structure of the input but it possesses the "lexems" of the semantic representation language as well as an explicit predicate-argument relation. This is the reason why we call this level of language the surface-oriented semantic representation language. It emerges without formal definition from LOL by the application of the partial mapping paz:

SOSRL := paz (LOL)

3.4.3. The transformational component - trans

The task of the transformational component trans is to transform the linear structures of the surface-oriented semantic representation language SOSRL into the hierarchically ordered structures of the semantic representation language. Thus the transformational component is target-oriented, i.e. it has to process the SOSRL expressions by transformation, in such a way that well-formed expressions of the target language SRL emerge. While the phases of translation - having been described above - are independent of the representation language with the exception of the requirement for an operator-operand structure, the transformations serve as a connecting link between the surface-oriented semantic representation language SOSRL and the syntax of the target language MSRL. The transformational process is performed by transformational rules and therefore allows the mapping into different languages and beyond this extensions of the scope of language of the input language to a restricted degree. The restriction is caused by the necessity to implement additional analyzing steps for more complex and new syntactic constructions.

---

[1] "KOSA" denotes complementary clauses. It is therefore a syntactic variable for embedded formulae.

The system of rules essentially represents a transformational component in the sense of Ginsburg/Partee(1969). Each rule consists of one part containing the structural description and another containing the structural change.

The set of rules is partially ordered with respect to the relations of substructures of the structural descriptions and (having priority) to an explicit hierarchisation of the rules. With respect to the relations of substructures the order of application within the various levels of hierarchies is arbitrary but it is fixed by the order within the lexicon of rules. Table 23 shows the lexicon of transformations.

```
OQEIN %% /TRUE/ = %
1PRED_Q002_OT %% KXX(OT) =<REST> PRED %
1= Q002_OT_%% .KXX(OT) = %
1Q002_OT_(1 %% KXX(OT) = OT (1<REL>)1 %
1Q002_OT_%% KXX(OT) = %
1Q001_OT FKTN %% FKTN =  <REST>%
1Q001 PRED %% PRED = %
1KT_(1 %%  .EX. OT ( KXX(OT) .EQ. 'KT' .AND. (1<REL> )1 .AND<REST>) %
1KT_%%  .EX. OT (KXX(OT) .EQ. 'KT' .AND.<REST>) %
2NEG1_ALLE_OT_(1 %% .NOT. .ALL. OT ( (1<REL>)1 .IMP.<REST>) %
2NEG1_ALLE_OT_%% .NOT. .ALL. OT (<REST>) %10*
2NEG1_PRED_%% .NOT. PRED %
2PRED NEG1 %% .NOT. PRED %
2NEG2 OT %% .NOT. .EX. OT %
2ALLE_OT_(1 %% .ALL. OT ( (1<REL>)1 .IMP.<REST>) %
2ALLE_OT_%% .ALL. OT (< REST >) %15 *
2NUR1_OT_(1 %% .ALL. OT ( (<REST>) .IMP. (1<REL>)1 ) %
2OT_(1 %% (1<REL>)1 .AND.<REST>%
3)1_# %% )1 .AND. # %
3.ALL. (_PRED_OT_) %% .EX. OT ( .ALL.<REST>( PRED ) ) %
3PRED_(1_%% PRED_.AND. (1<REL>)1 %
3)1_PRED %% )1 .AND. PRED %
4KOSA %%<KOMP>%
4= = %% = %
4PRED %% PRED %
/*
```

Table 23: The Lexicon of Transformations

Comments on table 23:

Table 23 contains the present state of the lexicon of transformational rules being used for the scope of language described in this paper:

- The numbering of the rules is only been given for the sake of better orientation.
- The first column of the lexicon of transformational rules contains the explicit ordering of the rules.
- The entry at the left side of the separating symbol "%%" corresponds to the structural description.
- The entry at the right side of "%%" consists of the structural change.
- Possibly at the right side of the symbol "%" (denoting the end of the structural change) numbers may occur referring to other rules which should first be tested for their applicability. Thus it is possible to also define another explicit order (see rule 9). Different numbers are separated from each other by " * ".
- The symbol '/* ' denotes the end of the lexicon.
- The symbols 'PRED', 'NUMR', 'OT', 'KT', 'FKTN', 'KOMP', 'REST', 'REL', '(1', '(2', ')1', ')2' are symbols of the meta-language of the transformational component.

The transformation of an expression of SOSRL is performed recursively per partial clause . Each rule is tried again as long as it is applicable, i.e. no change can be performed any longer. This rule will not be tried again within further transformations. By doing this the termination of the algorithm is ensured.

The rules are of different character: either they serve to ensure the syntactic correctness of the generated expression of the semantic representation language or they have the additional function of translating semantically relevant structures of natural language into equivalent structures of the target language. We have to mention that those are immanent within natural language, i.e. they are independent of the world of discourse.

The syntactic structure of the developed system of rules is of comparably small complexity. Besides the meta-symbols REL , KOMP , KOSA , REST , FKTN , PRED ,(the latter for functions and predicates) and syntactic variables like "OT" and "KT", only categorical symbols of the lexicon of word forms as well as symbols of the target language SRL occur. But these are only treated as strings and have no influence on the process of interpretation. Advantages in comparison with more powerful languages for systems of rules are the simple handling of the rules (insertion and update of rules for the sake of extension of the scope of language; readability of the rules) and the very simple and thus efficient mechanical interpretation of the rules.

Fears that the number of rules would - even at a relatively small processable scope of language - increase to such an extent that interdependencies between the rules were no longer transparent have, up to now, not been proved to be justified. Nevertheless, in comparison with other systems with a comparable scope of language BEAST needs only 25 rules for the above-mentioned scope of language (cf. table 23).

The transformational process does not cover all the bindings of implicitly bound variables of the input. In spite of this, a special algorithm has been implemented which binds more efficiently all the remaining unbound variables after the transformations have been performed.

As from predicate-argument assignment a set of alternative SOSRL representations (cf. fig. 21) may emerge, the transformational component is successively applied to these alternatives where after the generation of a semantic representation the user is offered this representation for control (cf. 2.2 and 3.1.2.).

As an example for a transformation let us consider the first alternative of example 21:

```
The SOSRL-string:
Q002 OT14 §REISENLAND(OT11,OT14) KT11'HANS'
Rule 5:
KXX(OT14) = §REISENLAND(OT11,OT14) KT11'HANS'
Rule 9:
KXX(OT14) = .EX. OT11 (KXX(OT11) .EQ. 'HANS' .AND.
            §REISENLAND(OT11,OT14) )
After rule 25 has been applied:
KXX(OT14) = .EX. OT11 (KXX(OT11) .EQ.'HANS' .AND.
             REISENLAND  (OT11,OT14) )
```

The "KXX" denotes one-place sorting functions[1] and depends on the sorted variable; in these cases "OT14" and "OT11", the following expression of SRL emerges after the substitution of functions

```
#LAND# (OT14) = .EX. OT11 (#PERSON#(OT11) .EQ.'HANS' .AND.
                 #REISENLAND# (OT11,OT14) )
```

The symbol "#" has been used for internal implementing reasons as well as "'" and ".".

Figure 24: A transformational process

Except for the queriable "OT14" which occurs on the left side of "=" as well, no other variable is free in the proposition. Therefore it is not necessary to apply the algorithm for binding variables.

---

[1] This form originates in the evaluation system ADIS used at first (cf. H. Engel 1976, Cherniavsky/Engel 1976 and Cherniavsky/Schneider 1978).
For the retranslation a substitution for the individual constants has already been implemented such that the SRL expression is:

```
LAND  (OT14) =  REISENLAND  ('HANS',OT14)
```

After the complete realization of SIREN (cf. 3.1.3) the substituted variant will directly be performed by trans.

Let us now consider the example 19b , then the SOSRL-string is:

QEIN KT11'MARIA' §GLAUBSACH(OT11,KOSA) (2 KT11'HANS' KT13'HAMBURG' §HALTVORTRAGORT(OT11,OT13))2

First the complementary clause is treated.

Rule 9:

.Ex.OT11 (KXX(OT11) .EQ. 'HANS' .AND. KT13'HAMBURG' §HALTVORTRAGORT(OT11,OT13))

Rule 9:

.EX. OT13 (KXX(OT13) .EQ. 'HAMBURG' .AND. .EX. OT11 (KXX(OT11) .EQ. 'HANS' .AND. §HALTVORTRAGORT(OT11,OT13)))

Rule 25:

.EX. OT13 (KXX(OT13) .EQ. 'HAMBURG' .AND. .EX. OT11 (KXX(OT11) .EQ. 'HANS' .AND. #HALTVORTRAGORT# (OT11,OT13)))

After copying the subclause into the remaining string, we have:

QEIN KT11'MARIA' §GLAUBSACH(OT11,KOSA) (2 .EX. OT13 (KXX(OT13) .EQ. 'HAMBURG' .AND. .EX. OT11 (KXX(OT11) .EQ. 'HANS' .AND. # HALTVORTRAGORT # (OT11,OT13))))2

Rule 1:

/TRUE/ = KT11'MARIA' §GLAUBSACH(OT11,KOSA) (2 .EX. OT13 (KXX(OT13) .EQ. 'HAMBURG' .AND. .EX. OT11 (KXX(OT11) .EQ. 'HANS' .AND. #HALTVORTRAGORT# (OT11,OT13))))2

Rule 9:

/TRUE/ = .EX. OT11 (KXX(OT11) .EQ. 'MARIA' .AND. §GLAUBSACH (OT11,KOSA) (2 .EX. OT13 (KXX(OT13) .EQ. 'HAMBURG' .AND. .EX. OT11 (KXX(OT11) .EQ. 'HANS' .AND. # HALTVORTRAGORT # (OT11,OT13))))2)

Rule 23:

/TRUE/ = .EX. OT11 (KXX(OT11) . EQ. 'MARIA' .AND. §GLAUBSACH (OT11,.EX. OT13 (KXX(OT13) .EQ. 'HAMBURG' .AND. .EX. OT11 (KXX(OT11) .EQ. 'HANS' .AND. # HALTVORTRAGORT # (OT11,OT13)))))

Rule 25:

/TRUE/ = .EX. OT11 (KXX(OT11) .EQ. 'MARIA' .AND. # GLAUBSACH (OT11, .EX. OT13 (KXX(OT13) .EQ. 'HAMBURG' .AND. .EX. OT11 (KXX(OT11) .EQ. 'HANS' .AND. # HALTVORTRAGORT# (OT11,OT13)))))

After the substitution of the functions and the instantiation of the individual constants we get the following result:

/TRUE/ = #GLAUBSACH# ('MARIA', #HALTVORTRAGORT# ('HANS', 'HAMBURG'))

The first lexem of the SOSRL-string "QEIN" is put in front always when we are dealing with declarative sentences. Rule 1 substitutes this by "/TRUE/" (resp. "!") which is the indicator for the corresponding illocution.

3.4.4. The paraphrasing in a quasi-natural language - rueck[1]

Within the scope of a precisification- and clarification dialog a disambiguated paraphrase of the input similar to natural language - a string of the quasi-natural language QNL - has to be given to the user (cf. 3.3.3.). Such strings are generated from strings of the semantic representation language by the system's component rueck (Rueckuebersetzung Retranslation) in two steps: after the syntactic analysis of the string of the semantic representation language being combined with its translation into an internal intermediate language having explicitly encoded the entire information of the syntactic analysis a translation from this intermediate language into QNL is performed.

The most important purpose of the syntactic analysis is to discover erroneous results of the transformational component trans. Syntactically incorrect expressions may emerge e.g. from a very high syntactic complexity of the input - with respect to the given set of transformational rules - or from missing entries in the lexicon of word forms. In this case the user is asked to reformulate the same fact using other words.

The expressions of the semantic representation language are analysed from left to right according to the system of syntactic rules for the description of well-formed expressions of MSRL. Additionally the sortal correctness with respect to the patterns of sorts is improved. According to their type the different kinds of operators (e.g. variable-binding operators, modal operators, propositional operators etc.) are encoded. Moreover a list of bound and free variables with respect to their sorting and the used constants is made up.

---

[1] For a more detailed description compare Wang (1979) and Wang/ Habel (forthc.)

After the first step of the translation into the internal intermediate language, expressions of the following form are generated (here we only give the "translation" of the proposition, i.e. we neglect the indicator for the illocution):

a. F3(K1,K2)

c. O2 (K1,F5(K2,K3))[1]

d. Q1 B1 (O3,B1,J1,F3(K1,K2))

Example 25: The intermediate language of the retranslation (according to example 15).

Comments on example 25:

- The operator constants are represented by encodings marking the type of the operator. The index distinguishes between the various operators:

F3	- Function no. 3	- "reisen" (travel)
O2	- (Modal) Operator no. 2	- "glauben" (believe)
Q1	- Quantifier no. 1	- existential quantifier
J1	- Propositional Operator no. 1	- negation

- Each constant is entered into a list of constants, e.g. for 25c:

1 - Maria

2 - Hans

3 - Hamburg

- The variables are entered into separate lists for bound ones "B" and free variables "V". To the variable B1 (from 25c) is assigned the sort "Person", with respect to the instantiation of the operator O3 (wissen), i.e. the sorting can be derived from the pattern of sorts of the operator.

---

[1] The processing of modal operators, i.e. the operators of type "O" operating over formulae and (!) terms has not been completely implemented in the component rueck at the present stage of implementation.

The second step of translation is controlled by the markings for the units of the intermediate language (e.g. 'F','K', .../cf. 25). On account of the marking a corresponding procedure is called to find out the substring to be processed, in the case of predicates the relevant substring consists of the coding of the predicate (or function) and the string of arguments.

After this, the translation is performed by using a lexicon of natural language patterns. As a result of this step we get expressions of QNL as have been listed in fig. 17.

4. Applications and prospects

4.1. Applications

The BEAST system is a system of the primary processing of natural language as explained in 2.4. Various applications may be considered if one thinks of linking it with systems of the secondary processing of language. Besides the conception of BACON (3.1.) two further applications are envisaged which will be outlined shortly in the following.

For very large data bases, i.e. in the applicational context of a natural language data base system it is important to have a truly efficient and powerful data base system with a natural language interface. Not only is the natural language communication one aspect of user-orientedness, but also the fast "reaction time" of the system[1].

On account of the similarity of the underlying concepts - even though on the one hand SIREN puts the main stress on the logical structure of natural language whereas on the other hand SIDAB puts the stress on the data base structure - BEAST is linked with the SIDAB system[2].

The SIDAB system and its underlying principles have been described in more detail by R. Munz (1976, 1978). Its data structures are given in the form of "WEBs", i.e. labelled edges and nodes.

A link between the two systems has been established by Huismann (1979).

---

[1]Beyond this a good data base system should also be economical from the commercial point of view.

[2]The SIDAB system has also been developed at the "Institut für Angewandte Informatik" at the Technical University of Berlin.

The entire system developed by linking both systems will be tested by the administration of the Technical University in the field of allocation of office space etc. This system seems to be applicable for further fields of business and administration.

The capability of the SIREN system to also handle logically complex semantic representations might prove necessary and useful for such fields of application where complex problem-solving and decision-making occurs. Particularly the use of modal particles in natural language serves for the description of more complex problems, e.g. the particles "may", "can", "must" etc. which in medical and legal texts determine a large part of the semantic substance. In the future it is planned to apply the BACON system to medical problems, with special stress being put on contra-indications and risks of drugs.

For the above-mentioned applications which could be subsumed under the term of natural language interfaces for information systems the performance of deviant sentences (cf. 2.3.) is a special advantage. Though natural language queries mean an easy access to computer assisted information systems for casual users they are, however, considered to be a nuisance by people well-versed in data processing, because natural language communication is much more extensive - due to the redundancy of natural language - than the communication by means of a formal data manipulation language. Due to the capability of accepting deviant sentences (and that is where the BEAST system differs from other natural language systems performing a test of the syntactic correctness) there exists a spectrum of various ways of formulating from natural language to ellipses. Each user can form his own "dialect" for the interaction with the system - within certain limits which can be discovered during the communication.

As variants for the natural language sentences of example 15a, 15b we have:

a) reisen Hans Hamburg. (travel Hans Hamburg
Hans reisen Hamburg. Hans travel Hamburg)

b) Wer reisen Berlin?	Who travel Berlin?
Wer reist Berlin?	Who travels Berlin?
reist nach Berlin?[1]	travels to Berlin?

Example 26: Acceptable "deviant utterances".

Besides the application of BEAST as a component for the primary processing of natural language for an information system it could be used also for the primary processing of a translation system. Then it would be that part which generates the semantic representation where SRL serves as interlingua of the translation. The secondary processing of natural language in this case is the translation of the semantic representation into another natural language. A revised version of the component rueck could be used for this.[2] If one uses appropriate lexica (lexicon of word forms, lexicon of operators and operands, lexicon of transformational rules and the lexica of the retranslation), then the application in the field of a multilingual information system for the world of discourse of 3.2. is already possible.

Translations having been supported by this system (it cannot be viewed as a system for automatic translation in its proper sense but it is a system for computer-aided translation[3]) will have the following characteristics emerging from the underlying principles. On account of the requirement for disambiguation and preciseness the translated text has also been disambiguated and made precise. This property of the system, acceptable - or even desirable - for scientific, technical as well as administrational and legal texts will not be acceptable for other texts, as e.g. literary ones.

---

[1] The supplementation of the interrogative pronoun "wer"(who) has to be performed algorithmically.

[2] A high quality translation from SRL into QNL is needed for the clarification/precisification dialog and the generation of answers, too.

[3] cf. the principles for a computer-aided translation being given by the principles of the BEAST system (Schmidt 1979).

Further considerations in this field[1] would surely lead to the task for characterization of that class of texts which are desired to be precise and disambiguated.

4.2. Prospects

To extend the processable scope of language and to improve the quality of the translation (i.e. to make it more adequate) it will be necessary to recover further information[2] from the natural language input and to process this together with the knowledge of the system.

In addition to the argument patterns for the recognition of the operator-operand relation the following phenomena of natural language can be used:

1. Prepositions[3]:

   e.g.: travel to Hamburg
   travel via Hamburg

without the consideration of prepositions a wrong translation would emerge. If prepositions are relevant for the assignment then they will be entered into the lexicon of operators and operands and will be considered when assigning the predicate and the instantiation of the argument places.

2. Surface case:

   Der Mann sieht Hans. (The man sees Hans).[4]
   Den Mann sieht Hans. (Hans sees the man).

---

[1]The development of such a system is a "waste product" of our research and thus cannot be followed up.

[2]This does not contradict the principle of minimal information as the minimal information necessary for the processing will be considered.

[3]The use of prepositions is realized in the OOL. Nevertheless a semantic analysis of different meanings of the same preposition is a problem occurring in the syntactic analysis as well as in the lexica for the individual elements of language.

[4]In German and other languages with relatively free word order (see below) case analysis can be very important.

The surface cases are matched against the argument places of the entries of the predicates in the lexicon of operators and operands by means of the deep cases. To do the case analysis more properly it is necessary to perform a much deeper syntactical analysis of the sentence. Besides the above-mentioned prepositions a morphological analysis is possible[1].

3. Word order:

In "Hans sieht Franz" (Hans sees Franz) a definite assignment based on the above-mentioned criteria is not possible. Languages with a relatively free word order can use normal word order only for an attempt to assign the most probable predicate. This could be the first alternative for the semantic representation. In our example this means that 'Hans' is the logical subject.

The first two criteria for the assignment of a predicate can solve most of the problems of assignment, although erroneous assignments can not always be avoided.

At present, according to the principle of minimal information, we do not use algorithms for the lemmatization. The lexical instantiation is only performed by the lexicon of word forms.

If we envisage in future the implementation of such algorithms they are essentially used for the recovery of the base lemma. Only if an explicit indication of the forms of inflexion should become necessary a sufficiently extensive analysis will be performed. This kind of processing promises a more efficient performance than the routine recovery of information which will perhaps not be used in the further processing.

---

[1] For the remarks on morphological and lemmatization algorithms: see below.

Another "source of information" for the processing of the assignment of meaning is the knowledge base of the system. Especially referential problems which may emerge in a sentence between main and subordinate clause[1] are more likely to be solved by means of the information of the knowledge base.

Besides this, the communicational context can be useful. It is well-known that it is of great significance for the processing of ellipses and anaphora.

The transition from a sentence-processing to a text-processing system will have effect in this field. Besides the "memory" for contexts the use of the knowledge base will enable BEAST to become a text-processing system. The textual interrelations are then given within the SIREN system by special operators between formulae.

A truly adequate solution of the problem of automatic text understanding can only be found parallel to the corresponding inquiry of text theory and discourse-analysis[2].

---

[1] For relative clauses a partial solution of referential problems between relative pronoun and the noun referred to has already been implemented.

[2] See Petöfi 1977 and Winograd 1977.

Bibliography

Austin, J.L. (1962): How to do things with words. Cambridge, Mass.

Bar-Hillel, Y. (1967): "Review: The structure of language, ed. by Fodor & Katz" Language 43.

Bartsch, R./Vennemann, T. (1972): Semantic structures, Frankfurt/M.

Belnap, N.D./Steel, T.B. (1976): The logic of questions and answers. New Haven.

Bloomfield, L. (1939): Linguistic aspects of science. Chicago.

Bobrow, D./Kaplan, R./Kay, M./Norman, D./Thompson, H./Winograd, T. (1977): "GUS, A frame-driven dialog system", Artificial Intelligence 8.

Charniak, E. (1977a): "Inference and knowledge in language comprehension" in: E.W. Elcock/D. Michie (eds.): Machine Intelligence 8. Chichester, Sussex.

----- (1977b): "Referenz und Fragebeantwortung in einfachen Erzählungen". in: P. Eisenberg (Hrsg.): Semantik und künstliche Intelligenz. Berlin.

Cherniavsky, V./Engel, H. (1976): "A data manipulation language". SNR 5/76.

Cherniavsky, V./Schneider, H.-J. (1978): "On data information systems". SNR 2/78.

Chomsky, N. (1967): "The formal nature of language". Appendix of: Eric H. Lenneberg: Biological foundations of language. New York.

Codd, E. (1974): "Seven steps to rendezvous with the casual user" in: J. Klimbie/K. Koffeman (eds.): Data Base Management. Amsterdam.

Engel, H. (1976): "A data query language". SNR 6/76.

Fillmore, C.J. (1968): "The case for case". in: E. Bach/R. Harms (eds.): Universals in linguistic theory. London.

Ginsburg, S./Partee, B. (1969): "A mathematical model of transformational grammars". Information & Control 15.

Habel, Ch. (1977): "BEAST - Ein semantik-orientiertes Paraphrase-System". CIS-Bericht 9/77.

Habel, Ch./Kanngießer, S. (1977): "Review article: Natürliche generative Grammatik". Lingua 42.

Habel, Ch./Rollinger, C.-R./Schmidt, A. (1978a): "Firsthand and secondhand knowledge - Processing of modal concepts". SNR 1/78.

Habel, Ch. /Rollinger, C.-R./Schmidt, A. (1978b): "Eine semantische Repräsentationssprache zur Darstellung modaler Konzepte." SNR 6/78.

----- (1978c): "Machine translation of natural language into a modal representation language". Vortrag: COLING 78 - Bergen.

Habel, Ch./Schmidt, A. (1978): "Eine modallogische Repräsentationssprache zur Darstellung von Wissen". CIS Bericht 14/78.

Habel, Ch./Schmidt, A./Schweppe, H. (1977a): "On automatic paraphrasing of natural language expressions". SNR 3/77.

----- (1977b) "BEAST - Ein Übersetzungssystem zur natürlich-sprachlichen Kommunikation mit Datenbasen". SNR 4/77.

----- (1978): "Zur automatischen Paraphrasierung natürlich-sprachlicher Sätze". in: M. Conte/A. Ramat/P. Ramat (Hrsg.): Wortstellung und Bedeutung. Tübingen.

Habel, Ch. et al. (forthc.): "Zur illokutiven Komponente der semantischen Repräsentationssprache MSRL" (tentative title).

Hintikka, H. (1969): "Semantics for propositional attitudes". in: J.W. Davis/D.J. Hockney (eds.): Studies in philosophical logic. Dordrecht.

Huismann, H. (1979): "Entwurf einer natürlich-sprachlichen Schnittstelle (Kopplung BEAST - SIDAB)" Diplomarbeit - TU Berlin.

Kalish, D./Montague, R. (1964): Logic - Techniques of formal reasoning. New York.

Kripke, S. (1972): "Naming and Necessity". in: D. Davidson/G. Harman (eds.): Semantics of natural languages. Dordrecht.

Minsky, M. (1975): "A framework for representing knowledge". in: P.H. Winston (ed.): The psychology of computer vision. New York.

Munz, R. (1976): Das WEB-Modell. Dissertation - Universität Stuttgart.

----- (1978): "The WELL-System". Information Systems 3.

Norman, D.A./Rumelhart, D.E. (1975): Explorations in cognition. San Francisco.

Partee, B.H. (1975): "Montague grammar and transformational grammar. Linguistic Inquiry 6."

Petöfi, J.S. (1977): "Textrepräsentation und Lexikon als semantische Netzwerke". in: K. Heger/J.S. Petöfi (Hrsg.): Kasustheorie, Klassifikation, semantische Interpretation. Hamburg.

Raphael, B. (1976): The thinking computer. San Francisco.

Rollinger, C.-R. (1978): "Zur Erschließung impliziten Wissens aus semantischen Netzen". CIS-Bericht 15/78.

v. Savigny, E. (1974): Die Philosophie der normalen Sprache. Frankfurt/M.

Schmidt, A. (forthc.): "Überlegungen zur desambiguierten Übersetzung" (tentative title).

Schmidt, A./Schneider, H.-J. (1978): Natürlich-sprachliche Frage-Antwort-Systeme /Bedeutung, Realisierung, Ausblick/", SNR 3/78.

Schneider, H.-J. (ed.) (1978): Automatische Erstellung semantischer Netze. Abschlußbericht für den Zeitraum 1975-1978. Berlin.

Searle, H. (1969): Speech acts. London.

Simmons, R./Bruce, B. (1971): "Some relations between predicate calculus and semantic net representations of discourse". Proceedings 2nd IJCAI.

Turing, A.N. (1950): "Computing machinery and intelligence". Mind 59.

Wang, J.-T. (1979): "Struktur-Computation and ATN-Formalismus" in: Christaller, T./Metzing, D. (eds.): Augmented Transition Network-Grammatiken (Band 1). Berlin.

Wang, J,-T./Habel, Ch. (forthc.): "Eine Muster-gesteuerte Übersetzung aus logischen Sprachen in die natürliche Sprache" (tentative title)

Weizenbaum, J. (1976): Computer power and human reason. San Francisco.

Wilks, Y. (1974): "One small head - Models and theories in linguistics". Foundations of Language 11.

Winograd, T. (1972): Understanding natural language. Edinburgh.

----- (1973): A procedural model of language understanding". in: R. Schank/K. Colby (eds.): Computer models of thought and language.

----- (1975): "Frame representations and the declarative/procedural controversy". in: D. Bobrow/A. Collins (eds.): Representation and Understanding. New York.

Winogard, T. (1977): "A framework for understanding discourse". Stanford AIM 297.

Abbreviations:

SNR = Report of the Project "Automatische Erstellung semantischer Netze" (Automatic Construction of Semantical Networks), Technical University of Berlin.

CIS = Research Group "Computergestützte Informationssysteme" (Computer-aided Information Systems), Technical University of Berlin.

THE ANATOMY
OF THE NATURAL LANGUAGE DIALOGUE SYSTEM
H A M - R P M

by

W. v. Hahn, W. Hoeppner, A. Jameson, W. Wahlster*

* Project 'Simulation of Natural-Language Understanding'
University of Hamburg. Germanisches Seminar
D-2000 Hamburg 13, Von-Melle-Park 6
Federal Republic of Germany

ABSTRACT: HAM-RPM is a dialogue system which converses with a human partner in colloquial German about limited, but interchangeable scenes. The objective of this report is to give a detailed, complete and self-contained description of the system in its present state of implementation. After a discussion of the goals and methodological principles which guide our research and a short introduction to the implementation language an overview of the system's architecture, of its knowledge base and of the domains of discourse is given. Then each processing phase from the analysis of natural-language input to the generation of a natural-language utterance is described in detail. The examples used during these descriptions are supplemented by transcripts of complete dialogue sessions. Finally HAM-RPM's programming environment is described.

1 THEORETICAL AND TECHNICAL BACKGROUND OF HAM-RPM

1.1 UNDERLYING ISSUES

HAM-RPM is a dialogue system which converses with a human partner in colloquial German about limited, but interchangeable scenes.

Recently, much AI research even in non-linguistic areas has been seeking contact with natural-language simulation systems. This interest has been motivated by many arguments, including the following:

- Natural language is a highly efficient means of interacting with non-linguistic AI systems.
- The other cognitive abilities, which are objects of interest of AI systems in general, are often directly or indirectly connected with linguistic abilities.
- Natural language systems are better suited to the expectations of naive users and can be managed by them better.

Most natural-language artificial-intelligence systems have been developed as interfaces to some sort of task-oriented system. Typical of this function are question-answering systems involved with information storage and retrieval or other documentation tasks (WALTZ 1977). In the research group 'Simulation of Language Understanding' at the University of Hamburg, we are investigating the feasability of computer simulation of natural-language structures and their communicative use in a systematic way. We are thus studying natural language as an object of interest in itself.

The overall goal of HAM-RPM can be characterized as the simulation of a natural-language dialogue partner on a computer. The three main components of this definition will now be described in more detail.

1.1.1 Simulation

The kind of simulation aimed at is simulation of function rather than that of performance; the degree to which this is achieved varies greatly from one component of the program to another.

The first direction of research on HAM-RPM involved an attempt to extend the breadth of the system so as to obtain a representative variety of linguistic features of performance. With respect to the function of language, this meant that we built up a sequence of communicative mechanisms extending as completely as possible from the analysis of an input sentence (more generally: a text) to the utterance of a response. We are convinced that a system is, in respect of methodology, the more interesting the more it generates or analyzes a really large number of performance features. First, such systems are realistic enough (reduction in the number of unsimulated features of the original, cf. Report No. 4). Much more importantly, these systems permit the investigation of the interactions among a large number of dynamic components. Incidentally, the performance of such systems is generally very difficult for the naive user to predict.

While we have been working in this first direction of research - the one which we have emphasized since the beginning of the project - some components have been represented only by provisional processes to mark the interfaces and to return acceptable values in standard situations.

It seems to us to be very important for sophisticated simulations that right from the beginning each new or modified process be testable in an existing and running program representing the communicative framework, so that each extension of the system takes place under comparable conditions and endless problems involving 'local correctness' of program components are avoided. With the aim of obtaining a realistic simulation of a dialogue partner, we have attempted to develop the different linguistic, communicative and cognitive abilities of the system as evenly as possible. Accordingly, we have developed individual parts of the system only to the extent which seemed sensible in view of the state of development of the system as a whole. We hoped thus to avoid both the dominance of one component or another (an often-criticized feature of earlier systems) and disadvantageous restrictions placed by one weak component on other components of the system.

1.1.2 Natural language

Our intention is that the linguistic behaviour of the system should exhibit the typical characteristics of natural-language dialogue behaviour. The features of special interest are:

- vague statements and inferences
- 'incomplete' syntactic structures
- implicit and redundant semantic structures.

While question-answering systems even today often proceed from the assumption that the best effects can be obtained using a restricted technical language like a subset of natural language, we try to adopt stylistic and pragmatic standards which are influenced as little as possible by the structures of technical language.

Furthermore, we intend that the internal structures used during the processing of a sentence remain as long as possible closely related to the structures of colloquial language, as we believe that colloquial language best exhibits the characteristics of natural language as a means of communication.

The efficiency of communication in colloquial language has undoubtedly been underrated by most application-oriented AI research. The work of HENDRIX 1977 and WALTZ 1978, among others, has shown, however, that the usefulness of such systems would be increased if they adopted some of the basic communicative and linguistic structures of this kind of language.

From a linguistic point of view, the combination - aimed at by HAM-RPM - of realistic natural-language utterances, an acting system, and a scene to which it can refer, is most interesting: Modern linguistics has been trying to establish a revised explication of language based on the notion of speech-action complexes and reference semantics. Traditional ways of proposing hypotheses or theories are in connection with this type of analysis less powerful with respect to:

- the assessment of the practicability of the underlying linguistic model
- the range of explanation
- the problems raised by interactions among the components of a complex system.

1.1.3 Communication

By speaking of a 'dialogue' partner we wish to emphasize that the spectrum of verbal actions performed by the system should be much wider than in question-answering systems. The sequences of verbal behaviour possible within dialogues with HAM-RPM are shown in Fig. 19. A prerequisite for such a breadth of simulation is the possibility of a uniform interpretation of all the system utterances as a simulation of natural behaviour. It is a part of our strategy in building the system, that no system messages, presentation of the system data, or the like are admitted when the system is in dialogue mode.

It is a further fundamental feature of more sophisticated artificial-intelligence systems to allow metacommunicative dialogues. This permits both partners to deal with problems involving the process of communication itself, giving them the opportunity to clear up misunderstandings, supply missing information, and so on. Here are two (independent) examples:

(1) AUF WAS BEZIEHT SICH 'ES'? (system)
What does 'it' refer to?

(2) WARUM WILLST DU DAS WISSEN? (partner)
Why do you want to know that?

1.1.4 Goals

By explaining how the system works and discussing the philosophy underlying the algorithms and their implementation, we hope to make a contribution to the following topics of research:

- the value of AI systems as a powerful scientific method of formulating hypothesis or theories, in particular as a way of operationalizing linguistic speech-act theories
- the extension of the scope of the simulation of natural language
- considerations of the communicative relevance of colloquial language in AI systems
- natural-language communication with computers.

Furthermore, HAM-RPM can be used as a testbed for the exploration of detailed theories about certain aspects of intelligent language behaviour.

Unlike many other workers in the field of AI, we try to take into account the results obtained by language researchers using other paradigms.

1.1.5 The aims of this report

Although the system HAM-RPM is described in this document in considerable detail, this document is not intended for use as a manual for the system; this function is rather fulfilled by HAM-RPM Memo No. 6.

On the other hand, relatively little is said here about the results of this research or the theoretical considerations underlying its design. Discussions of these issues can be found in the HAM-RPM Reports.

Although a great deal of work on the system is still planned, it is here described exactly as it is presently implemented, with the aim of presenting a complete picture of a large system, including both its strong and weak points. The examples of the system's behaviour presented are all excerpts from actual dialogues conducted with it. The English translations are as literal as possible within the bounds of acceptable English style.

1.2 THE PROGRAMMING LANGUAGE FUZZY

1.2.1 General characterization

HAM-RPM is implemented in FUZZY (LEFAIVRE 1977), a very-high-level artificial-intelligence language containing the most important mechanisms found in other languages in the tradition of PLANNER. Its distinguishing features are a set of mechanisms for dealing with fuzzy knowledge.

The description of FUZZY which follows is only detailed enough to permit an understanding of the rest of this document. All of the mechanisms mentioned are in fact more general and more powerful than the simplified descriptions given here suggest. Some features which appear in only one or two examples are not explained here, as it is assumed that their use will be understandable in context. FUZZY is embedded in Rutgers-UCI-LISP (LEFAIVRE 1978). Brief introductions to LISP can be found in SIKLOSSY 1976 and WINSTON 1977.

1.2.2 Pattern matching

FUZZY's pattern matcher uses 'FUZZY variables', which are independent of LISP variables. The prefix '?' indicates that a variable is to receive a value, whereas the prefix '!' causes the variable to be evaluated. Thus after the successful match

(1) (MATCH (A FORM OF ?STEM) (A FORM OF CHILD))

the FUZZY variable '?STEM' is bound to 'CHILD'. The expression

(2) (L STEM CHILDREN !STEM)

is then said to 'instantiate' to

(3) (L STEM CHILDREN (CHILD)) .

If the given pattern doesn't match the given structure, the match is said to 'fail', i.e. no FUZZY variables are bound and the special atom FAIL is returned. Otherwise the match is said to 'succeed'. The words 'fail' and 'succeed' are also used in this way in connection with data-base search (see 1.2.3) and the invocation of procedural knowledge (see 1.2.4).

A '?' standing alone matches anything. Segment variables are indicated by the double prefixes '??' and '!!'.

1.2.3 The associative net

FUZZY provides an assertional data base whose entries have the form

(4) ((D APPLE/ JUICE SWEET) . 0.7) .

The left-hand side is an arbitrary list structure. In (4), it is interpreted by HAM-RPM as ascribing sweetness to apple juice.

The number on the right is the 'z-value' which characterizes the assertions in FUZZY's data base. The z-value is often interpreted as a fuzzy truth value, but it is used in HAM-RPM in several other ways as well. In (4) the interpretation is in terms of frequency: apple juice is usually sweet. Note that the interpretation of the z-value within a particular context is specified only implicitly, by the procedures which make use of the assertion in question.

The FUZZY primitive for adding assertions to the associative net is ADD:

(5) (ADD (D APPLE/ JUICE SWEET) 0.7)

Assertions are retrieved using the primitive FETCH, whose first argument is a pattern. The command

(6) (FETCH (D ?OBJECT SWEET) 0.5)

will return an assertion which matches the pattern and which has a z-value equal to or greater than 0.5, such as the assertion in (4). Since the assertions are ordered according to z-value in the net, the appropriate assertion with the highest z-value is returned. If no such assertion is present in the net, the FETCH fails.

The associative net can be divided into any number of separate parts, called CONTEXTs, each of which has a name. The procedure CONTEXT is used to switch the FUZZY interpreter's attention from one CONTEXT to another. Thus the command

(7) (CONTEXT 'LEXIKON)

means that all following ADDs and FETCHes will refer only to the part of the net called LEXIKON.

The interpretation of the various CONTEXTs is up to the programmer. In HAM-RPM, the CONTEXT mechanism is often used simply as a way of avoiding having data which have nothing to do with each other shuffled together in a single part of the data base.

1.2.4 DEDUCE-procedures

Knowledge can be represented procedurally in FUZZY using DEDUCE-procedures, as exemplified by the following definition:

```
(8)  (PROC NAME: DRINK-TASTY
       (D (*R ?OBJECT (EQUAL (*TYPE !OBJECT 'DRINK))) TASTY)
              (FETCH (D !OBJECT SWEET))
              (FETCH (D !OBJECT NON-ALCOHOLIC))
              (SUCCEED))
```

This procedure could be invoked directly, for instance with the command

```
(9)   (DRINK-TASTY (D APPLE/ JUICE TASTY))
```

to check whether apple juice is to be considered tasty. If the interpreter could find assertions in the net to the effect that apple juice was sweet and non-alcoholic, the procedure would succeed. Usually however, DEDUCE-procedures are invoked not by name, but via their 'calling pattern'. In (8), this is the expression in the second line, which specifies that this procedure can be used to show that a particular object which is a drink is tasty. The command

```
(10)   (GOAL (D APPLE/ JUICE TASTY))
```

causes the interpreter first to perform a FETCH on the given pattern to see if such an assertion is stored in the associative net. If the FETCH fails, all DEDUCE-procedures whose calling patterns match the pattern passed as an argument to GOAL are invoked in turn, until one of them succeeds.

The primitive GOAL can thus be used to specify a condition without knowledge of how the fulfillment of the condition might be proved. For example, the definition (8) could be made more powerful by replacing the two FETCHes with GOALs. (The version of this procedure actually used in HAM-RPM is shown in section 2.12.3).

1.2.5 Procedure demons

Each DEDUCE-procedure has a procedure demon assigned to it by the programmer, which supervises the execution of the procedure: after the evaluation of each expression in the procedure, the value of the expression is passed to the responsible demon,which can then take appropriate action, such as aborting the evaluation of the procedure if the prospects of success appear too poor.

A typical activity of procedure demons is the updating of a special variable ZACCUM, which is usually a number. For example, FUZZY's default demon continually resets ZACCUM to the minimum of all the z-values which have been returned during the evaluation of the procedure. Thus if, during the evaluation of the procedure in (8) the first FETCH succeeded with a z-value of 0.7 and the second with 0.5, the value of ZACCUM at the end of the execution would be 0.5. This value could be used to estimate the reliability of the conclusion that the drink in question was tasty.

1.2.6 The language AIMDS

A powerful extension of FUZZY, called AIMDS, has been developed at Rutgers University (SRIDHARAN 1978). An important feature of this language is its implementation of the 'template' data structure. Templates are comparable to the data structures often referred to as 'frames' or 'schemata' (BOBROW/WINOGRAD 1977).

None of the mechanisms of AIMDS are used in the currently implemented version of HAM-RPM, but experiments are being performed in the following areas:

- the representation of semantic deep structure (see 2.11.1)
- the declarative representation of prototypical dialogue sequences
- the representation of complex actions.

2 PROCESSING STEPS IN HAM-RPM

2.1 OVERVIEW

2.1.1 Domains of discourse

The domains of discourse which will in most cases underly the examples in this report are a living room (WORLD3) and a traffic scene (WORLD2).

To give an impression of the kind of objects which are contained in these domains two graphic representations illustrate the scenes. These drawings are bird's-eye views, in which the locations of objects are represented by circles. Not all of the properties of the objects are represented in these figures.

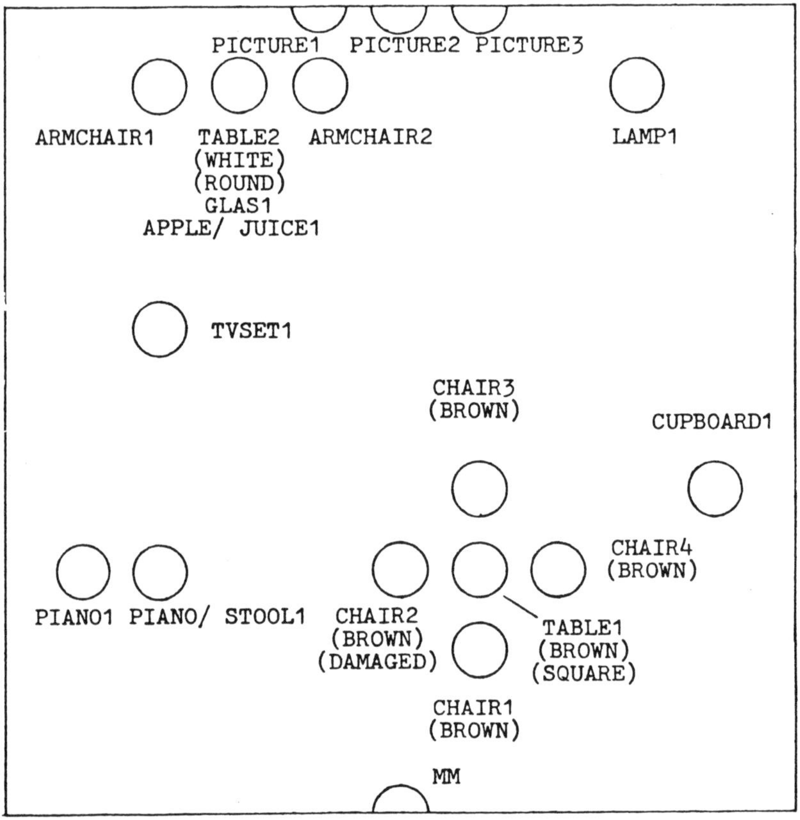

Fig. 1

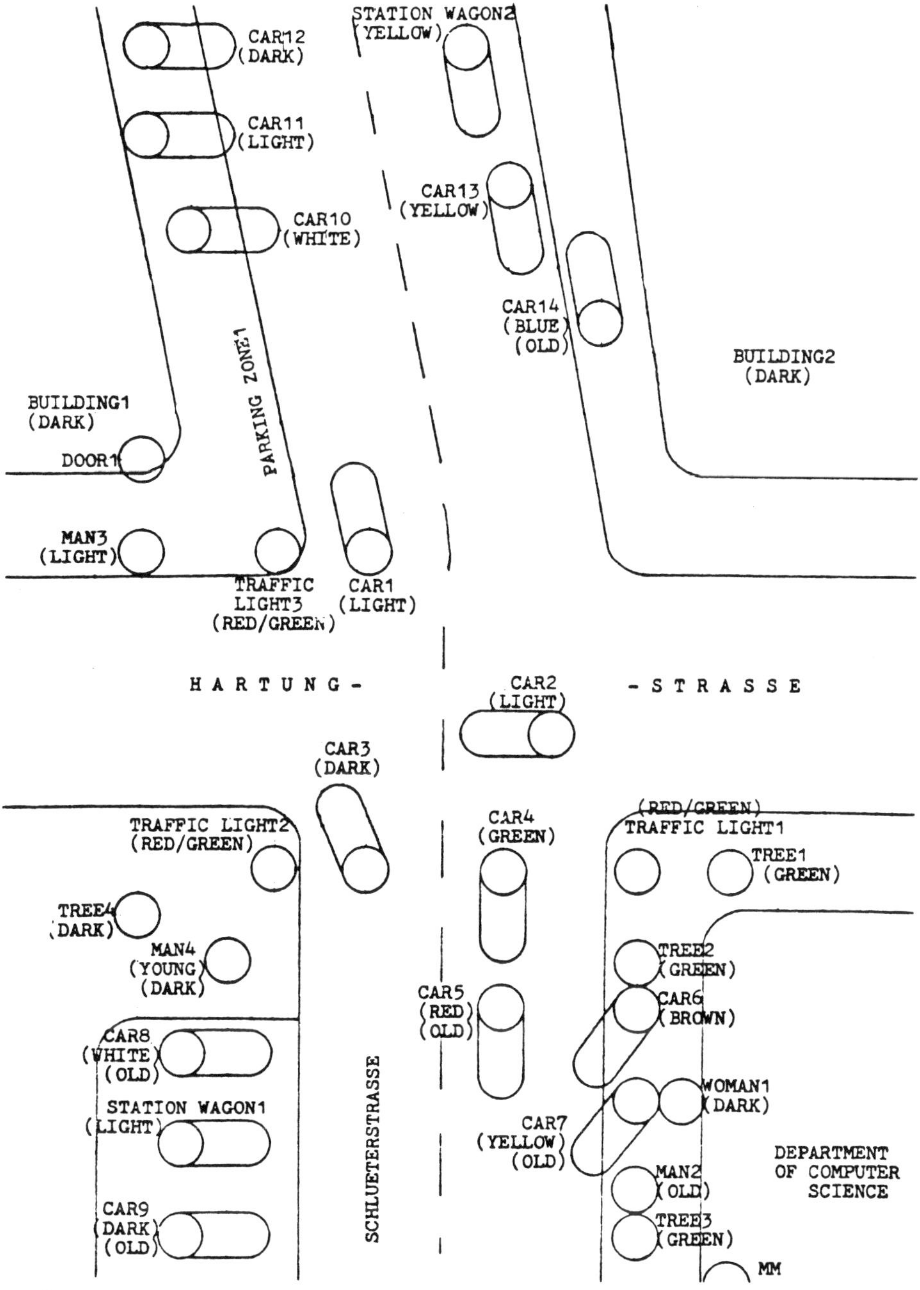
STATION WAGON2
(YELLOW)
CAR12
(DARK)
CAR11
(LIGHT)
CAR10
(WHITE)
CAR13
(YELLOW)
CAR14
(BLUE)
(OLD)
BUILDING2
(DARK)
BUILDING1
(DARK)
DOOR1
PARKING ZONE1
MAN3
(LIGHT)
TRAFFIC
LIGHT3
(RED/GREEN)
CAR1
(LIGHT)
HARTUNG-
-STRASSE
CAR2
(LIGHT)
CAR3
(DARK)
TRAFFIC LIGHT2
(RED/GREEN)
CAR4
(GREEN)
(RED/GREEN)
TRAFFIC LIGHT1
TREE1
(GREEN)
TREE4
(DARK)
MAN4
(YOUNG)
(DARK)
TREE2
(GREEN)
CAR5
(RED)
(OLD)
CAR6
(BROWN)
CAR8
(WHITE)
(OLD)
STATION WAGON1
(LIGHT)
SCHLUETERSTRASSE
WOMAN1
(DARK)
CAR7
(YELLOW)
(OLD)
DEPARTMENT
OF COMPUTER
SCIENCE
MAN2
(OLD)
CAR9
(DARK)
(OLD)
TREE3
(GREEN)
MM

Fig. 2

2.1.2 Processing phases

This section introduces the interaction between the components of HAM-RPM and the connections of processing modules and the knowledge base.

Fig. 3 represents the components in a linear order their functions being indicated by a few key words. The first two pages may be regarded as the environment of the system. On the following four pages components for the processing of single sentences in the context of a dialogue are illustrated. The names of components on the left-hand side of each page represent the call to components which deviate from the linear ordering. The numbers on the right refer to the sections of this report, in which the components are described in detail.

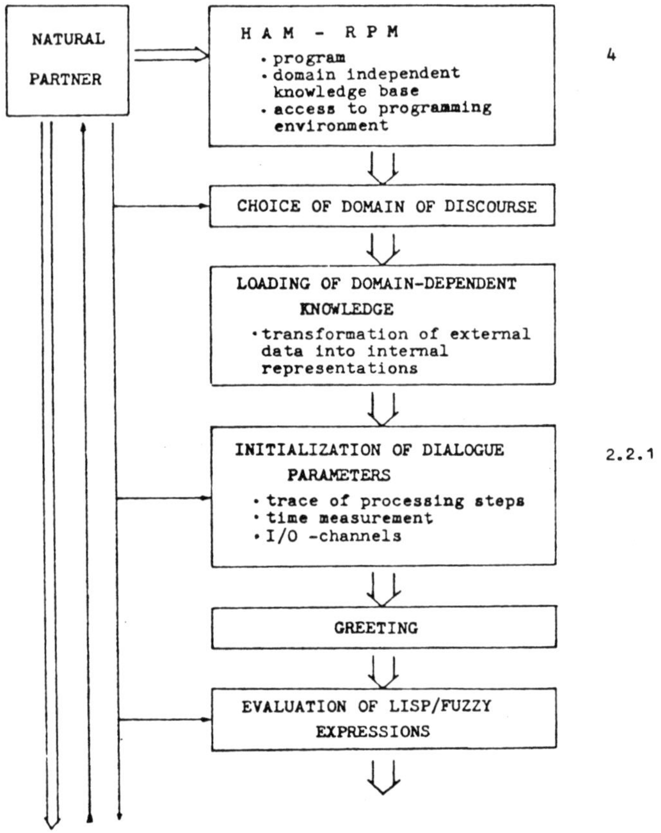

Fig. 3a

Fig. 4 lists the parts of the knowledge base whose external representation is introduced in section 2.1.3. Arrows pointing to names of processing components indicate the accessing of the corresponding part of the knowledge base by the component. Arrows the other way around represent the construction or modification of parts of the knowledge base by processing components.

In this report we do not distinguish the names of files containing domain-dependent knowledge with numbers, such as REF2.FUZ which is the actual name of the file on which the referential semantic network for WORLD2 is stored.

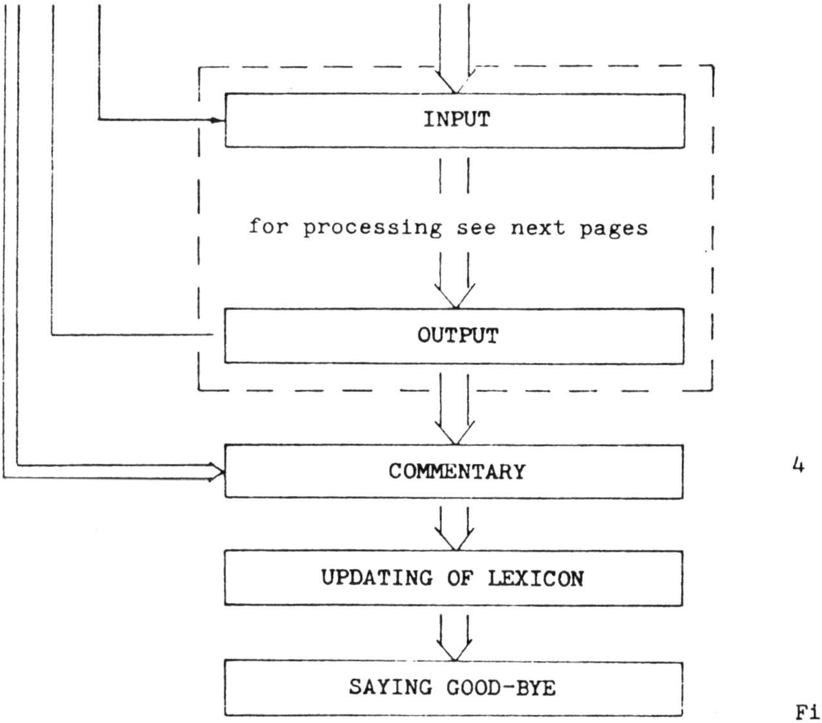

Fig. 3b

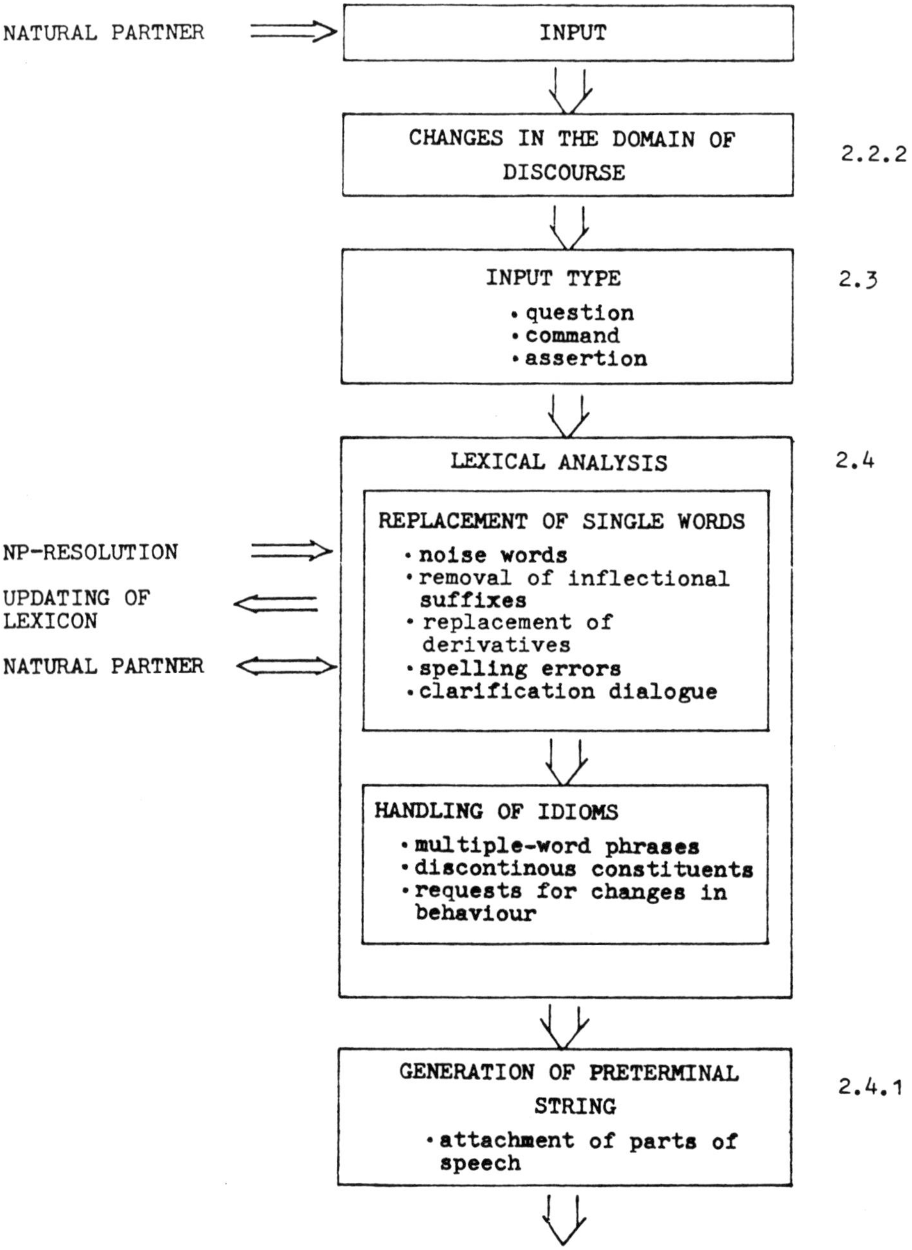
NATURAL PARTNER
INPUT
CHANGES IN THE DOMAIN OF DISCOURSE
2.2.2
INPUT TYPE
• question
• command
• assertion
2.3
LEXICAL ANALYSIS
2.4
NP-RESOLUTION
UPDATING OF LEXICON
NATURAL PARTNER
REPLACEMENT OF SINGLE WORDS
• noise words
• removal of inflectional suffixes
• replacement of derivatives
• spelling errors
• clarification dialogue
HANDLING OF IDIOMS
• multiple-word phrases
• discontinous constituents
• requests for changes in behaviour
GENERATION OF PRETERMINAL STRING
• attachment of parts of speech
2.4.1

Fig. 3c

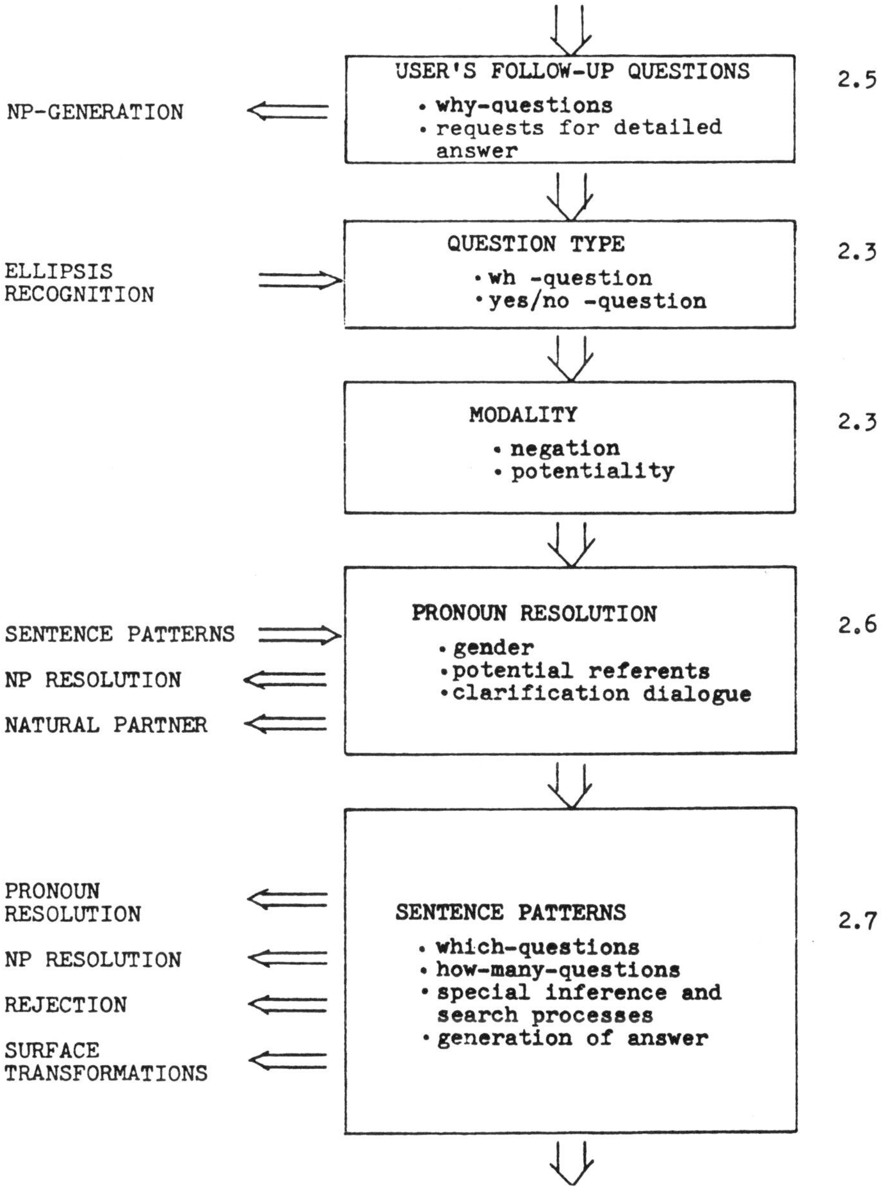
USER'S FOLLOW-UP QUESTIONS
• why-questions
• requests for detailed answer
2.5
NP-GENERATION
QUESTION TYPE
• wh -question
• yes/no -question
2.3
ELLIPSIS RECOGNITION
MODALITY
• negation
• potentiality
2.3
PRONOUN RESOLUTION
• gender
• potential referents
• clarification dialogue
2.6
SENTENCE PATTERNS
NP RESOLUTION
NATURAL PARTNER
SENTENCE PATTERNS
• which-questions
• how-many-questions
• special inference and search processes
• generation of answer
2.7
PRONOUN RESOLUTION
NP RESOLUTION
REJECTION
SURFACE TRANSFORMATIONS

Fig. 3d

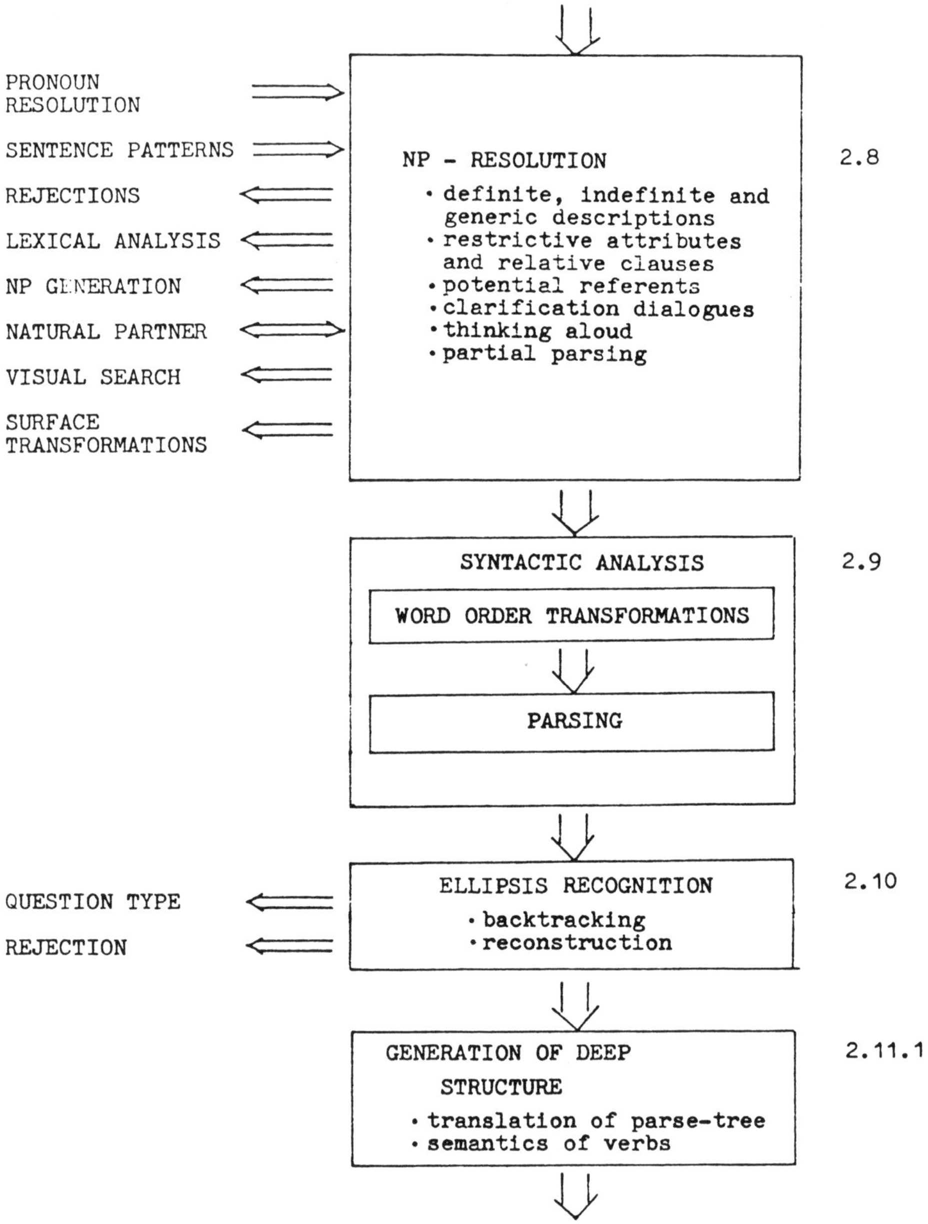
PRONOUN RESOLUTION
SENTENCE PATTERNS
REJECTIONS
LEXICAL ANALYSIS
NP GENERATION
NATURAL PARTNER
VISUAL SEARCH
SURFACE TRANSFORMATIONS
NP - RESOLUTION
• definite, indefinite and generic descriptions
• restrictive attributes and relative clauses
• potential referents
• clarification dialogues
• thinking aloud
• partial parsing
2.8
SYNTACTIC ANALYSIS
WORD ORDER TRANSFORMATIONS
PARSING
2.9
QUESTION TYPE
REJECTION
ELLIPSIS RECOGNITION
• backtracking
• reconstruction
2.10
GENERATION OF DEEP STRUCTURE
• translation of parse-tree
• semantics of verbs
2.11.1

Fig. 3e

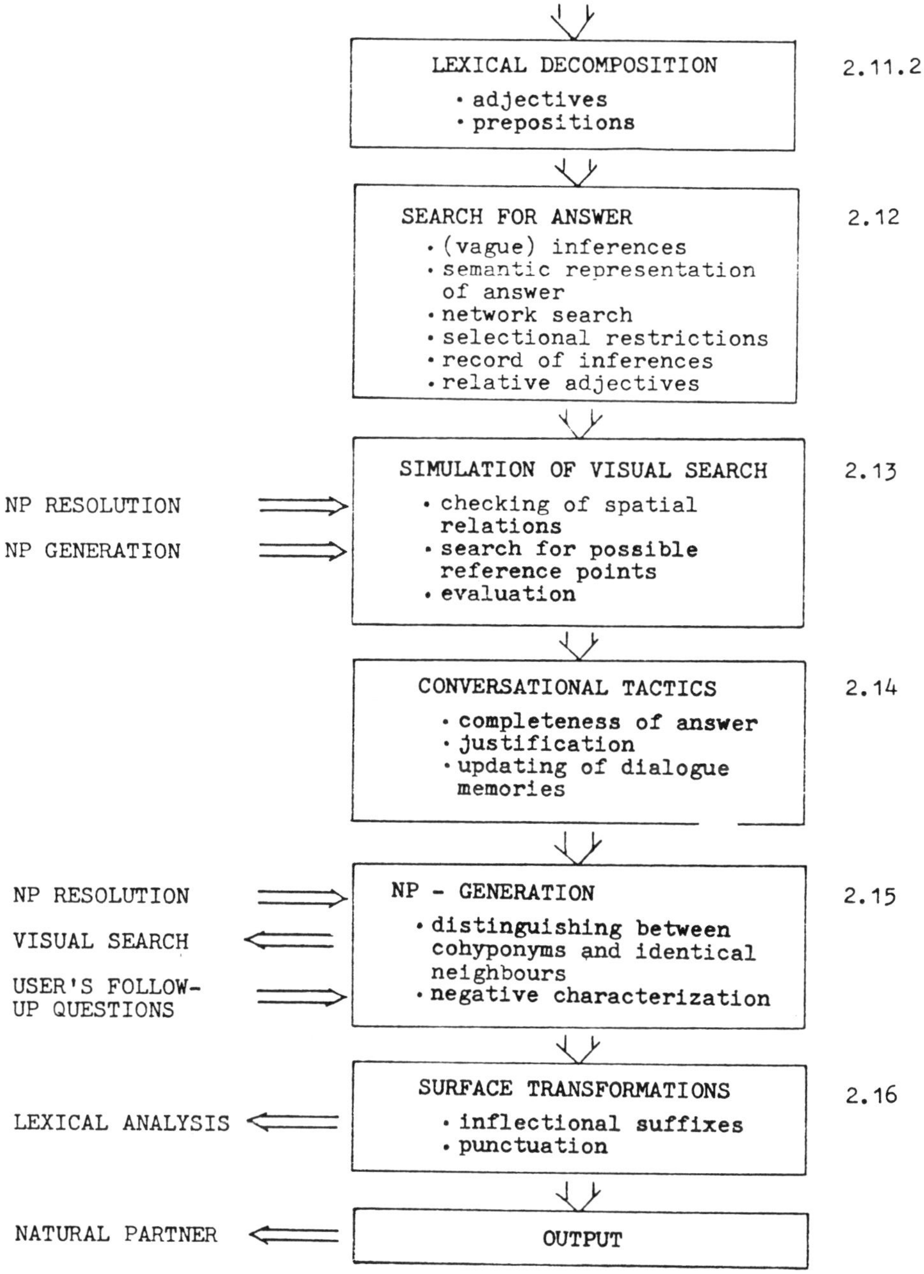
LEXICAL DECOMPOSITION
• adjectives
• prepositions
2.11.2
SEARCH FOR ANSWER
• (vague) inferences
• semantic representation of answer
• network search
• selectional restrictions
• record of inferences
• relative adjectives
2.12
NP RESOLUTION
NP GENERATION
SIMULATION OF VISUAL SEARCH
• checking of spatial relations
• search for possible reference points
• evaluation
2.13
CONVERSATIONAL TACTICS
• completeness of answer
• justification
• updating of dialogue memories
2.14
NP RESOLUTION
VISUAL SEARCH
USER'S FOLLOW-UP QUESTIONS
NP - GENERATION
• distinguishing between cohyponyms and identical neighbours
• negative characterization
2.15
LEXICAL ANALYSIS
SURFACE TRANSFORMATIONS
• inflectional suffixes
• punctuation
2.16
NATURAL PARTNER
OUTPUT

Fig. 3f

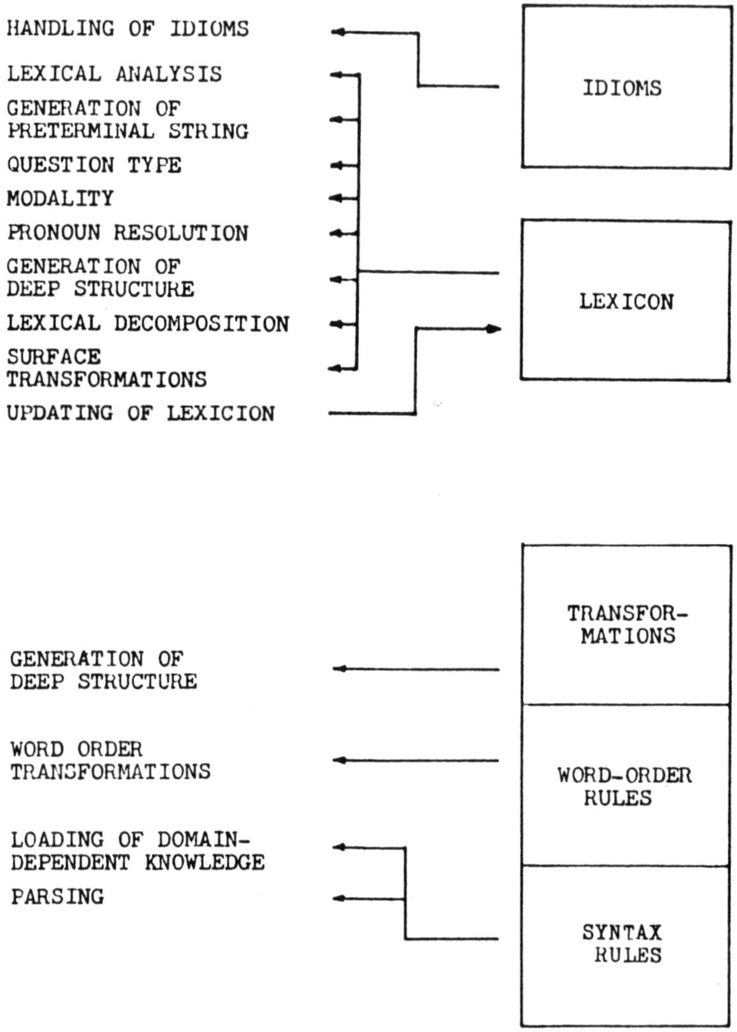
HANDLING OF IDIOMS
LEXICAL ANALYSIS
GENERATION OF PRETERMINAL STRING
QUESTION TYPE
MODALITY
PRONOUN RESOLUTION
GENERATION OF DEEP STRUCTURE
LEXICAL DECOMPOSITION
SURFACE TRANSFORMATIONS
UPDATING OF LEXICION
IDIOMS
LEXICON
GENERATION OF DEEP STRUCTURE
WORD ORDER TRANSFORMATIONS
LOADING OF DOMAIN-DEPENDENT KNOWLEDGE
PARSING
TRANSFOR-MATIONS
WORD-ORDER RULES
SYNTAX RULES

Fig. 4a

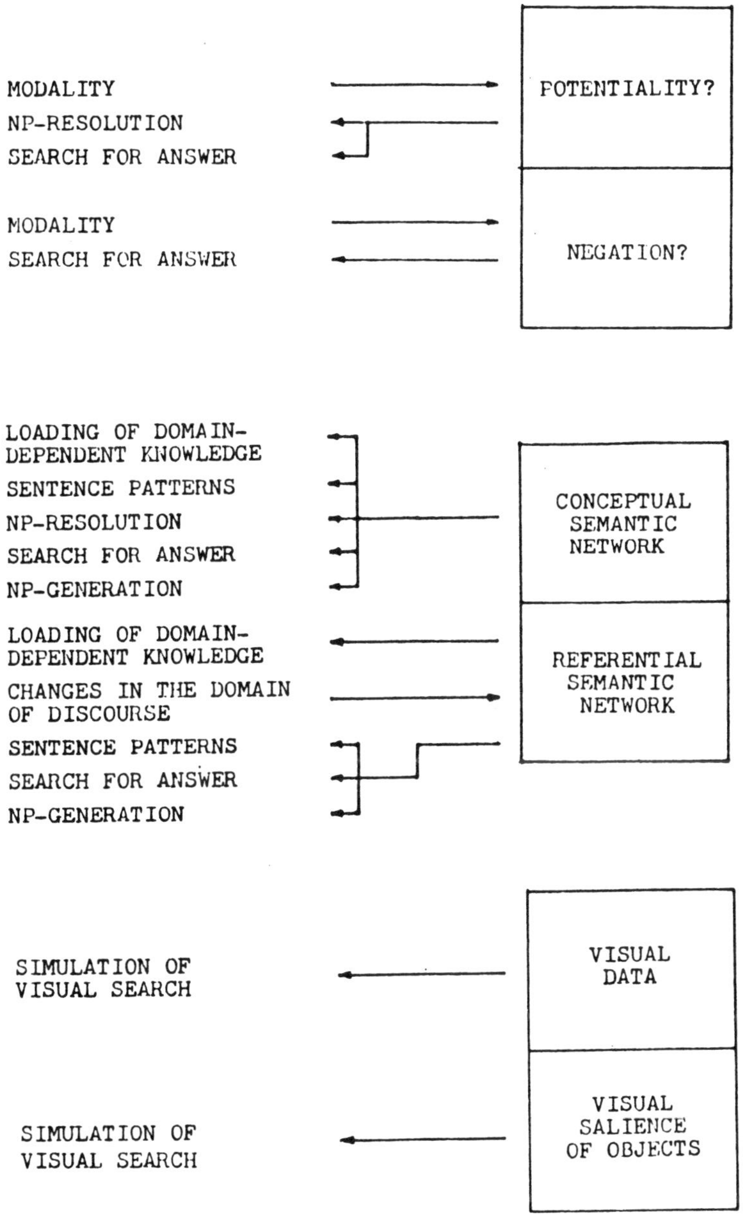
MODALITY
NP-RESOLUTION
SEARCH FOR ANSWER
POTENTIALITY?
MODALITY
SEARCH FOR ANSWER
NEGATION?
LOADING OF DOMAIN-DEPENDENT KNOWLEDGE
SENTENCE PATTERNS
NP-RESOLUTION
SEARCH FOR ANSWER
NP-GENERATION
CONCEPTUAL SEMANTIC NETWORK
LOADING OF DOMAIN-DEPENDENT KNOWLEDGE
CHANGES IN THE DOMAIN OF DISCOURSE
SENTENCE PATTERNS
SEARCH FOR ANSWER
NP-GENERATION
REFERENTIAL SEMANTIC NETWORK
SIMULATION OF VISUAL SEARCH
VISUAL DATA
SIMULATION OF VISUAL SEARCH
VISUAL SALIENCE OF OBJECTS

Fig. 4b

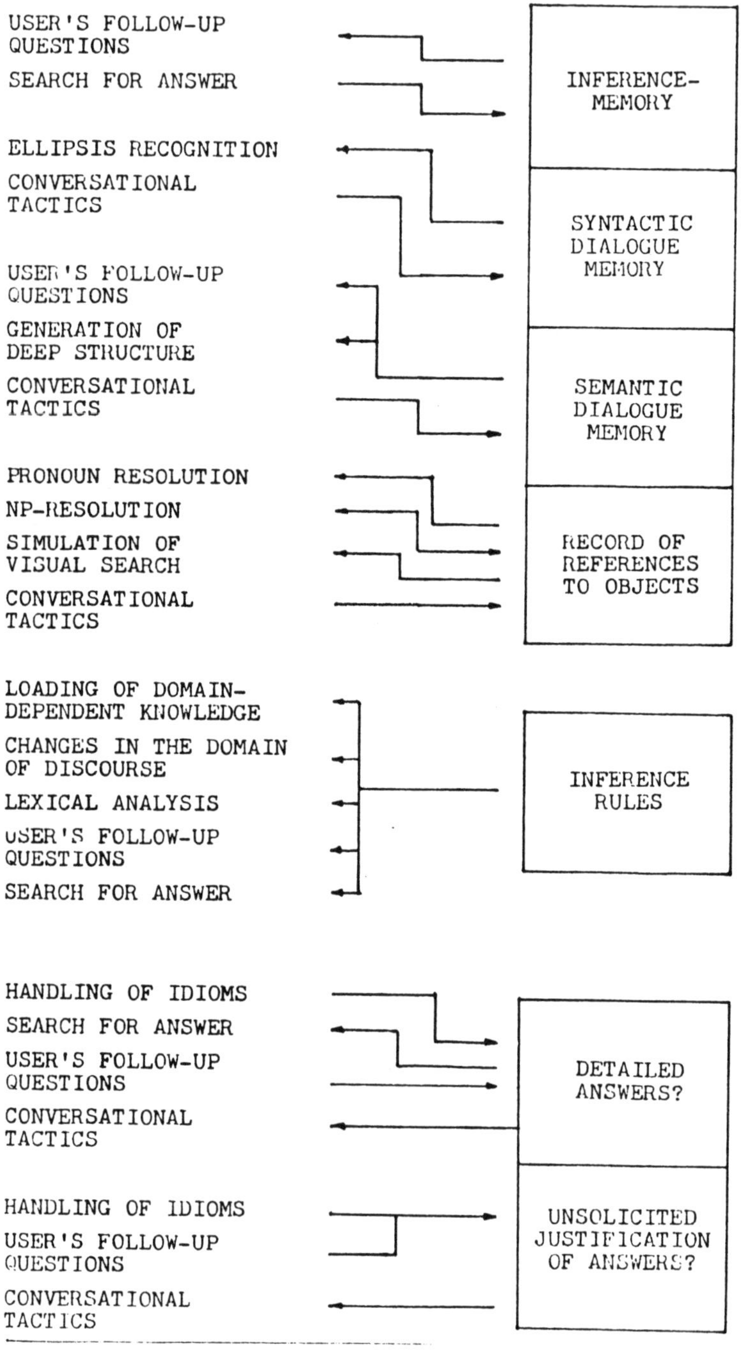
USER'S FOLLOW-UP QUESTIONS
SEARCH FOR ANSWER
INFERENCE-MEMORY
ELLIPSIS RECOGNITION
CONVERSATIONAL TACTICS
SYNTACTIC DIALOGUE MEMORY
USER'S FOLLOW-UP QUESTIONS
GENERATION OF DEEP STRUCTURE
CONVERSATIONAL TACTICS
SEMANTIC DIALOGUE MEMORY
PRONOUN RESOLUTION
NP-RESOLUTION
SIMULATION OF VISUAL SEARCH
CONVERSATIONAL TACTICS
RECORD OF REFERENCES TO OBJECTS
LOADING OF DOMAIN-DEPENDENT KNOWLEDGE
CHANGES IN THE DOMAIN OF DISCOURSE
LEXICAL ANALYSIS
USER'S FOLLOW-UP QUESTIONS
SEARCH FOR ANSWER
INFERENCE RULES
HANDLING OF IDIOMS
SEARCH FOR ANSWER
USER'S FOLLOW-UP QUESTIONS
CONVERSATIONAL TACTICS
DETAILED ANSWERS?
HANDLING OF IDIOMS
USER'S FOLLOW-UP QUESTIONS
CONVERSATIONAL TACTICS
UNSOLICITED JUSTIFICATION OF ANSWERS?

Fig. 4c

2.1.3 Knowledge base

The external representation of the system's knowledge apart from those memory structures built up in the course of a dialogue is distributed on nine files. The purpose of this section is to introduce the syntactic structure of the expressions on the files together with an outline of their semantics, which actually is defined by the procedures which interpret the internal representations.

The overall goal in designing the syntax of the files was to achieve a simple notation which permits the files to be understood and modified even by nonexperts. Therefore many external representations are transformed into internal structures better suited for manipulations by FUZZY and LISP. The internal representation of knowledge will be described together with the components of HAM-RPM which make use of it.

2.1.3.1 Lexicon

The lexicon consists of lexical entries stored on the file LEX.DTA. Each lexical entry has the following form:

(1) $(\langle word \rangle \ (\left\{ \langle relation \rangle \ \langle value \rangle \right\}^{1-n}))$

Here 'word' stands for the actual graphemic string of a word, 'relation' is one of six possible identifiers and 'value' indicates the actual property possessed by the word to be defined. (The curved brackets in (1) are not part of the lexical entry but stand for the fact that more than one relation-value pair is allowed for a single word.)

The six relations are WORTART (part of speech), STAMM (stem), SYNONYM, SEMANTIK (semantics), DEKOMPOSITION and ATT-DEKOMPOSITION (decomposition of attributively used words), each of which may be followed by certain values.

WORTART defines the part of speech of a word and thus is the basic property for generating the preterminal string of an utterance. The following abbreviations for parts of speech, which in terms of (1) were called values, are interpreted by HAM-RPM at present.

(2)

$(\text{NOM} \begin{Bmatrix} \text{MAS} \\ \text{FEM} \\ \text{NTR} \end{Bmatrix})$	Noun with gender (masc., fem., neuter)
$(\text{PRN} \begin{Bmatrix} \text{MAS} \\ \text{FEM} \\ \text{NTR} \end{Bmatrix}^{*})$	Personal pronoun with gender (potentially ambiguous; see 2.6)
(ADJ)	Adjective
(ADV)	Adverb
(VRB)	Verb
(MOD)	Modal verb
(IPRN)	Interrogative pronoun, standing for a noun phrase, e.g. who.
(IPRP)	Interrogative pronoun, standing for a prepositional phrase, e.g. where.
(DET)	Article
(NEG)	Negation particle
(KON)	Conjunction
(ITJ)	Interjection

An example of a lexical entry with only a WORTART specification is:

(3) (BODEN (WORTART (NOM MAS))) for the masculine noun 'floor'

The relation STAMM relates inflected words to their canonical form; thus the value for this relation is again a word, e.g.:

(4) (FAEHRT (STAMM (FAHR))) for the verb form 'drives'.

The canonical form of inflected nouns it is nominative singular, of adjectives it is the uninflected form and of verbs the infinitive stem. Articles, which differ in German according to gender, number and case, have the canonical form D- (definite article) and E- (indefinite article).

SYNONYM is used for replacing one word by one or more words, which already should exist as lexical entries. In the following example the contraction IM is to be expanded to IN DEM (in the):

(5) (IM (SYNONYM (IN DEM))).

Note that only the word(s) substituted is (are) used for further processing as for instance determining the parts of speech. To map words onto other words means to take over everything that is defined for these words.

It is also possible to delete words from the input string by means of the SYNONYM relation. For these purposes the value is NIL:

(6) (MMH (WORTART (ITJ) SYNONYM NIL))

The SYNONYM relation is only inspected in lexical analysis (see 2.4), not in surface transformations (see 2.16), so the WORTART value is not completely superfluous in example (6).

The remaining three relations (SEMANTIK, DEKOMPOSITION and ATT-DEKOMPOSITION) have a value which is the name of a procedure. This procedure is evaluated during the processing of the natural partner's input. In example (7) the procedure LEER-DEK is employed for generating an answer if the word LEER (empty) is used predicatively; in attributive use of this word the procedure LEER-ATTDEK would be evaluated in the NP-resolution component.

```
(7)  (LEER (WORTART (ADJ) DEKOMPOSITION (LEER-DEK)
            ATT-DEKOMPOSITION (LEER-ATTDEK)))
```

About 500 words are contained in the lexicon at present.

2.1.3.2 Idioms

The term 'idiom' is used very broadly within HAM-RPM to denote any pattern comprising several words which are treated by the system as a unit. The term thus covers the following sub-categories:

- idiomatic expressions

(8) WOHER WEISST DU DAS (replaced by WARUM)
What makes you think so why

- rigid multiple-word phrases

(9) FACHBEREICH FUER INFORMATIK (replaced by FBI)
Department of Computer Science

- conventional expressions

(10) ICH MOECHTE GERNE WISSEN ... (deleted)
I'd very much like to know ...

- clauses to which the system responds in a specialized manner

(11) WIE SPAET IST ES?
What's the time?

An idiom is defined in terms of one of the special procedures ERSETZEN (replace), KOMPRIMIEREN (compress) and ERWIDERN (reply), whose operation is described in detail in section 2.4.4. Each of these procedures takes as its first argument a pattern suitable for use by FUZZY's pattern matcher and specifies a certain type of action to be taken when this pattern is recognized within the input string.

Each idiom is stored on the property list of a 'key word' chosen at the time of its definition from among the words which are always present in an occurrance of the idiom (some words in an idiom may be optional, variable, or unspecified). Specifically, under the property IDIOME (idioms) of a word there is a list containing any idiom definitions for which that word has been chosen as a key word.

The idiom definitions - at present about 100 - are stored on a separate file called IDIOM.DTA. An entry on this file has the form which is exemplified in (12).

```
(12)    (DEFPROP WISS
           (ERSETZEN (WOHER WISS DU D-) (WARUM))
           (ERSETZEN (ICH MOEG (*OPT GERNE) WISS) NIL))
        IDIOME)
```

2.1.3.3 Word-order rules

Word-order rules are contained in the file TRANS.RUL and are used to transform shallow structures of questions or commands into the structure of an affirmative proposition (see 2.9.1). The syntax of each word-order rule is:

(13) (<structural change> <structural description>) .

The structural description is a list of the parts of speech of the whole structure to be transformed. The structural change is a list of integers specifying a rearrangement of the shallow structure.

(14) ((2 1 3 4) VRB NOM PRP NOM)

for instance transforms the shallow structure ((VRB (STEH)) (NOM (STUHL1)) (PRP (VOR)) (NOM (TISCH1))) according to the structural change into:

(15) ((NOM (STUHL1)) (VRB (STEH)) (PRP (VOR)) (NOM (TISCH1))) .

50 word-order rules are defined at present.

2.1.3.4 Syntax rules

The file BASIS.RUL contains rules which are interpreted by the parsing process (see 2.9.2). The notation for rules is similar to the one commonly used for context-free grammars. A category is expanded into dominated categories, the expansion being indicated by an arrow. Neither the number of the dominated categories nor their name are restricted in these rules. An example is:

(16) (S -> NP VP)

If the parts of speech are regarded as terminal symbols there are at present six preterminal categories (S, NP, VP, PP, VPA, AP). At present BASIS.RUL consists of 24 rules.

2.1.3.5 Transformation rules

Transformation rules for generating the semantic representation of an input are represented on the file SESY.PAT. This external knowledge base also contains patterns used by other components of HAM-RPM, such as the NP-pattern (see 2.8.2) and the patterns for 'which'- and 'how many'-questions (see 2.7). The syntax of transformation rules is described in section 2.11.1.

2.1.3.6 Inference rules

DEDUCE-procedures (see 1.2.4) and ASSERT-procedures (which correspond to the 'antecedent theorems' of PLANNER) of the programming language FUZZY are contained in the file INFER.PRC. The majority of these procedures are used in connection with changes in the domain of discourse (see 2.2.2), lexical analysis (2.4) and the search for an answer (2.12).

2.1.3.7 Conceptual semantic network

The conceptual semantic network is represented in the file BEGRI.FUZ. Each entry consists of an arc connecting two concept nodes. The general syntactic structure is shown in (17).

(17) ((<arc-name> <concept1> <concept2>) . z-value)

The six symbols which are defined as primitive arc-names are introduced in this section. The semantics of arcs is implicitly defined by the processes interpreting the network structure. The superset relation is represented by the U-arc:

(18) ((U <concept1> <concept2>) . z-value) .

Concept1 is the superset and concept2 the subset; the superset relation between 'thing' and 'object' would thus be represented by (19):

(19) ((U THING OBJECT) . 1.0)

Note that FUZZY's associative net (see 1.2.3) makes the separate representation of inverse relations - e.g. in this case, the subset relation - unnecessary.

Names of dimensions used to describe particular types of objects are introduced by the E-arc:

(20) ((E <type> <dimension>) . z-value)

Dimension is a linguistic variable (ZADEH 1974) which is also associated with particular properties via the V-arc:

(21) ((V <dimension> <property>) . z-value)

The assertions below represent the fact that objects have a colour and some properties on the dimension 'colour'.

```
(22)  ((E OBJECT COLOUR) . 1.0)
      ((V COLOUR BLACK) . 1.0)
      ((V COLOUR RED) . 1.0)
                 :
      ((V COLOUR BROWN) . 1.0)
```

Properties inherent to concepts or classes of concepts are attached to them by the D-arc:

(23) ((D <concept> <property>) . z-value) .

Examples are:

(24) ((D OBJECT SOLID) . 1.0)
((D PIANO BLACK) . 0.7)

The properties of concepts are mostly linked to a linguistic variable via the V-arc. The D-arc in the conceptual semantic network corresponds to the REF-arc of the referential semantic network (see next section).

Finally two arcs represent the relation between concepts and parts. The T-arc links parts to wholes, the z-value representing the degree of necessity of the assertion.

(25) ((T <concept> <part>) . z-value)

In HAM-RPM the z-value of the T-arc corresponds to a linguistic hedge (see Report No. 5).

The ANZAHL-arc (number-arc) is used to represent the number of parts of a concept, the degree of necessity again being expressed by the z-value.

(26) ((ANZAHL <T-arc> <value>) . z-value)

The value in (26) may be either a number or a natural-language quantifier. Using the knowledge of the examples (27) it can be inferred that a tree (BAUM) usually has branches (AST) and that, more often than not, it has many (VIELE) branches.

(27) ((T BAUM AST) . 0.8)
((ANZAHL (T BAUM AST) VIELE) . 0.6)

For a formal definition of the semantics of the primitive arcs the reader is referred to Report No. 5. For further examples and a discussion of part relations see section 2.7.2.

At the end of the next section Fig. 5 shows a section of the conceptual and the referential semantic networks of WORLD3.

2.1.3.8 Referential semantic network

The general structure of referential relations stated in the file REF.FUZ is the same as that of conceptual relations (see (17) in the previous section). Relations of the referential semantic network describe features of objects in the current state of the domain of discourse. Only relations in this network are subject

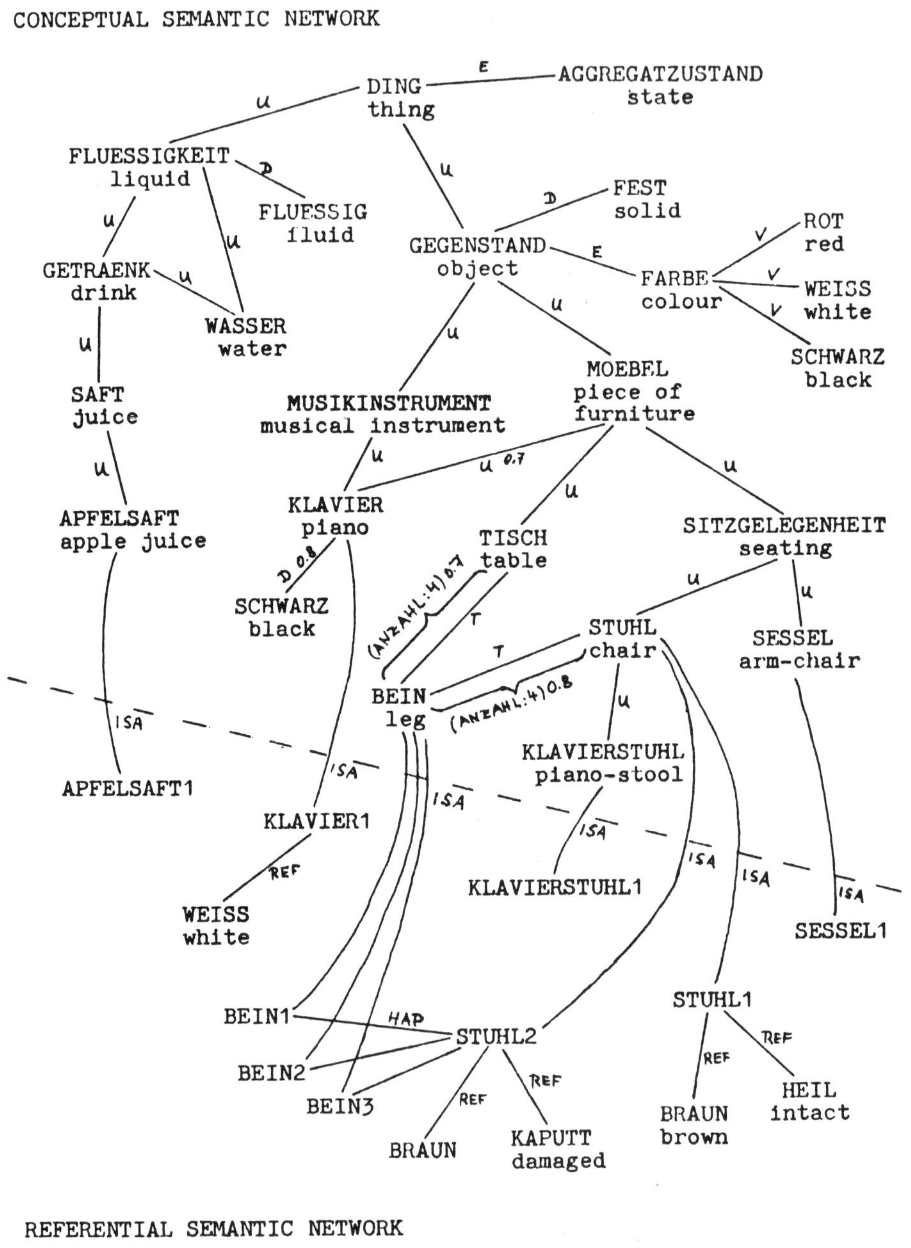
CONCEPTUAL SEMANTIC NETWORK
DING
thing
AGGREGATZUSTAND
state
FLUESSIGKEIT
liquid
FLUESSIG
fluid
FEST
solid
GEGENSTAND
object
ROT
red
FARBE
colour
WEISS
white
SCHWARZ
black
GETRAENK
drink
WASSER
water
SAFT
juice
MOEBEL
piece of
furniture
MUSIKINSTRUMENT
musical instrument
APFELSAFT
apple juice
KLAVIER
piano
TISCH
table
SITZGELEGENHEIT
seating
SCHWARZ
black
STUHL
chair
SESSEL
arm-chair
BEIN
leg
(ANZAHL:4)0.7
(ANZAHL:4)0.8
KLAVIERSTUHL
piano-stool
APFELSAFT1
KLAVIER1
KLAVIERSTUHL1
SESSEL1
WEISS
white
STUHL1
BEIN1
HAP
STUHL2
BEIN2
BEIN3
BRAUN
KAPUTT
damaged
BRAUN
brown
HEIL
intact
REFERENTIAL SEMANTIC NETWORK

Fig. 5

to change in the course of a dialogue (see 2.2.2).

The ISA-arc links each instance ('token') to its concept node ('type') in the conceptual semantic network.

(28) ((ISA <token> <type>) . z-value)

The REF-arc introduces referential properties of objects, such as a certain colour.

(29) ((REF <token> <property>) . z-value)

The properties are usually values of a linguistic variable in the conceptual network (see (21) in the preceeding section). A slightly different type of the REF-arc contains a numeric value which refers to a dimension introduced in the conceptual semantic network. An example of this arc type together with appropriate inference rules is given in section 2.12.3.

The third primitive symbol is the HAP-arc (has as parts) which links actual parts to actual objects.

(30) ((HAP <token> <part-token>) . z-value)

A part of the referential semantic network as specified in the file for WORLD3 is shown below:

```
(31)  ((ISA STUHL2 STUHL) . 1.0)
      ((REF STUHL2 BRAUN) . 0.8)
      ((ISA BEIN1 BEIN) . 1.0)
      ((HAP STUHL2 BEIN1) . 1.0)
```

Fig. 5 shows a graphic representation of sections of the conceptual and referential semantic networks taken from WORLD3.

2.1.3.9 Spatial data and visual salience

The entries on the file GEO.NET describe the position and the visual salience of all tokens in the current domain of discourse. The internal representations into which these data are transformed are described in sections 2.13.1 and 2.13.3.

An entry beginning with ORT (location) represents the position of an object in the horizontal plane:

(32) ((ORT <token> <coordinates>) . 1.0) .

Entries beginning with the word SENKRECHTE (vertical) describe vertical relations between tokens using natural-language relation words such as AUF (on):

(33) ((SENKRECHTE <relation> <token1> <token2>) . z-value) .

The visual salience of each token of the domain is represented by the AUFFAELLIG-arc (salient-arc):

(34) ((AUFFAELLIG <token>) . z-value) .

Here the z-value is interpreted as the degree of salience.

Example (35) is an excerpt from the external representation of such data for WORLD3.

```
(35)  ((ORT GLAS1 (3. 9.)) . 1.0)
      ((ORT TISCH2 (3. 9.)) . 1.0)
      ((SENKRECHTE AUF GLAS1 TISCH2) . 1.0)
      ((AUFFAELLIG GLAS1) . 0.2)
```

2.2 CONDUCTING A DIALOGUE WITH HAM-RPM

2.2.1 Starting the system

Human engineering has played a key role in the designing of the interactive software environment in which the natural-language dialogue processing of HAM-RPM is embedded. HAM-RPM has been designed to be a highly flexible on-line system. Some of the features provided include elaborate tracing and help facilities, error protection and error protocol mechanisms, batch-mode processing and time measurement.

The purpose of this section is to provide a short overview of the interaction with the user and the processing done by HAM-RPM before the actual natural-language conversation begins. The HAM-RPM user manual (Memo No. 6) provides detailed information on the operation of the system.

At present the user can converse with HAM-RPM about three different domains: two different interiors of living rooms (WORLD1 and WORLD3) and a natural traffic scene (WORLD2) which have been introduced in section 2.1.1. The user chooses a domain of discourse by typing on monitor level DO WORLD n (where n ranges from 1 to 3).

First the system types a list of the names of all files which are automatically included in all current versions of the system as domain-independent knowledge sources (e.g. idioms, transformations). Then the loading of files which contain domain-specific knowledge is protocolled. These protocolls enable the user to access the largely self-explanatory external representations of knowledge underlying the behaviour of HAM-RPM (see 2.1.3).

It should be emphasized that not all knowledge sources are actually loaded into core memory; instead, some are only indexed to permit random disc access during the conversation (see 2.4.3 and 2.13.3). This approach allows us to interface HAM-RPM to large domains of knowledge.

During the loading of the knowledge a good deal of processing is done, such as the mapping of the external data onto various internal representation structures and the extraction of specific information (e.g. a list of all physical objects in the domain, the maximal length of the right-hand side of a syntax rule) needed for efficient processing of the subsequent natural-language dialogue.

Having brought in the knowledge base the system interacts with the user in a menu-selection mode. In this dialogue the user can select certain options which specify the processing mode for the subsequent conversation. For example, the user can request that informative intermediate results be displayed to let him know how the processing of his input is proceeding. This is called the 'trace mode'. The user can choose to operate the system not in the usual interactive mode but in batch mode: a file prepared by the user containing a large number of test sentences is processed and the resulting dialogue is protocolled on a file. This is extremely useful for debugging and for verifying that particular changes that have been made in the program do not produce unexpected and undesirable side-effects.

All options may be changed during the conversation after the command (IO-OPTIONS) has been typed in.

When the user has specified his options, the system initializes all dialogue parameters and dialogue memories (see 2.14). Note, incidentally, that the user can re-initialize the system to the initial dialogue state by typing (HALLO!), if he wishes to undo certain effects of the conversation dynamics implemented in HAM-RPM. On the other hand, when the conversation has been interrupted, a command of the form (JETZT ... (Now ...)) (e.g. (JETZT GEHTS WEITER! (Now let's go on!))) allows the user to continue his conversation starting from the latest dialogue state.

HAM-RPM signals that it is ready to begin the conversation by greeting the user with an expression like GUTEN ABEND! (good evening!) depending on the time of day. When HAM-RPM outputs its prompt character '?', the user may type in natural-language expressions or LISP, FUZZY and AIMDS code. This means that a user who knows these programming languages and wishes to mix interactions with HAM-RPM and interactions with the programming system, can do so easily. This allows the system's designers to operate in an efficient extend-and-test-mode.

2.2.2 Changes in the domain of discourse

As MCDERMOTT 1978 has pointed out, many issues involving the organization of an episodic memory and the processing of temporal references are still open. Although the research reported in this document has up to now been focussed on conversations about static scenes, in the traffic scene (WORLD2) we have introduced dynamic elements, whose properties change with time independently of the actions of the participants in the dialogue.

Changing traffic lights and moving cars and persons can provide a framework for the development of a systematic representation of time. In HAM-RPM the time between the completion of the processing of a dialogue step and the complete input of the user's next utterance is used to evaluate the procedure STATE-TRANSITIONS-IN-DOMAIN-OF-DISCOURSE.

In the current version of HAM-RPM this procedure causes the changing of the traffic lights every two minutes in real-time. Hence, in the course of the dialogue the same question involving a traffic light may be answered differently by the system. Information about the dependencies between the traffic lights and their usual behaviour is stored in HAM-RPM as FUZZY antecedent procedures, so that the state of one single traffic light can imply the state of others in the scene.

2.3 CATEGORIES OF INPUT BY THE HUMAN PARTNER

Three types of initial utterances of the natural partner (as opposed to follow-up questions and answers to the system's questions) must be discriminated to guide the system's process of analysis: questions, commands and assertions. At present the understanding capability of HAM-RPM is largely restricted to an initial input of type 'question'.

These types of utterances can be distinguished by simple means as e.g. punctuation marks or by more sophisticated and linguistically justified criteria as syntactic structure or illocutionary verbs.

Apart from some patterns used for recognizing speech acts which directly influence the behaviour of the system (see 2.4.4) HAM-RPM interprets every initial utterance by the natural partner as a question, not caring about punctuation marks. Thus an input syntactically structured like an assertion is regarded as a question - which in spoken utterances would be marked by prosodic features. For instance the processing of IST DER STUHL BLAU? (Is the chair blue?) and DER STUHL IST BLAU? (The chair is blue?) will be identical, apart from word-order transformations (see 2.9.1).

Two minor components of HAM-RPM, which are not invoked until after the preterminal string has been generated (see 2.4), will be mentioned in this section because they categorize the complete utterance of the natural partner.

Two question types are established: wh-questions (including How ... ?) and yes/no-questions. This distinction predicts in several ways the process of finding an answer and the structure of the answer. In artificial-intelligence systems these two question types are used widely.

Furthermore input sentences are divided into a proposition and a modal component. 'Negation' and 'Potentiality' are analyzed in HAM-RPM as modal components ranging over the whole input sentence. Modality is detected on the basis of the parts of speech NEG and MOD.

Fig. 6 illustrates this for the sentence KANNST DU DAS WASSER NICHT TRINKEN? (Can't you drink the water?).

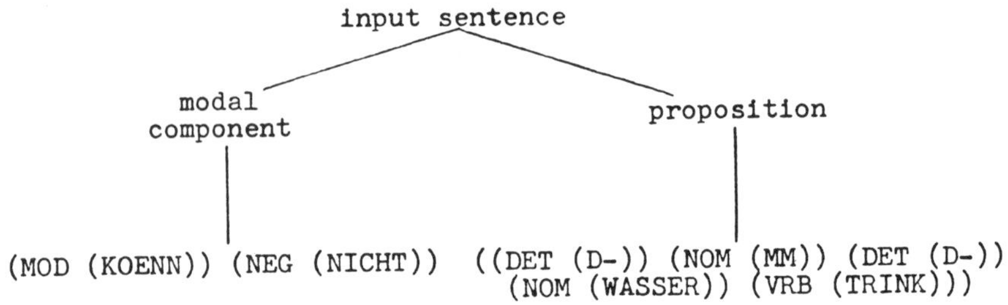

Fig. 6

Having recognized a modal word the input sentence is reduced by it and the kind of modality is bound to variables in the knowledge base of the system, thus allowing the use of modality as a processing parameter for the actual sentence.

At present modal expressions ranging over parts of the input sentence are not analyzed correctly. However, the system itself makes use of the restricted scope of modality (see 2.15).

2.4 LEXICAL ANALYSIS

2.4.1 The role of lexical analysis in HAM-RPM

The task of the component of HAM-RPM called 'lexical analysis' is twofold:

- to transform the string typed in by the user into a string of identical meaning which contains only canonical forms, i.e. words or other symbols about which the system has the information required by the process of syntactic and semantic analysis which are to follow.
- to construct the preterminal string in which these canonical forms are paired with their parts of speech.

The second of these two tasks is nearly trivial - the part of speech of a canonical form is easily determined - but HAM-RPMs handling of the first one will be described in some detail.

2.4.2 Types of lexical transformations of the sentence

Finding the canonical forms for an input sentence requires, among other things, the replacement of words which are not themselves canonical forms by other words. At present three categories of 'replacement' are defined in HAM-RPM. The categories STAMM (stem) and SYNONYM were described in section 2.1.3.1. Regarding the former, it should be noted that in the present version of HAM-RPM the information contained in an inflectional suffix is simply dropped.This is because at present the program's processes of syntactic and semantic analysis make no use of such information anyway. When these processes have been improved, a marker representing the information contained in the removed suffix will have to be associated with the stem of the word in question.

The third category, VERBESSERUNG (correction), involves the replacement of incorrectly spelled or typed words with their correct forms.

In addition to 'replacements', 'idioms' - as defined in section 2.1.3 - must be handled before the preterminal string can be created.

The next two sections describe in more detail than was possible in section 2.1.3 how these two types of transformations are realized.

2.4.3 The representation of 'replacemènts'

Information about the replacements admissible for specific words, e.g. irregular forms and synonyms, is stored declaratively on the file LEX.DTA, as is all other lexical information on particular words. Because this file is very large, it isn't loaded into working memory at the beginning of the dialogue. Rather, it is 'indexed', i.e. the byte address of each entry in the file describing a word is stored in working memory on the property list of that word so that the entry can be found quickly using the random-access facility of Rutgers-UCI-LISP.

On the other hand, the system often acquires new lexical information during the course of the dialogue, either deriving it itself by applying general rules, as described below, or getting it directly from the dialogue partner (see 2.4.5).

This new information is stored in a special CONTEXT of FUZZY's associative net called LEXICON. (It would be impractical to update the file LEX.DTA with each new piece of information acquired, and in any case it is useful to be able to use the more sophisticated mechanisms provided by FUZZY in dealing with this new information; this is easiest when the information is stored in the associative net.)

The form of these assertions is shown by the following examples:

```
(1)   (L VERBESSERUNG AGGREGATSZUSTAND (AGGREGATZUSTAND))
      (L STAMM BILDER (BILD))
      (L SYNONYM GREIS (ALTER MANN))
                         old man
```

A list is maintained of all new words learnt from the dialogue partner during the dialogue. After this interaction in natural language is over , these words are presented to the user individually for inspection, and he is asked to decide whether a word is worth saving or not. A fresh version of LEX.DTA is then made which includes the new words.

Almost all of the extensions to HAM-RPM's lexicon come about in this way - even the system's designers use this method rather than editing LEX.DTA directly.

Since a piece of specific lexical information may be stored in either one of the two places, a modified form of GOAL (FUZZY) (see 1.2.4), called LEX-GOAL , is used for determining the properties of words. LEX-GOAL first performs a FETCH in the CONTEXT LEXIKON of the associative net. If this FETCH fails, it LEX-GOAL checks whether the word has an address for the file LEX.DTA on its property list: if so, it reads the information on the word from the file. Only if the desired information is neither in the net nor on the file does LEX-GOAL try using DEDUCE-procedures. Incidentally, this checking in two places isn't as time-consuming as it might at first appear, since each of the checks fails very quickly if there is no information on the word in the place checked.

FUZZY DEDUCE-procedures (see 1.2.4)stored on the file INFER. PRC (see 2.1.3.6) are used to represent general knowledge about spelling correction and morphological analysis.

Their calling patterns have the same general form as the entries in the CONTEXT LEXIKON. For example, a procedure for removing certain adjective suffixes has the calling pattern

(2) (L STAMM ?WORT ?STAMM)

since what it can do is find a stem for a given word. A sucessful application of this procedure returns an instantiation of its calling pattern, e.g.

(3) (L STAMM BRAUNEM (BRAUN))

Similarly, there is a procedure for anylysing diminutive nouns such as BAEUMCHEN(little tree). Its successful application returns an expression like

(4) (L SYNONYM BAEUMCHEN(KLEIN BAUM))

So far little effort has been devoted to the extension of HAM-RPM's repertoire of lexical rules. As can be seen, however, this method of representing such knowledge permits it to be extended in a modular manner.

2.4.4 The implementation of 'idioms'

As was mentioned in section 2.1.3.2, an idiom is defined in terms of a call to one of three special procedures.

Calls to ERSETZEN (replace) have the form

(5) (ERSETZEN <old-pattern> <new-pattern> <LISP-expression>)

If 'old-pattern' can be matched against the sentence, the corresponding part of the sentence is replaced with 'new-pattern' (cf. the example in section 2.1.3).

If any 'LISP-expressions' are present, they are evaluated one after the other. This makes it possible for the use of certain expressions to have side-effects on the system's behaviour:

(6) (ERSETZEN (?? AUSFUEHRLICH ANTWORT) NIL (SETQ AUSFUEHRLICHKEIT 3))

The first part of the question

(7) BITTE AUSFUEHRLICHER ANTWORTEN: WAS STEHT HINTER DEM BAUM?
Please answer in more detail: what's behind the tree?

is deleted by the system, but it results in a resetting of the global variable AUSFUEHRLICHKEIT, which represents the partner's presumed interest in detailed answers (see 2.14.2). The system's answer to this and the succeeding questions would therefore be at its highest level of detail.

The procedure KOMPRIMIEREN (compress) is a simpler version of ERSETZEN for certain rigid, multiple-word phrases.

(8) (KOMPRIMIEREN <word>)

The concepts corresponding to such phrases are represented conveniently by single words consisting of the several words of the phrase compressed together with blanks between them. Thus the idiom

(9) (KOMPRIMIEREN RECHTS NEBEN)

results in the two words RECHTS NEBEN (to the right of) being replaced with the single word RECHTS/ NEBEN.

Finally, the procedure ERWIDERN (reply) permits the system to give quick responses to particular utterances which are conceptually simple, but difficult to recognize with the usual processes of analysis. Its second argument is a LISP-expression which evaluates to an answer which is passed directly to the surface-transformation component (see 2.16), bypassing all of the usual intervening processes.

(10) (ERWIDERN (WIE SPAET SEIN ES) (LIST (TIME-OF-DAY)))
What's the time

2.4.5 Clarification dialogues

Whenever a word in the sentence is not recognised as a canonical form and cannot be eliminated by any lexical operation, the system initiates a clarification dialogue with the human partner, typing a question of the form

(11) WAS HEISST '<word>'?
What's the meaning of '<word>'?

Since the partner's answers to such questions are invariably elliptical, they aren't subjected to the usual syntactic analysis described in section 2.9. Rather, the system attempts to match them against an (easily extensible) set of patterns, each of which has one of a limited number of consequences. The following three interchanges show how the three assertions listed in (1) above might be ADDed to the CONTEXT LEXIKON as a result of clarification dialogues:

(12) WAS HEISST 'AGGREGATSZUSTAND'? ICH MEINTE AGGREGATZUSTAND.
I meant Aggregatzustand.

(13) WAS HEISST 'BILDER'? EINE FORM VON 'BILD'.
A form of 'Bild'.

(14) WAS HEISST 'GREIS'? DASSELBE WIE 'ALTER MANN'.
The same thing as 'old man'.

If the user types something like NICHTS (nothing), NIL is recorded as a 'synonym' of the word in question, so that it will in the future be deleted from any sentence in which it occurs (unless it is recognized as part of an idiom: see 2.4.9). This is an important expedient for words like EIGENTLICH (actually) and DENN (then), which occur frequently in colloquial German but which could not at present have any effect on the way HAM-RPM answers a question.

If the partner's answer is something like

(15) LASSEN WIR DAS!
Forget it!

the system abandons the processing of the current question and asks for the next one.

Note that the replacements supplied by the human partner are not subjected to any analysis before they are ADD-- to the lexical data base. For example, the inflected form ALTER of the adjective ALT (old) in the definition of GREIS supplied in (14) is retained. The consequences of this are discussed at the end of section 2.4.9.

2.4.6 The control structure for 'replacements'

By 'control structure' is meant here a scheme which specifies the order in which the applicability of the various lexical operations is to be determined and the order in which they are to be carried out.

A different control structure is used for replacements than for idioms, because of an important difference between them: whereas the former only changes the sentence at one point, the latter may alter the form of the entire sentence.

A pass through the sentence making replacements involves the repeated execution of essentially the following loop until the end of the sentence has been reached:

(16) 1. Determine whether the next word in the sentence is:
A. a canonical form
B. a word for which a replacement has been found
C. neither of these, i.e. an 'unrecognized word'
2. If A, then pass over the word and go to 1.
If B, then substitute the replacement (which may consist of several words) for it, so that the next word is now the first word of the replacement, and go to 1.
If C, then ask the dialogue partner for help (see 2.4.7) and, after receiving it, go to 1, checking the same word again. (This time, the information just supplied will be available.)

Note that the words constituting a replacement are themselves subjected to analysis after they have been inserted. The necessity for this is clearest when the replacement has just been supplied by the dialogue partner, as in this sequence:

(17) IST DER STRASSENKREUZER ALT?
Is the 'street cruiser' old?

(18) WAS HEISST 'STRASSENKREUZER'?
What's the meaning of 'street cruiser'?

(19) DAS IST EIN GROSSES AMERIKANISCHES AUTO.
That's a big American car.

(20) WAS HEISST 'AMERIKANISCHES'?
What's the meaning of 'American'?

2.4.7 The control structure for 'idioms'

The control structure for idioms specifies a reprocessing of the sentence beginning with the first word as soon as an idiom has successfully been applied. It likewise involves the repeated application of a loop:

(21) 1. Check to see if the next word has any idioms on its property list (see 2.1.3.2).
2. If it doesn't, pass it over and go to 1.
3. Try each of the idioms to see if it can be applied successfully to the sentence; if one of them can, go to 1

and proceed from the beginning of the (now transformed) sentence.

4. (if none of the idioms listed for the word has succeeded:) Pass over the word and go to 1.

Note that if an idiom applied successfully in step 3 is of the type ERWIDERN (reply) (see 2.4.4), the process of lexical analysis is exited prematurely with a large jump to the surface-transformation component.

2.4.8 The automatic storage of derived results

As will become clear in the next section, it often happens that a piece of information derived using a general lexical rule is needed at some later point in the processing. Since the application of general rules is relatively time-consuming, it is important to store derived results so that they needn't be derived a second time.

FUZZY's procedure demons provide a simple means of accomplishing this: a special demon called MEMORY-DEMON is assigned to all lexical DEDUCE-procedures. This demon differs from FUZZY's default procedure demon (see 1.2.5) only in that, when the DEDUCE-procedure whose execution it is supervising succeeds, MEMORY-DEMON ADDs the result returned by the procedure to the CONTEXT LEXIKON of the associative net where it can be retrieved quickly by a future call to LEX-GOAL (see 2.4.3).

2.4.9 The overall control structure for lexical operations

In the course of the lexical analysis of an input sentence, three passes are made through the sentence in which individual words are replaced, and two in which idioms are handled. In these five passes, the control structures described in sections 2.4.6 and 2.4.7 are applied, with minor variations as described in the following sketch:

(i) a replacement pass

Recognized spelling errors and inflected words are replaced as a prerequisite to the handling of idioms, which can only be defined economically in terms of word stems. On the

other hand, any synonyms which are recognized are not replaced at this point: this can be done only after all idioms have been handled, since an idiom is defined in terms of particular words, not in terms of particular concepts. (The same is true in English: thus 'I'm ill and tired of this' is not recognizable as a use of an idiom even if the idiom 'to be sick and tired of something' is known. 'Sick' can therefore be replaced by 'ill' only after idioms have been handled.)
If a word is not recognized at all, an assertion to this effect is added temporarily to the lexical data base, so that the system will not try again in vain to analyse it, but the dialogue partner is not yet asked for a clarification of the word. This is because the word may yet be eliminated in the course of the handling of idioms which is to follow.

(ii) an idiom pass
Some of the words marked as 'unrecognized' during the first pass may prove to be words which are only recognizable as components of idioms; these will often be eliminated from the sentence if the corresponding pattern is in fact found. Other unrecognized words may be misspellings or unknown inflections of known words. If such a word forms an essential component of an idiom occurring in the sentence, this idiom will not be recognized during this pass (see, however, the fourth pass). Otherwise, all known idioms which actually occur in the sentence will be handled correctly within this pass.

(iii) a replacement pass
This pass differs from the first one only in that unrecognized words now lead to a clarification dialogue of the sort described in section 2.4.5. Aside from any such clarification dialogues, there is little to be done in this pass, as all words except any which may have been introduced during the second pass have already been analysed during the first pass.

(iv) an idiom pass
This pass is only necessary to pick any idiom whose recognition may have been made possible only by a clarification

dialogue concerning one of the words which it contains. It could be skipped if there were no unrecognized words left after the third pass.

(v) a replacement pass
This pass differs from the third one only in that any recognized synonyms are finally actually replaced in the sentence.

A complete exposition of the rationale for this relatively complicated control structure would exceed the scope of this report, but two of its distinguishing features should be mentioned.

First, a good deal of its complexity is made necessary only by the goal of robustness in dealing with words which can only be dealt with after a clarification dialogue. When no such words are present in the sentence, in effect only three passes are made.

Second, it is nowhere assumed that the words used in the definitions of replacements and idioms in the lexical data base are canonical forms, or even known stems: all words inserted into the sentence as the result of a lexical operation are analysed in just the same way as the words in the original input string (see 2.4.5, example (14)). This aspect of the control structure makes it possible to evade certain knotty problems that would be involved in any attempt to insure that the definitions in the knowledge base contained only the right sort of forms, the difficulties being aggravated by the fact that much of the updating of the data base is done in natural language by naive users. On the other hand, this relative lack of constraints on the lexical data base leads to inefficiency of processing, as the system must at some points be ready to deal with a much larger number of possibilities than it would otherwise have to take into account. It seems to us to be also psychologically less plausible. Work is in progress on an improvement of the lexical-analysis component which is more satisfactory in this respect.

2.5 ANALYSING FOLLOW-UP QUESTIONS

A typical feature of question-answer sequences in human dialogues is that some questions refer to questions just posed or to answers just given by the conversational partner. The handling of such follow-up questions is a major factor introducing dialogue coherence into conversations with HAM-RPM. In most cases such follow-up questions are elliptical and have a clear-cut illocutionary force, e.g. What else? or Why not? .

Some types of elliptical follow-up questions can easily be recognized via pattern matching without being processed by the general ellipsis-recognition process described in section 2.10. These follow-up questions are analysed in an early processing phase of HAM-RPM immediately after lexical analysis. The only two types of follow-up questions which have been implemented so far are 'why'-questions and requests for details. These are described in the following two sections.

2.5.1 'Why'-questions

Since expressions like AUS WELCHEM GRUND (for what reason) and WIE KOMMST DU DARAUF? (What makes you think that?) are transformed into the canonical form WARUM (why) by the lexical-analysis component (see 2.4.4) requests for a justification of a previously given response are recognized by simply looking for the word WARUM.

Two types of 'why'-questions are processed by the component described in this section. First, when a 'why'-question follows an answer to a user's question which resulted from failed selectional restrictions (see 2.12.3) the system explains which restrictions were violated. Second, when a 'why'-question follows an answer of the system which was derived by inferences, the system explains the reasoning underlying the answer. This is of great importance since in HAM-RPM most inferences are based on fuzzy or partial knowledge (see 2.12.3) and since the results of such reasoning are of limited use to the human dialogue partner unless the system is able to justify the underlying inference process.

A third type of 'why'-question, which occurs in clarification dialogues during NP-resolution, is described in section 2.8.7.

When selectional restrictions on predicates fail, the violated conditions are stored as the value of the global variable BEGRUENDUNG (explanation) for future use. This means that when BEGRUENDUNG is non-NIL the answer to a 'why'-question is constructed straightforwardly by passing BEGRUENDUNG to the language generation routines (for an example see 2.12.2 below). Finally BEGRUENDUNG is reset to NIL and the input sentence is marked as being incomplete, so that any elliptical inputs which may follow immediately are matched against the sentence preceding the follow-up question. When an answer cannot simply be retrieved from the knowledge base but must be derived using inference rules, a sort of trace of the inference process is stored in a separate data base called INFERENCE MEMORY while the reasoning is being performed (see Reports Nos. 5 and 7).

If BEGRUENDUNG is NIL when an explanation of a conclusion has been requested, the inference memory is traversed to find those assumptions used in the inference chain which are on a communicatively appropriate level of detail. This is accomplished by using meta-knowledge. A thorough discussion of this topic is contained in Report No. 9.

An interesting capability of the current version of HAM-RPM is that it is able to answer iterated 'why'-questions appropriately. For example consider the following dialogue fragment:

(1) MAGST DU DIESEN APFELSAFT GERNE?
Do you like this apple juice?

(2) ICH GLAUBE JA.
I think so.

(3) WARUM MAGST DU IHN GERNE?
Why do you like it?

(4) EIN APFELSAFTGETRAENK IST OFT SUESS UND EIN APFELSAFTGETRAENK IST ALKOHOLFREI.
Apple juice is often sweet and apple juice is non-alcoholic.

(5) WIE KOMMST DU DENN DARAUF?
What makes you think so?

(6) EIN APFELSAFTGETRAENK IST EIN SAFT UND EIN SAFT IST ALKOHOLFREI.
Apple juice is a juice and juice is non-alcoholic.

The 'why'-question (5) is interpreted by HAM-RPM as a request to explain further the explanans given for (2) in (4). Since the first conjunct of the explanans is not derived, but retrieved from the conceptual semantic net, the second conjunct, which results from a property-inheritance inference (see 2.12.2) is explained. As shown in sentence (4) HAM-RPM hedges its explanations according to the status of the knowledge used. In the current version of HAM-RPM explanations are modified by the linguistic hedges MEIST (mostly), OFT (often) and MANCHMAL (sometimes) depending on the z-value of the premises stored in the inference-memory.

When the dialogue partner has repeatedly requested explanations and the system has already mentioned all of the steps in the inference chain, the system finally outputs the message IST DOCH KLAR (It's obvious). The same response is generated when BEGRUENDUNG is NIL and the answer did not result from an inference process at all.

2.5.2 Requests for details

A variety of expressions like UND SONST (and what else) and WEITER NICHTS (nothing else) whose pragmatic meaning is a request for further information are recognized via pattern matching and are processed according to the following rather simple scheme.

When the semantic representation of an answer consists of a set of alternative items which is ordered according to relevance, usually only the item with the greatest relevance is verbalized, since the system is designed to act in accordance with the conversational maxims 'Don't make your contribution more informative than is required' and 'be relevant' formulated by GRICE 1975. This initial behaviour of the system is, however, subject to change during the dialogue (section 2.14.2).

All items not verbalized are stored under the variable RESTANTWORT (rest of the answer), so that follow-up questions which express a request for details are answered by passing RESTANTWORT to the language generation routines. As an example consider the following dialogue fragment:

(7) WAS STEHT IN DER NAEHE DES FERNSEHGERAETES?
What's near the TV set?

(8) DER COUCHTISCH.
The couch table.

(9) UND SONST?
And what else?

(10) DAS KLAVIER UND DER KAPUTTE STUHL.
The piano and the damaged chair.

After the answer (8) has been given, the value of the variable RESTANTWORT is the list (PIANO1 CHAIR2).

When the system has already verbalised all of the items contained in the semantic representation of the answer (see 2.15), it answers NICHTS (Nothing).

Finally, as with requests for justification, the follow-up question is marked as an incomplete input.

2.6 PRONOUN RESOLUTION

There are various types of pronouns which can be analysed or generated by HAM-RPM during the various processing phases.

Interrogative pronouns such as WER (who), WAS (what), and WO (where) are recognized early when the type of the question is determined (see 2.3). Later on, the semantics of these pronouns, which is encoded in translation rules (see 2.11.1), is used to construct a semantic representation of the question.

Relative pronouns such as WELCHER (who) and WELCHES (which) are processed by the NP-resolution component (see 2.8).

In this section we present our approach to the resolution and generation of non-reflexive personal pronouns. In the current version of the system, incidentally, demonstrative pronouns occurring alone as complete noun phrases -- for example DIESER (this) in WELCHE GROESSE HAT DIESER? (How big is this one?) - are treated exactly like the corresponding personal pronouns.

HAM-RPM has no trouble with the analysis of forms of the personal pronoun DU (you) or with the generation of forms of the pronoun ICH (I), as these forms in these cases always refer to the simulated dialogue partner. The generation of forms of DU is likewise straightforward, as these generated forms always refer to the human dialogue partner.

To find the antecedent of a personal pronoun, HAM-RPM uses a simple and efficient, but somewhat naive algorithm which makes use of the record of references to objects described in section 2.14.1. For every pronoun which occurs in the shallow structure of the sentence, the system performs a FETCH within the CONTEXT VORERWAEHNT which, if successful, returns an entry containing the name of the most recently mentioned object which satisfies the constraints on coreferentiality with the pronoun. This search is restricted to those objects which have been referred to during the previous six interchanges (clarification dialogues are not counted as separate interchanges). The name of the object found is substituted immediately for the pronoun in the shallow structure of the sentence; the NP-resolution process for the definite description which was the antecedent of the pronoun thus need not be repeated.

It is well known that in contrast to English in German the gender often can be used to constrain the set of potential referents of a pronoun drastically. As an example, consider the following dialogue sequence:

(1) IST DER BAUM, WELCHER RECHTS NEBEN DER AMPEL STEHT, GROSS?
Is the tree which is to the right of the traffic light big?

(2) JA.
Yes.

(3) WELCHE FARBE HAT SIE IM MOMENT?
What colour is it at the moment?

In German we know that SIE (it) which has the gender feminine, must refer to the traffic light, which has the same gender, because the gender of tree is masculine. In English the correct reference can only be determined using world knowledge. For example, the phrase 'at the moment' gives a hint that the colour of the object often changes. This would rule out the tree as a potential referent.

Since in a few cases the gender of some forms of a pronoun can be ambigous - e.g. IHM has the gender masculine or neuter - the algorithm only checks whether the intersection of the gender of the potential referent and the gender of the pronoun is non-empty.

Since objects referred to by answers of the system are also recorded, the pronoun DIESER (this one) in (6) below can be correctly replaced by the internal name of 'the brown chair':

(4) KANNST DU MIR SAGEN, WOVOR DER TISCH STEHT?
Could you please tell me what the table is located?

(5) DER BRAUNE STUHL.
The brown chair.

(6) UND WOVOR STEHT DIESER?
And what's that located in front of?

Expressions like DARAUF (thereupon) and DANEBEN (next to it) are transformed by the process of lexical analysis (see 2.4.2) into the expressions AUF IT and NEBEN IT, where IT is treated as an artificial pronoun which can refer to objects of all genders. As an example, consider:

(7) DER KLAVIERHOCKER STEHT WO?
The piano stool is where?

(8) VOR DEM KLAVIER.
In front of the piano.

(9) WAS STEHT DANEBEN?
What's next to that?

DANEBEN in (9) is interpreted as referring to the piano.

If the system cannot find a referent for the pronoun, it will behave cooperatively, asking the user with a metacommunicative question to provide the necessary information. As an example, consider the following dialogue sequence:

(10) STEHT SIE VOR DER AMPEL?
Is she standing in front of the traffic light?

(11) AUF WAS BEZIEHT SICH 'SIE'?
What does 'she' refer to?

(12) AUF DIE FRAU, WELCHE IN DER NAEHE DES GELBEN AUTOS STEHT.
To the woman who is standing near the yellow car.

The user's answer (12) to the question (11) is analysed by the NP-resolution component (see 2.8), which eventually returns a unique name which is then substituted for the pronoun.

The record of references to objects is updated as soon as an object has either been returned by the process of NP-resolution or included in the semantic representation of the answer. In particular, in the second case, some objects will be on record as having been referred to even though they were not included in the surface structure of the answer. This way of updating the record has two advantages:

First, the algorithm can find referents for pronouns which don't have explicit antecedents in the surface structure of any previous sentence. This is demonstrated by the following dialogue sequence:

(13) GIBT ES DENN UEBERHAUPT KEINEN AUFGEBROCHENEN SCHRANK?
You mean, there's no damaged cupboard here at all?

(14) DOCH.
Oh, yes, there is.

(15) WELCHE FARBE HAT DIESER DENN?
Well, what color is it?

The positive answer (14) implies that at least one damaged cupboard has been found. The name of this implied entity, which appeared in the semantic representation of the answer and was thus stored in the record of references to objects, is substituted for the pronoun DIESER in question (15).

Second, the system can cope with pronouns which have antecedents in the very sentence in which they themselves occur. For example, in the question

(16) STEHT DAS FERNSEHGERAET EIGENTLICH LINKS NEBEN DER LAMPE, WELCHE SICH IN DER NAEHE VON IHM BEFINDET?
Is the TV set in fact to the left of the lamp which is located near it?

IHM (it) is replaced by the result of the NP-resolution process applied to DAS FERNSEHGERAET (the TV set).

A problem in using the constraints of gender for the resolution of pronouns is that in German the gender which is associated with an object in a particular case is not determined once and for all by the gender of the lexical item that was used to refer to it, but may change during the course of the dialogue. For example, consider the following dialogue:

(17) SIEHST DU DAS FERNSEHGERAET (gender: neuter)?
Do you see the TV set?

(18) JA.
Yes.

(19) WELCHE FARBE HAT DIESER GEGENSTAND (gender: masculine)?
What color is this object?

(20) WEISS.
White.

(21) WO STEHT ER (gender: masculine)?
Where is it?

ER in (21) refers to the object first described as DAS FERNSEHGERAET in (17).This sort of phenomenon is what makes it necessary to store the gender of the lexical item which was used to refer to an object together with the name of the object, as is described in section 2.14.1.

At present HAM-RPM has no general procedures for the processing of reflexive pronouns, possessive pronouns, or pronouns which refer to events or whole sentences instead of to objects.

The experience of a large number of dialogue sessions with naive users has shown that the simple algorithm presented here works remarkably well. This is reminiscent of HOBBS' (1976) observation that in English about 90% of all pronoun references can be resolved using purely syntactic constraints. On the other hand it is clear, as CHARNIAK (1973) has demonstrated convincingly, that for difficult cases of pronoun resolution the full range of cognitive processes involved in understanding must be available, including complex common-sense inferences.

We have found that an algorithm similar to the one presented here for pronouns can also handle anaphoric noun phrases (see 2.8.6). This is indicative of the functional similarity of these two means of referring (cf. GROSZ 1976b).

The pronoun-resolution component is a major contributor to dialogue coherence in HAM-RPM.

2.7 UNDERSTANDING BY MEANS OF SENTENCE PATTERNS

Some frequent types of questions are not processed in the usual way described in the sections to follow, but rather are recognized, immediately after the resolution of pronouns, as instances of specific patterns on the basis of certain crucial syntactic categories. No complete syntactic analysis is attempted; rather, special search and inference processes are invoked to find an answer to these questions without generating a deep structure.

This short-cut processing of particular types of questions corresponds to the ability of human speakers to recognize and process frequently heard questions without going through a deep linguistic analysis each time.

In the current version of HAM-RPM certain types of 'which'- and 'how-many'-questions are handled in this manner. Several patterns specifying the position of certain characteristic syntactic entities -- in other words, a partially instantiated shallow structure -- are part of the knowledge base (see 2.1.3.5); these patterns match some simple 'which'- and 'how-many'-questions directly. There are, however, many more complex questions of these types which are not matched by these patterns, but which must be subjected to processing by the complete linguistic-analysis and inference components of HAM-RPM.

During the processing of those sentences which are matched by patterns, NP-resolution is carried out in the same way as for exhaustive linguistic analysis (see 2.8), though at present there are some differences. A characteristic feature of the short-cut method is the distinction between the generic and the definite or indefinite interpretation of noun phrases, which for experimental purposes is presently implemented only in this processing phase. For details on such differences, see section 2.8.9.

After each successful match with a sentence pattern, the shallow structure which has been generated is stored in the syntactic dialogue memory to permit the recognition of any elliptical sentences which might immediately follow (see 2.10).

2.7.1 'Which'-questions

Two patterns describe the shallow structures of some simple 'which'-questions:

(1) WHICH-PATTERN1:
((IPRN (WELCH)) ?? (NOM ?) (VRB ?) ?? (NOM ?) ??)

WELCH is the stem corresponding to the English 'which'. Here are some examples of sentences whose shallow structures would be matched by WHICH-PATTERN1:

(2) WELCHE GEGENSTAENDE SIND MOEBEL?
Which objects are pieces of furniture?

(3) WELCHE FARBE HAT DER STUHL, WELCHER RECHTS NEBEN DEM KLAVIER STEHT?
What color is the chair that's standing to the right of the piano?

(4) WELCHE BEQUEMEN SITZGELEGENHEITEN STEHEN IN DER NAEHE VOM TISCH?
What comfortable seats are near the table?

(5) WHICH-PATTERN2:
((IPRN (WELCH)) (NOM ?) (VRB ?) (ADJ ?EINGABEADJ))

(The FUZZY variable EINGABEADJ (input adjective) is referenced by the NP-generation routines described in section 2.15). An example which would be recognized via this pattern is:

(6) WELCHE MOEBEL SIND KAPUTT?
Which pieces of furniture are damaged?

The special search and inference mechanisms which were developed for analysing and answering the 'which'-questions which are matched by the above patterns will now be introduced.

Several types of question-rejections provide the human dialogue partner with information as to why an answer could not be found.

(7) WELCHE TISCHE SIND MOEBEL?
Which tables are pieces of furniture?

(8) UNSINNIGE FRAGE!
Meaningless question!

The question presupposes a superset relation between tables and pieces of furniture, whereas the actual relation is the other way around.

(9) WELCHE HAARFARBE HAT EIN TIER?
What is the colour of hair of an animal?

(10) WEISS ICH NICHT!
Don't know!

There is no conceptual property 'colour of hair' attached to animal or to a concept in the superset hierarchy of animal. Therefore the system cannot possibly answer the question on the basis of its present knowledge.

(11) WELCHE FARBE HAT EIN MENSCH?
What colour is a man?

(12) UNENTSCHEIDBAR!
Undecidable!

It is not possible to answer this question for one specific instance of man, but for certain subclasses various values (V-arcs) along the dimension 'colour' are stored. Thus for the superset 'man' no unique property of 'colour' can be determined. This rejection and the one in number (10) differ in that here some superset-concept of 'man' ('thing' in our case) is known to have the property 'colour' but there is no unique value of this property relatable to 'man'.

(13) WELCHES BILD IST GRUEN?
Which picture is green?

(14) KEIN BILD IST GRUEN.
No picture is green.

The question in (13) matches with WHICH-PATTERN2. In the current domain of discourse not even one possible referent can be discovered, nor is 'green' a conceptual property of the concept 'picture'.

Now let's turn to more positive and informative answers to 'which'-questions:

(15) WELCHE MOEBEL SIND SITZGELEGENHEITEN?
Which pieces of furniture are seats?

(16) STUHL UND SESSEL.
Chair and arm-chair.

A superset hierarchy can be established between 'pieces of furniture' and 'seat'. All subset nodes of the latter are taken to be the answer. This dialogue example contrasts with number (7). Note that in this case the question is interpreted as concerning only conceptual knowledge.

(17) WELCHER STUHL STEHT DIREKT LINKS NEBEN DEM TISCH?
Which chair is standing directly to the left of the table?

(18) DER KAPUTTE STUHL.
The damaged chair.

Detecting a preposition in the shallow-structure of a 'which'-question which matches WHICH-PATTERN2, the system assumes that a local relation between certain objects is asked for. The processes for finding the objects described are part of the NP-resolution component (see 2.8) and are likewise employed for 'how many'-questions (see 2.7.2). Roughly speaking the task is solved by finding all referents of the definite noun phrase 'the chair which is standing directly to the left of the table'.

(19) WELCHE FARBE HAT DER RUNDE TISCH?
What colour is the round table?

(20) WEISS.
White.

The system cannot establish a superset hierarchy between 'table' and 'colour' as in example (17) and therefore tries to interpret 'colour' as a conceptual dimension. An answer is found by looking for a referential property of that specific table which is a possible value of the concept 'colour'.

If this inference strategy had not been successful or the object had been interpreted generically the system would have tried to answer the question solely on the basis of its conceptual knowledge as in examples (22/23) and (24/25).

(22) WELCHEN AGGREGATZUSTAND HAT EIN TISCH?
What's the state of a table?

(23) FEST.
solid.

A superset concept of 'table' (for instance 'object') is known to be solid. Making use of inheritance hierarchy this is also true for the subsets.

(24) WELCHE FARBE HAT EIN KLAVIER?
What colour is a piano?

(25) NORMALERWEISE SCHWARZ.
Usually black.

If properties inferred from the conceptual semantic network are not true with absolute certainty, the extent of uncertainty is expressed by a linguistic hedge as in example (25). For a more detailed description of the use of linguistic hedges in generating answers see section 2.7.2 and Report No.7.

Modifying the answers to 'which'-questions according to the source of knowledge employed is analogously realized with shallow-structures matched by WHICH-PATTERN2:

(26) WELCHES MUSIKINSTRUMENT IST TEUER?
Which musical instrument is expensive?

(27) JEDES MUSIKINSTRUMENT IST TEUER.
Every musical instrument is expensive.

The concept of 'musical instrument' is known to have the conceptual property (D-arc) 'expensive'; thus the answer can be inferred from conceptual knowledge and is expressed as a general statement.

On the other hand properties attached to particular objects in the domain of discourse are presented in the referential semantic network; in the answer to a 'which'-question this is indicated by the complete enumeration of the objects in question:

(28) WELCHE MOEBEL SIND WEISS?
Which pieces of furniture are white?

(29) DAS KLAVIER UND DER KLEINE TISCH.
The piano and the small table.

2.7.2 'How many'-questions

As in the case with 'which'-questions two patterns are provided to identify simple types of 'how many'-questions:

(30) HOW-MANY-PATTERN1:
((IPRN (WIEVIEL)) ?? (NOM ?) (VRB ?) ?? (NOM ?) ??)
how many

Examples:

(31) WIEVIELE KAPUTTE MOEBEL SIEHST DU?
How many damaged pieces of furniture do you see?

(32) WIEVIELE BRAUNE SITZGELEGENHEITEN STEHEN IN DER NAEHE VOM TISCH?
How many brown seats are standing near the table?

(33) WIEVIELE BEINE HAT EIN MENSCH?
How many legs has a man got?

(34) HOW-MANY-PATTERN2:
((IPRN (WIEVIEL)) ?? (NOM ?) (VRB ?) ?? (ADJ ?))

Examples:

(35) WIEVIELE GEGENSTAENDE SIND HEIL UND WEISS?
How many objects are intact and white?

The analysis algorithm for simple 'how-many'-questions distinguishes between two semantic groups: One asking for the number of objects with certain properties or relations to other objects, the other one asking for the number of parts of objects.

All question types of the first group are handled with processes which are part of the NP-resolution component (see 2.8). Roughly speaking these question types are transformed into definite noun phrases whose scope of extension, i.e. the number of possible referents, is the answer. As with 'which'-questions noun phrases occuring in the shallow structure of 'how many'-questions are resolved beforehand. The entire analysis capacity of the NP-resolution component is therefore employed twice during the processing of these question types.

Examples of the transformation of 'how many'-questions into definite noun phrases:

(36) WIEVIELE HEILE GEGENSTAENDE HIER SIND BRAUN?
How many intact objects here are brown?

--> scope of extension of DER HEILE BRAUNE GEGENSTAND
The intact, brown object

(37) WIEVIELE STUEHLE STEHEN DIREKT NEBEN DEM TISCH?
How many chairs are standing directly next to the table?

--> scope of extension of DER STUHL, WELCHER DIREKT NEBEN DEM TISCH STEHT.
The chair which is standing directly next to the table.

Special search and inference processes are at present being developed for the second group of 'how many'-questions, questions about parts of objects. Here the representation of parts in the knowledge base of HAM-RPM (see 2.1.3) will be described along with algorithms implemented so far. Then problems arising with the interpretation of the parts representation will be discussed.

Three types of arcs represent the relation between concepts or objects and their parts in the semantic networks of HAM-RPM.

The conceptual semantic network contains two of these arcs

(38) ((T <concept> <part of concept>) z-value)

(39) Example: ((T MAN LEG) . 1.0)

(40) ((ANZAHL (T <concept> <part of concept>)<quantity>) z-value)

(41) Example: ((ANZAHL (T MAN LEG) 2) . 0.9)

Using these representation constructs, part relations are established on the conceptual level which allow inferences about compound objects and the number of their parts, each associated with a z-value (for further inferences on the T-arc see Report No. 5).

The third type of arcs belongs to the referential semantic network. It links special instances of parts to objects in the domain of discourse:

(42) ((HAP <object name> <part name>) z-value)

(43) Example: ((HAP MAN2 LEG1) . 1.0)

A HAP-arc will only be stated in the referential network where it may be necessary to address oneself to specific parts of specific objects, or if the number or the properties of specific parts differ from the default values in the conceptual knowledge. For example one of the chairs in the living-room scene is broken. It has only three intact legs, although four legs are said to be parts of the concept 'chair'. The discrepancy is represented with four HAP-arcs linking the object name to four instances of 'leg', three of these with the referential property 'intact' and to one with the property 'broken'.

Answering 'how many'-questions which concern parts of objects is achieved by determining the component of the knowledge base presumably containing relevant information. If the NP-resolution component decided to interprete the object noun phrase (i.e. the last noun phrase) as generic (see 2.8.9) the conceptual network is searched for suitable T-arcs. T-arcs are involved in superset inheritance-hierarchy, so supersets of the concept are inspected if the direct attempt fails. If an appropriate T-arc is found the number value of the ANZAHL-arc, which may be either a number or a quantifying word such as VIELE (many), answers the question. As it was found in the conceptual semantic network the z-value of the ANZAHL-arc is interpreted as a degree of certainty. This degree is expressed by linguistic hedges (see above example (25)), which are assigned to possible subranges of the z-value. For instance NORMALERWEISE (usually) represents the interval [0.8, 0.9] of z-values; MANCHMAL (sometimes) represents the interval [0.4, 0.5].

Here is an example of a 'how many'-question answered by conceptual knowledge:

(44) WIEVIELE BEINE HAT EIN STUHL?
How many legs has a chair?

(45) NORMALERWEISE VIER.
Usually four.

When the NP-resolution has assumed that the last noun phrase refers to a specific object, the HAP-arcs of the name of this object are examined. The number of HAP-arcs - if there are any - satisfying the attribute restrictions is the answer.

Here is an example of a 'how many'-question answered by referential knowledge:

(46) WIEVIELE HEILE BEINE HAT DER STUHL, WELCHER LINKS NEBEN DEM TISCH STEHT?
How many intact legs has the chair which is standing left to the table got?

(47) DREI.
three.

It may be the case that there are no corresponding HAP-arcs associated with the object name. Parts of objects may be concealed by other objects in the domain of discourse. The system then backs up and tries to find an answer on the basis of its conceptual knowledge as described above, using instead of the object names the concept, which is linked to the object name by an ISA-arc.

One major problem with inferences about parts involves the part-inheritance hierarchy: How should parts of parts of objects be represented and what is to be inferred using a given representation scheme?

A second question is: is the transitivity of parts hierarchies limited to a certain degree? For example, all subparts of objects relatable to an object via T-arcs might not represent a single quantifying assertion. Third, how can parts hierarchies, which are embedded in superset-inheritance hierarchies, be verbalized if the system is required to reason about its inferences?

Finally, it seems that the use of specific linguistic hedges expressing the degree of certainty of an assertion has to be dependent on the concepts involved. For example, to say 'a passenger car nearly always has four wheels' sounds perfectly normal, whereas 'a man nearly always has two legs' is at best somewhat awkward. Partitioning the semantic networks for special purposes - for example, into 'object concepts' and 'living beings' - and interpreting degrees of certainty according to this partitioning may be helpful, not only where part relations are concerned.

Future work within HAM-RPM on parts representation and inferences will include the topics just sketched and might produce a more elaborate structuring of the semantic networks.

2.8 NP-RESOLUTION

2.8.1 Objectives

In HAM-RPM semantic, pragmatic and syntactic processes cooperate closely in analysing the natural partner's input. One major component which attempts to interpret parts of the input chiefly by means of semantic and pragmatic knowledge is the one responsible for NP-resolution.

The first task of this component is to determine whether a given noun phrase is used as a generic, a definite or an indefinite description (cf. OOMEN 1977, NORMAN/RUMELHART 1975, ch. 3). After having made sure of the type of determination or - if that is not possible - after a hypothesis about it has been put forth, all of the knowledge available to the system at the moment is employed to determine the reference of the noun phrase.

The reason for analysing noun phrases before the complete input sentence is parsed is that a natural partner does not necessarily wait for a whole utterance which might be syntactically analysable before trying to process the parts of the utterance already perceived (cf. GERSHMAN 1977, in contrast to WINOGRAD 1972, RITCHIE 1977). This is often observed in natural dialogues (cf. GROSZ 1976a), when either an utterance is not completed at all or the speaker hesitates while looking for an appropriate continuation. The listener in these cases is able to detect semantically or pragmatically ill-formed or ambiguous noun phrases and interrupt the discourse with rejections, reassurances or clarification questions.

We do not claim that noun phrases necessarily and always have to be or even can be resolved before the whole sentence has been parsed; but rather that the referential analysis of partial sentences is one characteristic feature of natural dialogue behaviour. This ability has to be taken into account in the simulation of a natural dialogue partner.

2.8.2 Definite descriptions

Now let's take a closer look at the analysis of noun phrases in HAM-RPM. In this section we shall restrict ourselves for the sake of simplicity to the assumption that the noun phrase to be analysed is a definite description (for indefinite and generic descriptions see 2.8.8 and 2.8.9).

Input to the NP-resolution component is the shallow structure generated so far in the course of the analysis. In a first step noun phrases are looked for using the following pattern:

(1) (?? DET ?? NOM ??)

This pattern describes any segment between an article (DET) and a noun (NOM). If it matches a segment of the input sentence, a relative clause directly following the noun is looked for. Thus the structure of a noun phrase identified by the NP-resolution is represented in (2). With definite descriptions the article is assumed to be definite, i.e. 'D-'.

(2) $$\text{NP ::= DET} + \left(\left\{\text{ADJ}\right\}\right) + \text{NOM} + \left(\text{RELCL}\right)$$

The structure of a relative clause is characterized by (3):

(3) $$\text{RELCL ::= } \underset{\text{which}}{\text{(IPRN (WELCH))}} + \begin{pmatrix} \left\{\text{ADJ}\right\} \\ \left(\text{ADV}\right) + \text{PRP} + \text{NP} \end{pmatrix} + \text{VRB} .$$

Before going into detail concerning the further processing we shall illustrate the definition of noun phrases with some examples of noun phrases identified by partial parsing:

(4) DAS FERNSEHGERAET
the TV set

(5) DER BRAUNE, KAPUTTE STUHL
the brown, damaged chair

(6) DER RUNDE TISCH, WELCHER WEISS IST
the round table which is white

(7) DER BRAUNE STUHL, WELCHER DIREKT RECHTS NEBEN DEM TISCH STEHT
the brown chair which is standing directly to the right of the table

In German relative clauses are not marked with respect to restrictiveness (RITCHIE uses punctuation marks to discriminate restrictive relative clauses from non-restrictive ones). No syntactic features indicate the type of a relative clause. To interpret it as non-restrictive would entail adding new information to the knowledge base and proving its consistency with the knowledge already present. This is not done in HAM-RPM at present. Relative clauses, like attributive adjectives, are always regarded as being restrictive.

While relative clauses are identified according to the syntactic structure of (3) by a process similar to that used by GERSHMAN 1977 they are transformed into an internal representation associated with the noun phrase they refer to. Subsequently the relative clause is eliminated from the shallow structure.

If the relative clause introduces attributive adjectives, as in example (6), these adjectives are added to the attributes of the dominating noun phrase. Under certain conditions the system comments on this transformation by 'thinking aloud' (see 2.8.5).

The second syntactic type of a relative clause (example (7)) essentially consists of a prepositional phrase which may be modified by an adverb. This prepositional phrase is bound to a name of the dominating noun phrase (a quoted description, which is a compressed version of its words) and is analysed later on in connection with that noun phrase. At this stage a relative clause which was part of the first noun phrase has disappeared from the shallow structure.

After this syntactically guided identification process the noun phrase is now subjected to semantic and pragmatic analysis.

In German a proper name may be preceeded by an article. Thus if the noun of the NP is already a proper name such as 'Marilyn Monroe' (who, incidentally, is represented in the pictures of WORLD3) the noun phrase in the shallow structure is replaced by it and in the remaining shallow structure further NPs are looked for. The same applies to noun phrases of the structure (DET NOM) having only one possible referent in the domain of discourse. Thus example (4) would be replaced by FERNSEHGERAET1 (TV set1).

The system does not attempt to establish sets of potential referents for nouns representing property dimensions in the conceptual semantic network (linked to concepts via the E-arc), such as 'D- FARBE' (the colour).

2.8.3 Attributive adjectives

Attributive adjectives, as in example (5), are analysed using the knowledge stored in the semantic networks. There are three ways in which properties of concepts or of objects are represented: denotative properties belong to the conceptual semantic network (D-arc, see 2.1.3.7), decomposed properties are defined by specific procedural knowledge (see 2.12.2) and referential properties are stated in the referential semantic network (REF-arc, see 2.1.3.8).

In the analysis of noun phrases each attributive adjective is examined to see whether it is a denotative property of the concept, i.e. the noun of the NP, or one of its supersets. All of HAM-RPM's deductive mechanisms (see 2.12) are employed in this process. If this is the case the denotative attribute is eliminated from the set of adjectives preceding the noun and the next adjective is inspected. Thus the system itself will never mention denotative attributes, which actually are inherent properties of concept classes, as for instance 'fluid water', in asking for additional information (see 2.8.7).

If, however, a denotative property is not applicable to the concept the whole utterance containing the actual noun phrase is rejected, as illustrated in the following example:

(8) IST DER FLUESSIGE STUHL ROT?
Is the fluid chair red?

⋮

EIN STUHL IST GRUNDSAETZLICH NICHT FLUESSIG!
A chair is by definition not fluid!

After the system has looked for properties of concepts and analysed them, the set of relevant tokens is created. All tokens linked to the noun of the NP by ISA-arcs - whether directly or indirectly via inheritance - are contained in the set of tokens. For example, the set of tokens of the noun MOEBEL (pieces of furniture) will be:

(9) (SESSEL1 SESSEL2 TISCH1 TISCH2 STUHL1 STUHL2 STUHL3 STUHL4 KLAVIER1 KLAVIERSTUHL1)
(arm-chair1-2, table1-2, chair1-4, piano1, piano stool1)

This set of tokens is the basis for determining whether one of its elements is the referent of the given definite description.

As in the lexical-decomposition component (see 2.11.2) attributive adjectives may be reduced to semantic primitives by decomposition procedures. The lexicon entry of these adjectives contains the keyword ATT-DEKOMPOSITION linked to the name of a procedure. There is, for instance, a procedure for the adjective LEER (empty), if it is used attributively, which evokes processes similar to the one described in section 2.12.3 for predicative use. The decomposition procedure yields a set of tokens which will consist of fewer elements than initially if the decomposed attribute only applies to a subset of the initial set of tokens.

All the remaining adjectives of the NP under investigation are assumed to be referential properties. Going through the set of tokens, each single token whose referential properties do not fit the adjectives of the NP is removed from the set. With definite descriptions an exhaustive search has to be performed, as GROSZ 1976a,b has already stressed. During the checking of referential properties all of the deductive mechanisms of the inference component, such as the handling of relative adjectives (see 2.12.3; cf. RITCHIE 1977) are employed.

The analysis of attributive adjectives finally yields a set of tokens. This set may be empty, which means that there is no appropriate object in the domain of discourse:

(10) DAS KAPUTTE KLAVIER
The damaged piano

⋮

ES GIBT HIER KEIN KAPUTTES KLAVIER.
There is no damaged piano here.

Here, as in example (8), the analysis of the whole utterance is rejected.

Having successfully analysed the attributes of an NP the initial set of tokens (9) has been reduced to a single element:

(11) NP: DAS BRAUNE, KAPUTTE MOEBEL
The brown, damaged piece of furniture
set of tokens: (STUHL2) .

2.8.4 Relative clauses

If the set of tokens consists of one or more elements, a previously transformed relative clause might help to confirm the analysis if a unique token has already been found or it might disambiguate the set if more than one token has remained so far. The type of relative clause whose analysis has not yet been described consists of a - possibly modified - prepositional phrase (see 2.8.2). The noun phrase which is part of this prepositional phrase is analysed in the same way as was described in the previous section. If there are no rejections, for example an existential presupposition is violated, a set of tokens is determined to represent the extension of the NP of the relative clause. The analysis so far has yielded two sets of tokens. The preposition of the relative clause specifies a relation between elements of these two sets.

An example will illustrate this:

(12) DER BRAUNE STUHL, WELCHER VOR DEM TISCH STEHT
The brown chair which is standing in front of the table

The set of tokens of DER BRAUNE STUHL is determined to be (STUHL1 STUHL2 STUHL3 STUHL4); the set of tokens of DER TISCH turns out to be (TISCH1 TISCH2). Some element of the STUHL-tokens is said to be in the relation VOR (in front of) to an element of the TISCH-tokens. At present prepositions in HAM-RPM have only locative meaning. Therefore the procedure used for checking spatial relations (see 2.13.1) is called to yield those pairs of tokens which stand in the proper relation to one another.

An adverb possibly modifying the scope of the relation determines the range of the domain of discourse which has to be inspected. At the moment four ranges are discriminated, each of which may be referred to by adverbs interpreted as linguistic hedges (cf. LAKOFF 1975).

(13)

linguistic hedge (adverb)		range
DIREKT, GENAU, DICHT, UNMITTELBAR directly, precisely, closely, immediately	-->	very narrow
BEINAHE, MEHR ODER WENIGER almost, more or less	-->	rather narrow
IN ETWA, UNGEFAEHR about, roughly speaking	-->	very broad
no adverb present	-->	medium

Note that some of these adverbs are used similarly for the generation of definite descriptions of objects (see 2.15).

2.8.5 Thinking aloud

As the checking of spatial relations usually takes some time the system tells the partner what it is doing at the moment and - more important - that it is doing something. This strategy of 'thinking aloud' is often observed in natural dialogues. Longer breaks, which are not understandable for the partner, violate a communicative convention. In a system which is supposed to behave cooperatively, such pauses should be avoided.

Hendrix' LIFER system (HENDRIX 1977) holds the attention of the user by printing a protocol - not in natural language - of the processing of his query. In HAM-RPM, messages not in natural language are permitted only in the trace mode (see 2.2.1). Its thinking aloud, like all other utterances intended for the dialogue partner, is in natural language.

A number of different syntactic frames are provided which are filled with actual words characterizing the current processes. The degree of detail of the utterance chosen is to represent the degree of ambiguity in the sets of tokens and thus gives an impression of the time presumably needed for the checking of spatial relations. Example (14) is an utterance when only two tokens are to be inspected, example (15) an utterance for highly ambiguous sets of tokens.

(14) DIE LAMPE, WELCHE SICH UNGEFAEHR HINTER DER SCHRANKWAND BEFINDET
The lamp which is situated roughly behind the cupboard

. . . UNGEFAEHR HINTER DER SCHRANKWAND . . . EINE LAMPE . . .
. . . roughly behind the cupboard . . . a lamp . . .

(15) DER STUHL, WELCHER HINTER DEM BRAUNEN MOEBEL IST
The chair which is behind the brown piece of furniture

. . . ES SOLL HIER HINTER EINEM BRAUNEN MOEBEL EINEN STUHL GEBEN . . . DA MUSS ICH MAL GENAUER HINSEHN . . .

. . . behind a brown piece of furniture there's supposed to be a chair . . . I've got to take a closer look . . .

A different step in the analysis which produces thinking-aloud utterances is the transformation of relative clauses containing only adjectives (see 2.8.2). Out of a set of several syntactic frames one or perhaps none are selected at random as shown in example (16).

(16) DAS FERNSEHGERAET, WELCHES WEISS IST
The TV set which is white

. . . HMM . . . EIN WEISSES FERNSEHGERAET . . .
. . . hmm . . . a white TV set . . .

2.8.6 Potential referents

Let's now return to the process of disambiguating sets of tokens by means of relations between them. The checking of spatial relations has yielded either nothing or a set of pairs of tokens. In the first case the relation specified could not be found between any pair of tokens in the domain of discourse. The whole utterance is therefore rejected:

(17) DAS BILD, WELCHES HINTER DEM BRAUNEN TISCH HAENGT
The picture which is hanging behind the brown table

HINTER DEM BRAUNEN TISCH SEHE ICH KEIN BILD.
Behind the brown table I do not see a picture.

If only one pair has been found, the complex definite description under inspection is successfully disambiguated and is replaced by the appropriate token. Thus a unique pair has been found in the domain of discourse, although each of the NPs, the one from the relative clause and the one from the dominating proposition,may have been highly ambiguous. In the example above, there may have been several pictures and several brown tables, but only one picture behind a brown table.

If there are more than one pair of tokens then even the relation has not been precise enough to identify a single object. In these cases the record of references to objects (see 2.14.1) is inspected to see whether one of the tokens in question has recently been in the focus of attention (cf. GROSZ 1976b). If a suitable token is found, this is taken to be the one meant by the natural partner. If this still does not single out a unique pair, a clarification dialogue is initiated (see 2.8.7) to get more details about the object described by the NP of the relative clause.

The same processes as described for disambiguating the definite NP of the relative clause are carried out for the NP of the main proposition. The record of references to objects is inspected and clarification dialogues are initiated in case of ambiguity.

Finally, if no rejections have terminated the further processing, the definite NP is replaced by the token it referred to. A corresponding entry is added immediately to the record of references to objects; this may be required for pronoun resolution in a later part of the sentence (see 2.6).

The rest of the utterance is then searched for further noun phrases, which will be subjected to the same process of reference analysis. The output of the NP-resolution is the shallow structure with each NP replaced by a token. As NP-resolution always analyses the whole shallow structure and yields a modified one, it may be employed in different steps of the analysis; this actually is the case in HAM-RPM (see 2.1.2). An input to HAM-RPM consisting only of one noun phrase - as do the examples in this section - is also analysed until, if it is not interpreted as an elliptical utterance, the parsing component rejects it as an ill-formed sentence (see 2.9.2). Further commented examples of NP-resolution are contained in Memo No. 5.

2.8.7 Clarification dialogues

Whenever the reference of a noun phrase cannot be disambiguated the system does not give up and do nothing (WINOGRAD 1972) but rather asks the natural partner for further discriminating features. Such clarification dialogues are freqently used in natural dialogue situations, when the referential assumptions of the two partners are not identical (cf. DEUTSCH/CLAUSING 1979).

Two types of clarification dialogues are provided in the NP-resolution of HAM-RPM. If the number of potential referents is small, i.e. the set of tokens consists of only two elements, the system takes one of them and asks whether this one was the object meant. As the system on principle uses natural language to interact with the dialogue partner, it generates a noun phrase representing the internal object name (see 2.15). The natural partner may now accept or reject the system's choice. If he rejects it, the remaining token is regarded as the referent of the noun phrase and the partner is informed of this decision.

The second type of clarification dialogue is initiated if there are more than two potential referents. The system asks the partner to supply more distinctive features. The features already analysed are mentioned in the system's question. The response to such a question may be a more specific noun phrase, an elliptical one, such as DEN ROTEN (the red one), or a relative clause. Embedding the new information into the already analysed restrictions for the noun the system attempts to find a unique referent in the way described above. Recursive reference (a brilliant example is given in MORTON 1976) is thus modelled by clarification dialogues.

A complex noun phrase with a relative clause may contain two nouns, which may happen to be identical, as in DER SCHRANK, WELCHER NEBEN DEM SCHRANK STEHT (the cupboard which is standing next to the cupboard). In clarification dialogues the partner is informed which of the nouns could not be resolved uniquely. If it is the noun in the relative clause which is ambiguous, the whole prepositional phrase is asked for.

Clarification questions posed by the system are explained to the natural partner if he requests this by asking a 'why'-question (cf. Report No. 9). The system justifies its speech act by naming the quantity of potential referents established so far, as illustrated in (18) below.

Many features of the clarification dialogues appear in the example (18). The user's question is the first one of a dialogue sequence, so the record of references to objects is empty.

The answer to the original question is not only 'yes'; rather, the transformed shallow structure, which was the input of the parsing, is added to the reply. This is done because the extensive clarification dialogue may have made the partner forget the original question. For another example of this kind see section 2.16.

(18)

KANNST DU DAS BRAUNE DING DA ANFASSEN?
Can you touch the brown thing there?

WELCHES BRAUNE DING MEINST DU? WIESO FRAGST DU MICH DAS?
Which brown thing do you mean? Why do you ask?

WEIL ES SIEBEN DAVON GIBT!
Because there are seven of them!

WELCHES DING MEINTEST DU? DAS, WELCHES NEBEN DEM TISCH STEHT.
Which thing did you mean? The one standing next to the table.

. . . MOMENT, EIN BRAUNES DING ALSO . . . UND ZWAR NEBEN EINEM TISCH . . .
. . . just a moment, a brown thing . . . next to a table . .

MEINST DU NEBEN DEM COUCHTISCH? WESHALB FRAGST DU MICH SCHON WIEDER?
Do you mean next to the couch table? Why do you ask me again?

WEIL ES ZWEI GIBT!
Because there are two!

MEINTEST DU NEBEN DEM COUCHTISCH? NEE!
Did you mean next to the couch table? No!

NEBEN DEM ESSTISCH ALSO.
Next to the dining table then.

MEINST DU DEN KAPUTTEN STUHL? GENAU.
Do you mean the damaged chair? Exactly.

JA, ICH KANN DEN KAPUTTEN STUHL GREIFEN.
Yes, I can touch the damaged chair.

2.8.8 Indefinite descriptions

A noun phrase is interpreted as an indefinite description if the indefinite article 'E-' ('a') was used and a generic interpretation is not possible (see 2.8.9). The analysis of these noun phrases is similar to the one described for definite NPs. At present there are only two differences.

If the modality of an input is 'potential' (see 2.3) ,violated decomposed or referential properties of objects do not lead to the rejection of the whole utterance. Properties known to be represented in referential knowledge are also known to be subject to change. In questions of the modality 'potential' the referential attributes of indefinite noun phrases do not have to agree with the current state of the domain of discourse, but are rather interpreted as questions concerning possible domains. In the example below there is no lilac picture to be seen in the domain.

(19) KOENNTEST DU EIN LILA BILD AUF DEN BODEN LEGEN?
Could you place a lilac picture onto the floor?

JA.
yes.

The second difference between the handling of indefinite and definite noun phrases concerns the postulate of uniqueness. Indefinite NPs do not have to refer to one specific referent but rather can refer to any member of the set of tokens. Therefore in HAM-RPM one of the appropriate tokens is selected and replaces the indefinite NP. This solution clearly does not in all cases do justice to the meaning of an indefinite noun phrase, as demonstrated in the following example.

(20) STEHT EIN STUHL NEBEN DEM ESSTISCH?
Is there a chair standing next to the dining table?

NEIN.
No.

The reason for the wrong answer 'no' is that just one token has been picked from the set of chairs and this one does not happen to be next to the table. It would be a somewhat more adequate method to generate the set of tokens of the indefinite NP and proceed to analyse the question. This is planned as an improvement of the NP-resolution component. Problems arising with indefinite noun phrases are discussed in more detail in Memo No. 2.

2.8.9 Generic descriptions

Generic or intensional descriptions (NORMAN/RUMELHART 1975) do not refer to objects but to concepts or classes of concepts. Generic noun phrases are syntactically similar to definite or indefinite ones, i.e. they may have either the definite or indefinite article.

In HAM-RPM criteria are being developed to distinguish generic descriptions from definite and indefinite ones. The presently existing criteria are only applied within a limited context, namely the analysis by sentence patterns (see 2.7), which handles simple types of 'which'- and 'how many'-questions. For experimental purposes just this part of the understanding capabilities has been chosen, because here special search and inference procedures are closely connected with the syntactic structure.

At present five rules indicate generic interpretation of noun phrases. An NP is regarded as being generic, if

- the noun is neither a proper name nor an internal name of an object,
- there are no attributive adjectives,
- there are no restrictive relative clauses attached to the noun,
- the definite article is present and no potential token of the concept represented by the noun is in the focus of attention (see 2.8.6),
- the question does not specify any local relations.

If all these criteria are satisfied by an NP of a 'which'- or 'how many'-question, it is regarded as a generic NP and replaced by the noun, which for further processing represents the name of a concept. In trace mode the user is informed of the generic interpretation of the noun phrase, as illustrated in this example:

(21) WIEVIELE RAEDER HAT DAS AUTO?
How many wheels has the car?

⋮

(DAS AUTO WIRD GENERISCH INTERPRETIERT)
(The car is being interpreted generically)

⋮

MEISTENS VIER.
In most cases four.

(22) WIEVIELE RAEDER HAT DER GELBE KOMBI?
How many wheels has the yellow station wagon?

⋮

VIER.
Four.

Obviously the criteria for identifying generic noun phrases are not adequate in every respect. More powerful methods would presumably include the use of verb frames and tenses, the postponement of the decision until the sentence has been parsed and, as a last resort, asking the natural partner directly about the intended type of reference. Together with the analysis of indefinite noun phrases, the handling of generic ones will be a major topic in the improvement of HAM-RPM's NP-resolution component.

2.8.10 Extensions of the NP-resolution

Apart from topics already mentioned in the preceeding sections future research on NP-resolution in HAM-RPM will mainly be concentrated on five points.

First the syntactic structure of a noun phrase has to be extended to provide for genitive attributes, transformed relative clauses such as 'the chair standing to the left of the table', modified attributes such as 'the slightly damaged cupboard', and negative characterizations (which are already used in NP-generation; see 2.15).

Second, plural and conjoined noun phrases have to be analysed in respect to their referential function (cf. GERSHMAN 1977).

Third, nonrestrictive relative clauses and attributes have to be identified and processed as new information (cf. RITCHIE 1977).

Fourth, 'foregrounding' (see GROSZ 1976b, NORMAN/RUMELHART 1975) has to be employed in solving reference relations in tightly coherent dialogue sequences.

Fifth, any change of topic has to be noticed and have an impact on the resolution of noun phrases (cf. GROSZ 1976a).

2.9 SYNTACTIC ANALYSIS

The syntactic-analysis component in HAM-RPM dates from the beginning of our research on the simulation of a natural dialogue partner in 1975 and has not undergone major changes since that time. It was originally implemented to yield the phrase structure of simple sentences without spending much effort on solving more sophisticated syntactical problems such as structural ambiguity.

Syntactic sentence analysis consists of two successive processes: word-order transformations create a canonical shallow structure which is the input to the actual parsing of the sentence.

2.9.1 Word-order transformations

The objectives of HAM-RPM do not restrict the natural partner to questions (see 2.3). Therefore the component responsible for syntactic sentence analysis has to handle various types of input.

To limit the number of necessary syntax rules for all sentence types the shallow structure which has been generated and modified so far is transformed into a canonical structure. This canonical shallow structure resembles the structure of affirmative propositions (a similar approach was taken by BORGIDA 1975).

The transformation rules are formulated as is usual in a transformational grammar. A structural description (SD) of a preterminal string is associated with instructions on how to rearrange the string (SC: structural change). An example is given in (1).

(1)	Input:	WO STEHT DER BRAUNE STUHL? Where is the brown chair standing?
		⋮
	shallow structure:	((IPRP (WO)) (VRB (STEH)) (NOM (STUHL1)))
	SD:	IPRP VRB NOM
	SC:	(3 2 1)
	transformed shallow structure :	((NOM (STUHL1)) (VRB (STEH)) (IPRP (WO)))

The internal representations of word-order rules in HAM-RPM are stored on the property list of the identifier TRANS. The structural change of a shallow structure is stored as the value of a property which is a compressed version of the structural description.

(2)

identifier	value	property
TRANS	(3 2 1)	IPRP VRB NOM (actually: IPRPVRBNOM)
	(2 1 3 4)	VRB NOM PRP NOM
	⋮	⋮
	(2 1 3)	VRB NOM ADJ

This internal representation is generated while the word-order rules are being read from the file TRANS.RUL (see 2.1.3.3).

On the one hand this method enables a user to add new rules or modify existing ones without detailed knowledge about the system's internal design. On the other hand the whole set of rules does not have to be searched for a suitable one but rather an applicable rule is accessed directly.

When HAM-RPM is operating in trace mode, a message is printed whenever a word-order rule is applied to the shallow structure showing its effect. For example, suppose the input sentence KANNST DU MIR SAGEN, OB DER TISCH VOR DEM STUHL STEHT? (Could you tell me whether the table is standing in front of the chair?) has been reduced to the shallow structure in (3):

```
(3)   ((NOM (TISCH1)) (PRP (VOR)) (NOM (STUHL2)) (VRB (STEH)))
      (PRAETRANSFORMATION:)
      ((NOM (TISCH1)) (VRB (STEH)) (PRP (VOR)) (NOM (STUHL2)))
                           :
```

If no word-order rule for a given shallow structure exists a corresponding message is typed: (KEINE PRAETRANSFORMATION MOEGLICH) (No word-order transformation possible). Examples of this type are questions syntactically structured as assertions, which in speech would be marked by intonation:

```
(4)   DER BRAUNE STUHL IST BEQUEM?
      The brown chair is comfortable?
                       :
      ((NOM (STUHL1)) (VRB (SEIN)) ((ADJ (BEQUEM)))
      (KEINE PRAETRANSFORMATION MOEGLICH)
                       :
```

When they leave this component, the shallow structures of questions and commands have been unified to the structure of affirmative propositions, which will be parsed in the next processing step.

2.9.2 Sentence parsing

Syntax rules are stored internally in a way similar to that just described for word-order rules. A constant identifier called SYNTAX has one property for each syntax rule. Each property is a compressed version of the dominated categories; its value is the dominating category together with the dominated categories put in brackets.

(5) identifier	value	property
SYNTAX	(S (NP VP))	NP VP (actually: NPVP)
	:	:
	(PP (PRP DET NOM))	PRP DET NOM

The internal representation is constructed while the syntax rules are being read from the file BASIS.RUL (see 2.1.3.4). The same advantages as stated for the internal representation of word-order rules (see 2.9.1) apply to syntax rules.

As shown in the examples above, the rules are not restricted to a normal form, i.e. the quantity of dominated categories is not limited to a fixed number. Thus no difficulties arise with uninterpretable auxiliary categories, which become necessary if e.g. Chomsky normal-form is used. (The most extreme rule utilizing the nonstandard form would be the domination of a whole preterminal string by the category 'S', which obviously is inadequate.)

The maximum number of dominated categories appearing in a set of syntax rules is determined when the internal representation has been set up. This numerical value is used by the parsing process.

Having described the syntax rules let's now turn to the process which makes use of them.

The syntactic analysis of a sentence proceeds from left to right in the preterminal string (i.e. parts of speech in the beginning). The concatenation of as many preterminal symbols as the maximum of dominated categories indicates is constructed to see whether there exists a suitable syntax rule. If there is none, the length of the preterminal string just inspected is reduced by one element at a time until either the preterminal string is empty or a syntax rule can be applied.

If no applicable rule is found in the first attempt, the first element of the preterminal string is ignored temporarily and the remaining part is handled by the same procedure as described above. For the sake of simplicity we are calling the string to be analysed 'preterminal string', although this is not quite accurate. In the course of the analysis the relevant string consists not only of parts of speech, but also of dominating categories such as 'NP'.

If, however, a rule can be applied, the dominated categories in the preterminal string are replaced by the value of the syntax rule. Thus the categories replaced do not disappear, but are pushed down one level. The analysis which follows does not take notice of them, for it always regards the first level of the preterminal string as the object to be analysed.

Having reached the end of the preterminal string the analysis starts again at the left margin of the whole string which has been modified by the application of syntax rules.

The analysis terminates if the first level of the complete preterminal string consists only of the symbol 'S'. In this case the shallow structure of the input sentence has been syntactically accepted. In trace mode the system types the message (SATZ AKZEPTIERT:) (Sentence accepted:) and prints the structure which has been built up in the course of the parsing process. The parse tree is also printed - in a slightly distorted manner (see Fig. 7 below) - if the user requested at the beginning of the dialogue that this be done (see 2.2.1).

A shallow structure is syntactically not well formed if no further rule can be applied to a preterminal string which does not consist of the single symbol 'S'. In this case ellipsis recognition is tried (see 2.10) and if that also fails, the sentence is rejected by the system, which types BITTE FRAGE NOCHMAL ANDERS FORMULIEREN! (Please express the question differently!). In trace mode additional information is typed: (SATZ NICHT AK-

ZEPTIERT:) (Sentence not accepted:) followed by the preterminal string constructed so far.

To illustrate the algorithm described above, the steps of the analysis are shown in Fig. 7 on the next page. Here the maximum number of dominated categories was three.

As the analysis does not keep track of which rules have already been applied it has no way to detect more than one structural description of a given shallow structure. But up to now this limitation has not appeared to be particularly disadvantageous. Nevertheless, together with a new concept of the semantic representation of a sentence (see 2.11), a more ambitious parser which can cope with structural ambiguities will be necessary for analyzing more complex sentences.

Experiments are to be made with the replacement of the syntactic sentence analysis in HAM-RPM by already implemented versions of an ATN parser (see BATES 1978). Parts of this parser might equally be employed in components with integrated partial parsing, such as NP-resolution (see 2.8). If the use of an ATN parser turns out to be too painstaking or too rigid for our purposes (see Report No. 9) the possibility still remains of improving the existing parsing component of HAM-RPM.

Natural partner's input:

WAS STEHT HINTER DEM GROSSEN TISCH?
What is standing behind the big table?

⋮

shallow structure:

((IPRN (WAS)) (VRB (STEH)) (PRP (HINTER)) (NOM (TISCH1)))
(KEINE PRAETRANSFORMATION MOEGLICH)

applicable rule	inspected section of preterminal string
-	(IPRN VRB PRP)
-	(IPRN VRB)
NP -> IPRN	(IPRN)
-	(VRB PRP NOM)
-	(VRB PRP)
-	(VRB)
PP -> PRP + NOM	(PRP NOM)
-	(NP VRB PP)
-	(NP VRB)
-	(NP)
VP -> VRB + PP	(VRB PP)
S -> NP + VP	(NP VP)
	(S)

```
(SATZ AKZEPTIERT:)
(S (NP (IPRN (WAS))) (VP (VRB (STEH)) (PP (PRP (HINTER))
                                          (NOM (TISCH1)))))
```

```
S
      NP
              IPRN
                        WAS
      VP
              VRB
                        STEH
              PP
                        PRP
                                 HINTER
                        NOM
                                 TISCH1
```

Fig. 7

2.10 ELLIPSIS

HAM-RPM handles some kinds of elliptical expressions; this is of great importance in natural conversations, where utterances are by no means always complete. As for the resolution of anaphoric references (see 2.8.6), the dialogue context of an utterance provides a framework for the interpretation of sentences in which some elements are omitted.

In HAM-RPM ellipsis may occur on three levels: questions posed by the user, the user's responses to questions posed by the system, and the system's answers.

In most cases, the user's elliptical responses can be analysed straightforwardly, because the syntactic form of the system's question implies a certain syntactic form of an elliptical response. For example, the response to a question like

(1) WELCHEN STUHL MEINST DU?
Which chair do you mean?

will often be an isolated noun phrase, which might itself be elliptical. Elliptical responses of this sort are handled by the components of the system which generate the corresponding questions, as, for example, in a clarification dialogue (see 2.8.7).

Since HAM-RPM in general answers the user's question as concisely as possible - unless requested to do otherwise by the dialogue partner (see 2.14.2) - it usually outputs expressions which are not complete sentences, for example isolated noun phrases or prepositional phrases:

(2) WAS STEHT VOR DER AMPEL?
What's in front of the traffic light?

(3) DER ROTE PERSONENWAGEN.
The red car.

Information which was already contained in the question is not mentioned in the answer; indeed, it is not even contained in the semantic representation of the answer.

This section will focus on the processing of elliptical questions posed by the dialogue partner.

If the system's attempts to parse a question as a complete sentence fail, it backs up and starts an ellipsis-recognition process. Incidentally, a simple improvement of this strategy could provide faster recognition of relatively obviously elliptical inputs: If the system has noticed a tendency on the part of the human dialogue partner to use ellipsis, it first checks for ellipsis using certain simple criteria such as the absence of a verb; only if this fails does it attempt to parse the input as a complete sentence.

The ellipsis routines match the syntactic structure of the input, in which all pronouns and noun phrases have been resolved, against the shallow structure of the last complete input, which is stored in the value of the variable SHALLOW-ALT (shallow-old), as described in section 2.14. The following dialogue sequence represents a simple example of this approach:

(4) IST ER KAPUTT?
Is it damaged?

(5) NEIN.
No.

(6) DAS HEISST ALSO, HEIL?
Aha! Intact then?

(7) JA.
Yes.

(8) UND DER STUHL, WELCHER IN DER NAEHE DES FERNSEHGERAETES STEHT?
And the chair which is near the TV set?

From the shallow structure of (6), ((ADJ (INTACT))), the ellipsis routines construct the pattern

(9) (??BEGINNING (ADJ ?) ??END)

which is then matched against the shallow structure of (4),

(10) ((VRB (IS)) (NOM (TABLE1)) (ADJ (DAMAGED)))

Since the match is successful, the variable bindings are used to expand the shallow structure of (6) to

(11) ((VRB (IS)) (NOM (TABLE1)) (ADJ (INTACT))) .

An analogous process underlies the expansion of the shallow structure of (8), namely ((NOM (CHAIR4))), into

(12) ((VRB (IS)) (NOM (CHAIR4)) (ADJ (INTACT))) .

We see from this example that when the sentence preceding an elliptical input is itself elliptical, its expanded shallow structure is used. Incidentally, the conjunction 'and', which often appears at the beginning of elliptical questions, is deleted when the system tries to analyse the input as an ellipsis.

In contrast to the ellipsis facility designed by GROSZ (1976c) for the SRI Speech Understanding System, the routines sketched here can cope with sentences in which more than one constituent is present in the incomplete input. For example, consider the sequence:

(13) STEHT DIE FRAU JETZT VOR DEM FACHBEREICH FÜR INFORMATIK?
Is the woman now standing in front of the Computer Science Department?

(14) JA.
Yes.

(15) UND DER MANN RECHTS NEBEN DER AMPEL?
And the man to the right of the traffic light?

(16) NEIN.
No.

(17) DAHINTER?
Behind it?

When operating in trace mode, (see 2.2.1), HAM-RPM types the message ELLIPSE ERKANNT (ellipsis recognised) and the expansion of the elliptical input. In general, all decisions previously made concerning the type of question and the modal component (see 2.3) of the input are revised as soon as it is recognised as being elliptical.

It seems to be a certain improvement over the ellipsis facilities of LIFER (HENDRIX 1977) and PLANES (WALTZ 1978) that for the construction of the semantic representation of the expanded sentence full parsing and semantic translation are not performed; instead, on the basis of a comparison of the shallow structure of the previous sentence with the expanded ellipsis, particular constituents are projected onto the semantic representation of the previous sentence, which has been stored just as the previous shallow structure has (see 2.14.1). Consider the following dialogue sequence:

(18) PARKT DER WAGEN AUF DER PARKZONE?
Is the car parked in the parking zone?

(19) NEIN.
No.

(20) VOR DEM BAUM, WELCHER IN DER NAEHE DES GROSSEN GEBAEUDES STEHT?
In front of the tree which is near the large building?

To construct the semantic representation of (20), the predicate ON in the semantic representation of (18), namely

(21) ((CAR4) (PARKING/ ZONE1) (ON))

is replaced by IN/ FRONT/ OF, and the argument PARKING/ ZONE1 is replaced by TREE3. This produces

(22) ((CAR4) (TREE3) (IN/ FRONT/ OF)),

which is the semantic representation of the elliptical input (20).

One limitation of the current ellipsis routines stems from the assumption that the shallow structure of the elliptical utterance must be similar to some part of the last successfully analysed input. This is not always the case, as is shown by the following example:

(23) HAT DIE STRASSE ZEBRASTREIFEN?
Has the street got zebra stripes?

(24) JA.
Yes.

(25) WIEVIELE?
How many?

The major limitations of the current version of the algorithm are due to the fact that HAM-RPM's ellipsis routines use only syntactic clues. By contrast, the mechanisms of LIFER (HENDRIX 1977) and PLANES (WALTZ 1978) for handling ellipsis rely heavily on the notion of a 'semantic grammar'. This means that a certain amount of semantic information is encoded in the syntactic categories (see Report No. 11), so that similarity of 'syntactic' structures implies semantic similarity. We could easily introduce semantic categories into our grammar, and this would improve the performance of our ellipsis routines considerably. But we think that from a theoretical point of view such 'semantic grammars' are awkward because of their lack of generality and economy of description.

Although the simple but efficient approach described here works remarkably well, a notion of semantic closeness such as the one used by GROSZ (1976c) to select from among the different candidates for the substitution and semantic checks on the suitability of a projection are under exploration so that HAM-RPM's treatment of ellipsis may be improved.

2.11 GENERATION OF THE SEMANTIC REPRESENTATION

2.11.1 The translation component

The input to the search and inference component of HAM-RPM is a semantic representation of the user's question. The propositional part (see 2.3) of this semantic representation is constructed by a translation component which we will describe in this section. The source language of the translation component consists of syntax trees resulting from the parsing process described in section 2.9.2. The target language consists of semantic representation constructions which in general are ordered sets of triples. The semantics of this representation construction are defined in section 2.12.1. As described in section 2.10 the translation process is skipped when the input is an expanded ellipsis; instead a projection is performed, which uses the semantic representation of the previous sentence.

The general scheme of the translation process is first to match the parse tree against an ordered set of patterns and then to use the variable bindings resulting from these matches to construct the semantic representation.

As we will show below by examples, the whole matching process is controlled by the semantic definitions of the main verb of the analysed sentence. In the lexicon entry for each verb (see 2.1.3.1) a pointer is attached to the keyword SEMANTIK, which allows the translation component to retrieve the semantic definition of the verb. For example, consider the lexicon entry for the verb 'to drink':

(1) (TRINK (WORTART (VRB) SEMANTIK (TRINK-SEM))) .

Here TRINK-SEM is the name of a piece of knowledge which procedurally represents the semantics of 'to drink'.

The pattern matching is organized in the following way: For each position of the triple an ordered set of transformation rules is stored in the knowledge base of the system (see 2.1.3.5). Each transformation rule is an arbitrarily complex FUZZY pattern containing only one open variable ?A. A successful match causes the insertion of the value of the variable ?A into the corresponding slot of the triple. If all matches fail, NIL is inserted into the corresponding slot.

Let us examine this process in detail by discussing three simple examples. Suppose that after a successful parsing of sentence (2) the syntax tree displayed in Fig. 8 is to be transformed by the translation component.

(2) KANNST DU DAS GETRAENK, WELCHES SICH AUF DEM COUCHTISCH BEFINDET, TRINKEN?
Could you drink the drink which is located on the couch table?

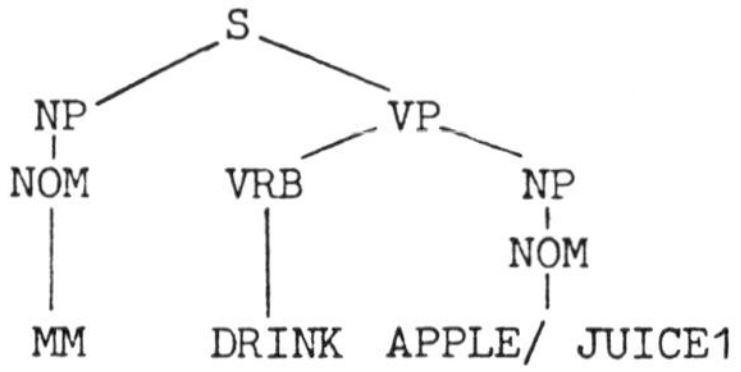

Fig. 8

First the pattern displayed in Fig. 9 is matched against the structure in Fig. 8. As a side effect of this successful match,

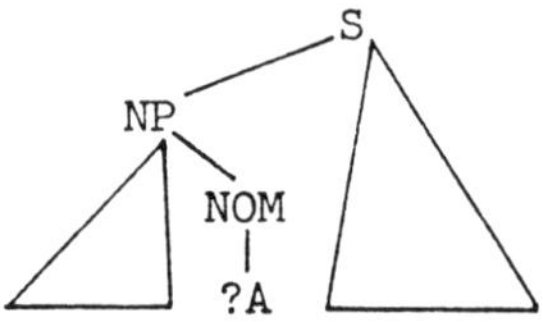

Fig. 9

the variable ?A is bound to the value MM. This value is inserted into the first slot of the first triple. Fig. 9 shows the graphic representation of the pattern, which in linearized form is represented as (3):

(3) (S (NP ?? (NOM ?A)) ??)

Note, incidentally, that this is also the form in which the patterns are stored on the file SESY.PAT. This file can easily be updated to include further transformation rules if the scope of the grammar stored on the file BASIS.RUL (see 2.1.3.4) is expanded.

The second slot of the triple is filled with APPLE/ JUICE1.

This is accomplished by unifying Fig. 8 with the pattern

(4) (S ?? (VP (?? (NP ?? (NOM ?A)) ??))) .

Having filled the third slot of the triple with DRINK the semantic definition of the verb 'to drink' causes the translation process to stop without producing further triples. In summary, the result obtained by the translation component for this simple case is the triple:

(5) ((MM) (APPLE/ JUICE1) (DRINK))

Let us consider another example, in which a NIL slot is generated. Suppose (7) is the linearized form of the parse tree for (6).

(6) WOVOR STEHT DAS FERNSEHGERAET?
The TV set is located in front of what?

(7) (S (NP (NOM (TVSET1))) (VP (VRB (LOCAT)) (PP (PRP (IN/ FRONT/ OF)) (IPRN (WHAT)))))

The first slot of the triple is filled in the same way as in the previous example, this time with TVSET1. All patterns defined for the second slot fail to match. Thus the value NIL is inserted into this slot. This signals to the search and inference component of HAM-RPM that a value has to be found which fills the slot. The semantic definition of LOCAT causes a match of (7) with the pattern (8).

(8) (S ?? (VP ?? (PP (PRP ?A) ??) ??))

Since this is a successful match, the third slot is filled with IN/ FRONT/ OF resulting in the triple (9):

(9) ((TVSET1) NIL (IN/ FRONT/ OF)) .

To give an idea of the more general capabilities of the translation component let's finally consider a slightly more complicated example. The parse tree (11), which is derived from the surface structure (10), contains the verb PLACE, which in this case takes three arguments: You, TV set, couch table. Since the predicate and its three arguments obviously cannot be represented by one triple, successively the two triples in (12) are generated.

(10) KANNST DU DAS FERNSEHGERAET AUF DEN COUCHTISCH STELLEN?
Could you place the TV set on the couch table?

(11) (S (NP (NOM (MM))) (VP (VPA (VRB (PLACE)) (NP (NOM (TVSET1))) (PP (PRP (ON)) (NP (NOM (TABLE2))))))

(12) ((MM) (TVSET1) (PLACE))
((TVSET1) (TABLE2) (ON))

The order of the triples reflects a logical dependency: First it must be checked whether MM is able to manipulate the TV set at all and then whether he can place it on the couch table.

When operating in trace mode HAM-RPM types the triples generated by the translation component for inspection by the user.

This notation for the semantic representation of a sentence is inadequate for representing the meaning of very complex sentences. In fact it represents a sort of bottleneck within HAM-RPM as a whole: a number of important types of questions and some interesting inference processes have had their implementation delayed because the corresponding deep structure could not be represented.

Work is in progress on a richer notation for representing deep structures which uses the template construct provided by the language AIMDS (see 1.2.6). The meaning of a particular sentence, e.g. 'Where are you?' is represented by a specific instance of a general template representing a certain type of sentence, e.g. 'request for description of location'. Templates similarly represent other complex structures such as indefinite noun phrases. Each general sentence template contains slots which must be filled in order to represent the meaning of a certain type of sentence, as well as information on how to fill the slots using various kinds of knowledge.

Here are three strong points of this approach:

- Since the slots in a template can be filled with other templates, the meaning representation can be arbitrarily deeply nested.
- The important differences between various types of sentences can be done justice to by defining the corresponding templates accordingly, there being no need to squeeze all meaning representations into a single format.
- The generation of the meaning representation needn't proceed strictly bottom-up: once the sentence type has been determined, the construction of the semantic representation is

guided by the corresponding general templates.

2.11.2 Lexical decomposition

The output of the translation component, which was outlined in the previous section, in general consists of an ordered set of triples. This set undergoes a process of lexical decomposition, which we will sketch in this section. The purpose of this component is to map the semantic representations constructed by the translation component onto 'deeper' representations, in which elements of a set of semantic primitives are used. This mapping is essential, since inferences are only defined for semantic primitives, whose formal properties are known to the system. The user can easily extend the set of semantic primitives, for instance by introducing new relations into the semantic networks or adding the appropriate inference rules. It is not our intention here to discuss the strengths and limitations of approaches which make heavy use of semantic primitives, such as the system of SCHANK 1975.

In the current version of HAM-RPM only adjectives are decomposed. Since these linguistic entities always occur in the third slot of a triple, the lexical-decomposition routine checks whether the knowledge base provides a decomposition procedure for the item in the third slot.

This is done by consulting the lexicon (see 2.1.3.1), where for each decomposable word a pointer to a decomposition routine is attached to the keyword DEKOMPOSITION. For example, this is the lexicon entry for LEER (empty):

(13) (LEER (WORTART (ADJ) DEKOMPOSITION (LEER-DEK))) .

The evaluation of LEER-DEK triggers transformations in the modal (see 2.3) and the propositional part of a semantic representation which includes the adjective 'empty'. Suppose that sentence (14) was mapped onto the triple (15).

(14) IST DAS GLAS LEER?
Is the glass empty?

(15) ((GLAS1) NIL (LEER))

When the lexical-decomposition procedure for 'empty' is executed, LEER in (15) is replaced by the semantic primitive CONTAINS and in the modal part of the semantic representation the value of the variable NEGATION is changed from T to NIL or vice versa. This means that actually HAM-RPM tests whether a container is empty by checking whether anything is contained in it. One advantage of lexical decomposition is that other surface predicates can also be decomposed using the predicate CONTAINS. For example, in HAM-RPM the adjective VOLL (filled) is in effect mapped onto 'includes something'.

When operating in trace mode the system types the message DEKOMPOSITION and the transformed triple. For example, after the decomposition of LEER in (14) the system types:

```
(16)   (DEKOMPOSITION ((GLAS1) NIL (ENTHAELT)) NEGATION: T)
                                    contains
```

In the current version of HAM-RPM little use is being made of the decomposition capabilities, so that most semantic representations constructed by the translation component are passed on to the answer-generation routines without any change.

2.12 THE INFERENCE COMPONENT

The task of the inference component is to build up a semantic representation of an appropriate response to a given question. The problem of how to formulate this response in natural language for presentation to the dialogue partner can then be handled by the components described in sections 2.15 and 2.16.

The inference component accepts as input a semantic representation of the user's question, which has been generated by the translation component (see 2.11.1).and possibly modified by the decomposition routine (see 2.11.2). It is capable of retrieving information explicitly stored in the referential and the conceptual semantic networks and of deriving information not explicitly represented in the knowledge base by invoking inference rules coded as FUZZY DEDUCE-procedures (see 2.1.3.6).

It is clear that even during the language-understanding process which has been described up to this point the system must be able to make inferences concerning the content of the dialogue partner's utterances, for example when determining the referent of a noun phrase (see 2.8). Even the language-generation components must perform inferences. In other words, the derivational and retrieval machinery contained in HAM-RPM is employed in almost every processing phase.

But what we shall describe in this section is only the inference processes involved in the derivation of the semantic content of an appropriate answer to a given question. Although both read-time and question-time inferences, as defined by CHARNIAK (1976), are used, we shall deal in this section only with question-time inferences.

Before describing the various types of inference processes used in HAM-RPM, we shall show how the semantic representations of the input sentences are interpreted by the inference component.

2.12.1 The semantics of the semantic representations

Apart from the modal part of the semantic representation of an input sentence, the triples generated by the translation component are interpreted as logical expressions of the Predicate Calculus. Since a list of triples is treated by the infer--ce component as an abbreviation for an extended conjunction of logical expressions, we shall confine our discussion to the semantics of single triples.

All NIL slots of a triple are interpreted as distinct variables. A NIL in the third slot of a triple is a variable ranging over the set of all primitive predicates known to the system. Variables in the first two slots range over individual constants of the domain of discourse. The third slot is thus the predicate position, the first two slots the argument positions. The second slot is disregarded by the inference component when the third slot contains a one-place predicate, as is the case with the triple ((CHAIR4) NIL (RED)).

When the triple is fully instantiated, as is ((TV/ SET1) (TABLE2) (ON)), the truth of the predication is tested against the domain model encoded in the knowledge base.

The interpretation of the variables contained in the triples depends on whether the triple is interpreted as representing a yes/no-question or a wh-question (see 2.3). For yes/no-questions, all of the variables are interpreted as being existentially quantified with immediate scope. In the case of the triple ((GLASS1) NIL (CONTAINS)), for example (see 2.11.2), the truth value of

(1) $(\exists x)$ CONTAINS (GLASS1,x)

is checked. For wh-questions, on the other hand, all variables are taken to be universally quantified. For example, for the triple ((TV/ SET1) NIL (IN/ FRONT)), the set of all x such that

(2) IN/ FRONT (TV/ SET1,x)

is true represents the complete answer to the question. (In fact, only a particularly relevant subset of this set is found and mentioned in the answer; see 2.13.4.)

Variables can range over predicates, as well as over tokens, as in the example ((TV/ SET1) NIL NIL), which is the semantic representation of the question

(3) WO STEHT DAS FERNSEHGERAET?
Where is the TV set?

This sketch of the semantics of triples has been simplified in many respects. For example, when 'potentiality' has been recorded as the modal part of a yes/no-question, the system checks whether the formula denoted by the triple is true in some possible world. An example of such a sentence is

(4) KOENNTEST DU DAS GETRAENK TRINKEN?
Could you drink the drink?

whose semantic representation is ((MM) (APPLE/ JUICE1) (DRINK)).

An important feature of our approach, which distinguishes it from most others, is that it is based on fuzzy set theory and fuzzy logic. This means that the predicates in the third slot are interpreted as fuzzy predicates, that the truth values computed are fuzzy truth values, and that the sets derived by the inference component are fuzzy sets. For the sake of clarity we have disregarded these facts in the informal presentation of the semantics just given. Thorough discussions of this topic are contained in WAHLSTER 1977 and HAM-RPM Report No. 5.

2.12.2 The general structure of the inference process in HAM-RPM

The first task of the inference component is to determine which inputs are requests involving spatial relations and which are requests for network search and deduction. In this section only the latter case is discussed, the treatment of spatial relations being described independently in section 2.13.

Before actually performing any inferences, the system checks for possible selectional restrictions on the predicates contained in the triple. For example, consider the triple ((MM) (CHAIR4) (DRINK)). The semantic definition of TRINKEN (drink) contained in the knowledge base specifies as a selectional restriction that the object of drinking must be a fluid. When a selectional restriction is violated, the input sentence is rejected and the reasons for the rejection are recorded, so that any follow-up-questions posed by the user asking for a justification of the rejection can be answered (see 2.5.1). For the present example, the system generates the justification:

(5) EIN STUHL IST NICHT FLUESSIG.
    A chair isn't fluid.

Note that the checking of selectional restrictions may itself require complex inference processes.

Ultimately any question is transformed into one or a series of GOAL-expressions, which trigger search and inference processes. All triples containing a one-place predicate for which no specific semantic definition is stored under the property SEMANTIK are transformed into GOAL-expressions which inspect REF-arcs (see 2.1.3.8). For example the triple

(6a) ((CHAIR3) NIL (BROWN))

is transformed into

(6b) (GOAL (REF CHAIR3 BROWN)).

Suppose the assertion used as an argument for the GOAL-expression is present in the referential network. Then we have the trivial case, since the GOAL succeeds immediately when a matching assertion is found.

Now let's discuss a slightly more interesting example, in which an inference rule must be applied. Suppose in the inference component the expression

(7) (GOAL (REF PIANO1 EXPENSIVE))

is evaluated and the referential network contains only (ISA PIANO1 PIANO) as an assertion referring to PIANO1. Furthermore suppose that the assertions (U MUSICAL/ INSTRUMENT PIANO) and (D MUSICAL/ INSTRUMENT EXPENSIVE) are stored in the conceptual semantic network. Property inheritance, namely the transitivity of D-arcs over U-arcs, is defined via a DEDUCE-procedure with the calling pattern (D ?X ?Y). In the body of this rule, which is one of the general inference rules stored on the file INFER.PRC, the two conjoined expressions (GOAL (U ?Z !X)) and (GOAL (D !Z !Y)) are evaluated.

Since the evaluation of (7) failed HAM-RPM tries a generic interpretation of the piano in (7) evaluating:

(8) (GOAL (D &(*TYPE PIANO1) EXPENSIVE))

*TYPE is one of a large number of general service functions working on the networks and gives back the name of the superset of its argument using the ISA-arc in the referential semantic network. Since no matching assertion for (D PIANO EXPENSIVE) is found in the conceptual semantic network, inference rules are automatically fired by FUZZY's pattern-directed procedure invocation mechanism. In our example the variables ?X, ?Y and ?Z are assigned to PIANO, EXPENSIVE and MUSICAL/ INSTRUMENT respectively. Since the evaluations of (GOAL (U MUSICAL/ INSTRUMENT PIANO)) and (GOAL (D MUSICAL/ INSTRUMENT EXPENSIVE)) succeed, the GOAL in (8) succeeds. Actually, inferences in HAM-RPM are usually far more complicated than this, because in the average inference chain many different inference rules have to be applied and a good deal of backtracking must be done (see Report No. 5 for such examples).

Having sketched the general framework within which the inference component works, in this paper we only discuss in more detail the handling of fuzzy predicates, which is one of the distinguishing features of HAM-RPM's inference component.

2.12.3 Inferences based on fuzzy knowledge

The use of terms with vague meanings and of fuzzy inferences is a typical feature of non-technical communication. As the objective of our research is to reconstruct the communicative and cognitive competence of a human dialogue partner in a simple everyday situation, in the design of HAM-RPM we have considered the human ability to deduce useful information even in case of vague or partial knowledge by approximative and common-sense reasoning.

As a typical example of our approach to vagueness let us first consider the representation of the referential meaning of vague, relative adjectives and its use in the inference component of HAM-RPM. The use of relative adjectives like 'old', 'big', 'narrow' always implies a context-dependent comparison with an expected norm. Furthermore, such predicates in most cases fit only to a certain degree to a given object. Hence we represent the referential meaning of relative adjectives in HAM-RPM as a set of implicitly defined fuzzy sets (see ZADEH 1978) whose members correspond to the possible reference sets. As an example, consider the referential meaning of 'big' for the reference set 'trees' in (9):

```
(9a)   (PROC (REF _>TREE  BIG)
(9b)         (FETCH (REF !TREE ?HEIGHTVALUE INST HEIGHT)
(9c)         (SUCCEED (REF !TREE BIG) (SFUNK !HEIGHTVALUE 10 20)))
```

Suppose the assertion (10) is stored in the referential net, de-

```
(10)   ((REF TREE3 15 INST HEIGHT) . 0.8)
```

noting the fact that the height of TREE3 is about 15 meters. Furthermore suppose in the inference component the GOAL-expression (GOAL (REF TREE3 BIG) 0.2) is evaluated. When no matching expression is found in the referential net, the DEDUCE procedure displayed above is invoked. _>TREE is an implicitly typed variable. This means that it can only be assigned to names of objects of type TREE; this insures that this definition of 'big' is used only for the appropriate reference set. With (9b) the system retrieves the height of TREE3. The degree of 'bigness' of TREE3 is computed in (9c) as a fuzzy set membership value via the standard function SFUNK introduced by Zadeh. In the second and third parameter of SFUNK the expected norm of 'bigness' is encoded. The value of the GOAL-statement above is then ((REF TREE3 BIG) . 0.5). Note that the GOAL-statement has as its second argument a threshold, so that assertions derived by the inference component don't succeed if their z-value is smaller than this threshold. This is important, because in the semantic networks negation is represented by the z-value 0.

Finally, let's consider a derivation in which both fuzzy and highly subjective knowledge are involved. Suppose that the assumptions (11) - (14) are represented in the semantic networks.

(11) ((ISA APPLE/ JUICE1 APPLE/ JUICE) . 1.0)
(12) ((U JUICE APPLE/ JUICE) . 1.0)
(13) ((D JUICE NON-ALCOHOLIC) . 1.0)
(14) ((D APPLE/ JUICE SWEET) . 0.6)

(14) represents the subjective experience that apple juice is often sweet, but sometimes sour. Suppose the question 'Do you like this apple juice?' is finally transformed into the expression (GOAL (REF APPLE/ JUICE1 TASTY) 0.2). The 'subjective meaning' of 'tasty' is defined by the inference rule displayed in fig. 10.

```
META-KNOWLEDGE:
     Apply the control knowledge coded in
     TRACE-PROCEDURE-DEMON8.
     Don't use instantiations of premises with degrees of
     belief lower than 0.3.
     The degree of informativeness of this rule is 0.5.
RULE:
     If you want to show that (X is a tasty drink)
                    show that (X is sweet)
                     and that (X is non-alcoholic).
```

Fig. 10

This inference rule is coded in FUZZY as follows:

```
(15) (PROC DEMON: TRACE-PROCEDURE-DEMON8 ZVAL: '(0.3 0.8)
      (D _>DRINK TASTY)
      (FOR GOAL: (D !DRINK SWEET)
           (FOR GOAL: (D.!DRINK NON-ALCOHOLIC) (SUCCEED?))))
```

Meta-knowledge is associated with each inference rule which is available to the system. This meta-knowledge plays an essential role in the generation of explanations of inferences (see 2.5.1). It is also used by the inference component. For example, when the calling pattern of more than one inference rule matches the pattern in a GOAL-expression, the conflict is resolved by preferring the inference rule with a higher degree of informativeness.

Since in the given dialogue situation the system is unable to taste APPLE/ JUICE1, it derives an answer on the basis of general knowledge, evaluating the expression
(GOAL (D APPLE/ JUICE TASTY)). Applying the inference rule (15) and the general rule for property inheritance described above, the system builds up the goal tree shown in Fig. 11.

The z-value 0.6 of the conclusion is verbalised by the output routine of the system by the hedged affirmative ICH GLAUBE JA (I think so). The goal tree and some additional information are recorded in a separate CONTEXT of the assertional data base called INFERENCE-MEMORY by TRACE-PROCEDURE-DEMON8, a procedure demon which differs from the one normally used in that it makes a note of each step in the inference process. The information in this CONTEXT is the basis for HAM-RPM's explanation capability (see 2.5.1).

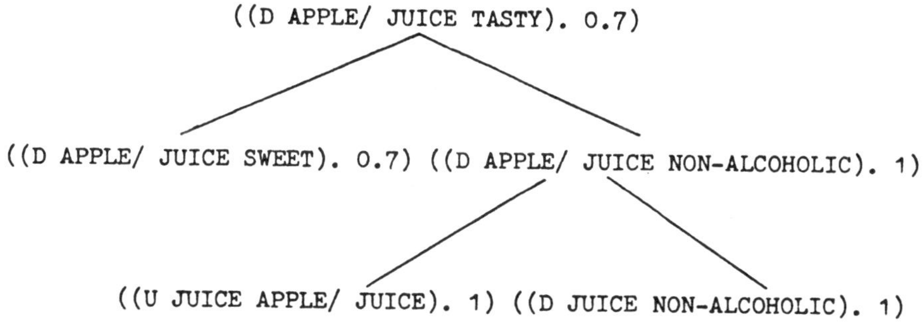

Fig. 11

2.13 SPATIAL RELATIONS AND THE SIMULATION OF VISUAL SEARCH

Spatial relations play an important role in conversations about HAM-RPM's scenes. On the one hand, some questions focus on spatial relations directly, for example

(1) WORAUF STEHT DAS FERNSEHGERAET?
What's the TV set standing on?

On the other hand, both the natural dialogue partner and the system itself often refer to objects in the scene in terms of spatial descriptions, using noun phrases such as

(2) DER SESSEL, WELCHER DIREKT HINTER DEM COUCHTISCH STEHT
the armchair that's directly behind the couch table

(see sections 2.8.4 and 2.15).

Two kinds of tasks which must be performed by the component of HAM-RPM responsible for spatial relations may be distinguished:

- the checking of spatial relations, i.e. the determination of the degree to which a given spatial relation holds between two given objects
- the search for objects which stand in a given spatial relation to a given object.

The former task, which will be discussed first, involves little more than the application of the definitions of the various spatial relations to particular objects.

2.13.1 The definitions of spatial relations

The locations of most of the objects in HAM-RPM's domains of discourse are represented by pairs of integers between 1 and 30 corresponding to points in the horizontal plane (see 2.1.3.9). This information permits an adequate description of the spatial relations between objects for HAM-RPM's purposes, except in the case of very large objects such as the streets in the traffic scene. Such objects could be represented by sets of coordinate pairs, but the definitions of the spatial relations involving such objects are complicated and have not yet been worked out within the context of HAM-RPM. The coordinates of each object, which are loaded from the file GEO.DTA at the beginning of each dialogue, are placed on the property list of the object's name to permit quick retrieval.

The spatial relations in the plane which are presently defined in HAM-RPM are: VOR (in front of), HINTER (behind), NEBEN (next to), RECHTS/ NEBEN (to the right of), LINKS/ NEBEN (to the left of), and IN/ DER/ NAEHE (near).

The procedure PRUEFEN (check) takes as arguments two object names and the name of a spatial relation. It checks to see whether the given relation holds between the two objects by first computing the vector which points from the first object to the second and then comparing this vector with the definition of the spatial relation. These definitions are essentially mappings from vectors onto z-values. Figure 12 illustrates the definition of VOR (in front of) by showing which z-values between 0 and 1 are associated with various vectors.

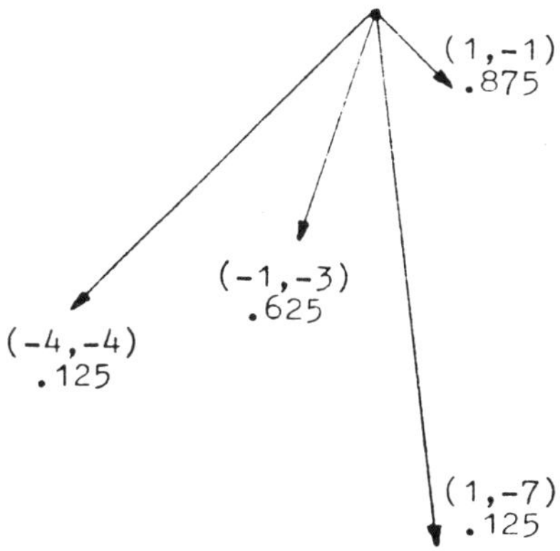

Fig. 12

The definitions presently being used were developed on the basis of intuition and with a view to simplicity; they could certainly be improved upon with respect to their psychological realism.

The procedure PRUEFEN fails if the vector it computes doesn't lie within the area for which z-values are provided by the definition. Otherwise, it returns essentially the z-value found.

The definitions of the individual relations are contained directly in the definition of PRUEFEN. It would have been more consistent with HAM-RPM's overall design philosophy to store them separately so that they could be easily understood and modified by naive users. This wasn't done because such definitions would be difficult to express in a self-explanatory notation and because the number of relations of this sort is very limited in any case.

As described in section 2.1.3.9, spatial relations involving the vertical dimension are stored directly in the knowledge base. One reason for this is that the small number of vertical relations existing between pairs of objects in HAM-RPM's domains makes this simplification feasible. Another reason is that vertical relations tend to depend more heavily than plane relations on the shape of the two objects and the nature of the contact between then (compare, for example 'on' and 'above'), so that deriving them from coordinates would entail the addition of more detailed information on the position of the parts of the objects.

When the relation name passed to PRUEFEN as its third argument belongs to the vertical dimension, PRUEFEN first checks whether the vector between the two objects is (0 0). If so, it tries to FETCH the corresponding assertion - for example
(SENKRECHTE AUF GLAS1 TISCH2) ('(horizontal on glass1 table2)')
from the associative net which was initially loaded directly from the file GEO.NET. If it finds such an assertion, it returns its z-value; otherwise it fails.

2.13.2 The role of the simulation of visual search

In a number of different cases the system must search for objects standing in a given relation to a given object. One such case is when it is answering a question like (1) above. Another is when it is generating a definite description of an object in terms of the object's spatial relations to other objects (see 2.15).

In contrast to the checking of spatial relations described in the last section, the answer returned by such a search process, which is essentially a list of objects, is not determined solely by the position of the objects in the scene and the definition of the spatial relation in question. This is because there are usually more objects present which fit the given description than it would make sense for the system to mention. The system must therefore select certain objects over others on the basis of several criteria, two of which are:

- proximity to the given object
- salience of the object found.

The objects which rate high in these two respects are, generally speaking, the ones which would tend to be found first by a human being looking in the neighbourhood of the given object. The corresponding search processes in HAM-RPM have therefore been designed to simulate to a certain degree the way in which a human being performs such a search. (A more detailed discussion of the motivation underlying this simulation is contained in Report No. 3.)

2.13.3 The data structures used by the search processes

The key notion involved in this simulation is that of a 'glance': when looking at a certain point in a scene, a human being is aware of certain objects, but not others; some of the objects he can see are more salient than others, this salience depending not only upon the appearance of the object itself, but also on its distance from the point being looked at. Since the processing which actually takes place in a human being during a glance does not lend itself to simulation on a digital computer, the essential points just mentioned are reproduced in HAM-RPM by having the system rather laboriously compute the content of each possible glance in advance, at some time at which it isn't engaged in a dialogue.

The content of each possible 'glance' is stored in a separate FUZZY CONTEXT. There are as many CONTEXTs as there are points with integer coordinates in the scene in question, each CONTEXT bearing a name constructed from the coordinates of the corresponding point, e.g '/ 4/ 16'. An entry in such a CONTEXT has the form

(3) ((AUFFAELLIG <token>) . z-value)

where the z-value represents the 'relative' salience of the object, i.e. its salience with respect to a glance at the point corresponding to the CONTEXT in question, as opposed to its 'intrinsic' salience, stored on the file GEO.NET, which it has only in the CONTEXT corresponding to its own location.

To compute the contents of all of the possible glances, the system determines for each object in the scene the names of the CONTEXTs in which it should be represented and the relative salience it should have in each of these. This is done using a simple, intuitively defined function of the location of the object and its intrinsic salience. For example, most objects of low salience are represented only in the CONTEXT corresponding to their own location, in which they have their intrinsic salience, and in the CONTEXTs corresponding to the four points nearest to them, in which they have an even lower salience.

Once the contents of all of the CONTEXTs have been determined, all of this information is dumped onto the file BLICK.DMP (glance.dmp) . This file is used during the dialogue instead of the CONTEXTs in the assertional data base themselves to save space in working memory. At the beginning of the dialogue BLICK.DMP is indexed for random access in roughly the same way as the lexicon file LEX.DTA (see 2.4.3). The FUZZY primitive FETCH can't be used to retrieve data from a file, but an analogous procedure is used. (For the sake of clarity of exposition we shall speak below as if the CONTEXTs were all present in working memory during the dialogue and as if they were accessed using FETCH.)

2.13.4 The search processes

The way in which the data structures just described are used can best be illustrated using the example of a question like

(4) WAS STEHT HINTER DEM JUNGEN MANN?
What's behind the young man?

in which the system is explicitly requested to describe the objects which stand in a certain relation to a given object. Let's suppose that the NP-resolution component (see 2.8) has determined that MANN4 is the referent of the noun phrase 'the young man' and that its location, retrieved from its property list, is (3 15).

There is a FUZZY procedure called WAS (what) which specialises in generating objects which fit such descriptions. Its arguments are essentially the name of an object and the name of a spatial relation. First, WAS calls the procedure BLICKE (glances), which is passed (3 15) and HINTER (behind) as arguments; BLICKE computes a list of 'glances', i.e. CONTEXT names, which correspond to points 'behind' (3 15) in the coordinate system. The CONTEXT names returned by BLICKE do not correspond to all of the points which satisfy the definition of HINTER, but rather to a subset of them large enough to ensure that all but the least salient objects will be contained in at least one of the CONTEXTs. At present about every fourth CONTEXT is sampled. (It would be possible to implement BLICKE in such a way that it derived its sample of points directly from the definition of the spatial relation in question, but at present the procedure simply uses a stored list of vectors corresponding to each relation.)

The procedure WAS enters these CONTEXTS in the order in which they were returned by BLICKE, namely the ones closest to (3 15) first. Within each CONTEXT it FETCHes successively any entities of the form ((AUFFAELLIG <object>) . z-value) which it may contain, finding them in decreasing order of z-value, which here - as described in section 2.13.3 above - represents relative salience.

All of the objects found in this way will rate fairly high according to the two criteria mentioned in section 2.13.2, but they must still be regarded as mere 'candidates' which must be evaluated and compared according to a more complete set of criteria.

The following criteria, which include the two mentioned in section 2.13.2, are at present incorporated in the definition of WAS:

(5) i: The degree to which the object satisfies the given spatial description. This is computed by calling PRUEFEN (see 2.13.1 above) and taking the z-value of the result.

ii: The intrinsic salience of the object. This is FETCHed from the associative net originally loaded from GEO.NET.

iii: The prominence of the object in the dialogue so far. This is a function of how often and how recently it has been referred to, and is computed as described in section 2.14.1.

The measures obtained by applying these criteria are combined according to the following formula to yield a measure of the mentionability of each object found:

(6) i • (ii + iii)

Note that even an object which fulfills the spatial description with a z-value of 1.0 may receive a low mentionabiliby rating if it has a low intrinsic salience and hasn't played an important role in the conversation so far. On the level of performance, this is reflected in the fact that small objects in the scene are in general only mentioned spontaneously by the system if they have already played a role in the conversation.

A general procedure called FIND controls the search for relevant objects wherever visual search is simulated. FIND keeps track of the mentionability ratings associated with each object, determines when a sufficient number of mentionable candidates have been found, and selects a certain number of them to be finally mentioned. Applied to our present example, FIND directs the search according to the following instructions:

(7) Continue calling WAS with the arguments MANN4 and HINTER until 4 candidates have been generated with a mentionability rating of at least 0.2, or until no more can be found. Then return the 3 most mentionable of these candidates, in the order of their mentionability.

The list of objects returned by FIND is the semantic representation of the answer. It is transformed by the generation routines (see 2.15 and 2.16) into a natural-language description of the objects.

The three numbers 4, 0.2, and 3 in (7) can be viewed as resource-allocation parameters: the higher they are, the more thorough and selective the search will be, the longer the answer will be - and the more processing time will be required. These parameters are at present fixed for each type of question whose processing involves a call to FIND, but it is planned to make them depend on such factors as the interest the partner has expressed in spatial descriptions and the motivational state of the dialogue partner. This will permit a more sophisticated simulation of the dependence of resource allocation on dialogue context than that which is presently implemented (see 2.14.2).

Clearly, neither the set of criteria (5), the formula (6) for combining them, nor the selection strategy (7) can be claimed to be complete or final. Their use in HAM-RPM has, however, shown that some such rules are essential if a system is to generate easily understandable, natural-sounding spatial descriptions, and that the rules described here serve their purpose quite well. The implementation in HAM-RPM is designed so as to facilitate experimentation with different sets of rules.

Other types of requests involving searches for objects are handled with the help of specialized procedures structurally similar to WAS, and the searches are also controlled by FIND. Thus the answering of questions like

(8) WO STEHT DIE ALTE FRAU?
Where's the old woman standing?

differs from the process just described mainly in that

- objects are found which stand in the relation IN/ DER/ NAEHE (near) to the object named
- not only the names of the objects found are kept track of by FIND, but also the names of the more precise relations in which the named object stands to them.

Thus an element of the semantic representation of an answer to such a question would be

(9) ((HINTER 0.9) AMPEL2)

The number 0.9 associated with HINTER (behind) is the degree to which this relation holds between the object originally given and AMPEL2 (traffic-light2). These numbers are translated into hedges such as DIREKT (directly) and IN/ ETWA (roughly) if they lie within certain ranges (cf. 2.15).

All of the major general procedures used in this component have now been described, and examples have been given of the specialized procedures which are used in connection with particular types of requests involving search. It remains to be explained how the system recognizes which type of request is being made of it. This is accomplished straightforwardly by the procedure STEHT (stands), which is passed as arguments a triple of the sort used to represent the meaning of questions (see 2.11.1). In fact, except when STEHT is being called by the components responsible for the resolution and generation of noun phrases (see 2.8.4 and 2.15), its arguments are just the elements of the semantic representation of the question. For the examples (4) and (8) respectively, the arguments to STEHT would be:

(10) NIL (MANN4) (HINTER)

(11) (FRAU2) NIL NIL

The request's type is determined uniquely by which slots of the triple are NIL and which are not. If none of the slots are NIL the triple represents a yes-no question which can be answered straightforwardly with a call to PRUEFEN. All other cases involve search. In these cases, STEHT calls FIND, specifying the name of a particular procedure such as WAS.

A major extension of the simulation of visual search processes is planned: The information presently contained in the referential semantic network (see 2.1.3.8) could be distributed among the many 'glance'-CONTEXTs just as the information on saliences is. This would mean that in all cases where the system has to look for objects with particular properties - for example, in resolving the noun phrase DER OFFENE SCHRANK (the open cupboard) - it would have to enter various CONTEXTs, instead of simply accessing the referential semantic network, as it does at present (see, for example, 2.8.3).

This would provide some interesting, psychologically interpretable effects. For example, the noun phrase 'the truck' would be resolved much faster than 'the poster': since the property of being a truck is visually much more salient than that of being a poster, the corresponding entries about trucks, for example

(12) ((ISA TRUCK1 TRUCK) . 1.0)

would be present in many more CONTEXTs than the corresponding statements about posters. The system would thus have to enter fewer CONTEXTs when looking for entries about trucks than it would for posters.

In an effort to minimize the number of 'glances' it cast when looking for an object, the system would occasionally overlook an object with an unexpectedly low visual salience, thus reproducing some typically human errors.

2.14 CONVERSATIONAL TACTICS

HAM-RPM's behaviour at any given point in a dialogue is determined in many cases to a large degree by the course of the dialogue up to that point. In particular, the system adapts to a certain extent to the interest expressed by the dialogue partner in

- certain parts of the scene being discussed, and
- certain types of behaviour on the part of the system itself.

The precise nature of these adaptations, as well as the way in which they are realized, is described in the two sections to follow.

2.14.1 The record of references to objects

Each time an object is referred to, either by the human dialogue partner or by the system itself, a corresponding entry is ADDed to a special CONTEXT of the assertional data base called VORERWAEHNT (already mentioned). The entries in this CONTEXT have the following form:

(1) ((<token> <gender> <sum-of-references>) . <last-reference>)

for example,

(2) ((MANN2 MAS 22.5) . 17.5)

'last-reference', the z-value, is the sentence-number of the 1 st sentence in which the object was referred to (the system's answers are assigned numbers 0.5 greater than the numbers of the questions which evoked them). 'Gender' is the gender of the noun or pronoun which was used when this latest reference was made.

Both of these pieces of information are used by the pronoun-resolution component, which, when trying to determine the referent of a given pronoun, looks for the most recently mentioned object which was last referred to using a lexical item of a certain gender (see 2.6). The component which resolves noun phrases uses this information in a roughly similar way when trying to resolve ambiguous noun phrases (see 2.8.6).

The number 'sum-of-references' in (1) is the sum of the numbers of all the sentences in which the object has been referred to. As it reflects the number of times the object has been mentioned during the entire conversation, but gives a greater weight to recent references, it can be used to construct a rough measure of the prominence of the object at a given point in the conversation. The system requires such a measure when deciding what refe ference points to mention in an answer to a question.(see 2.13.4). 2.13.4).

If the prominence of an object is to be determined at a time when the sentence number is N, the assertion beginning with the object's name is FETCHed from the CONTEXT VORERWAEHNT. (Actually, as explained in 2.6, two or three such assertions may be present, differing in the slots 'gender' and 'last-reference'; but the value of 'sum-of-references' will be the same for all of them.) The number 'sum-of-references' is normalized by being divided by N, and the quotient is taken to represent the prominence of the object. If no assertion containing the name of the object is found - i.e. if the object has not yet been referred to - its prominence is taken to be 0.

The ellipsis-recognition component (see 2.10) requires semantic and syntactic dialogue 'memories', but the storage of the necessary information is a simple matter, as only the last complete input is taken into account. Before the system prints its response, it checks to see whether the input was flagged as being complete. If so, it records the shallow structure and the semantic representation of the input as the values of two global variables; otherwise, the values of these variables remain unchanged.

2.14.2 Spontaneous justifications and detailed answers

In general, HAM-RPM justifies its answers to questions only when asked to do so in a particular case (see 2.5.1). It does, however, keep track of the number of times the dialogue partner has requested a justification by incrementing the global variable BEGRUENDUNGSFORDERUNG (request for a justification) after each such request. The value of this variable is checked each time an answer is generated: if it has reached the threshold of 3, any justification which the system has noted is appended to the answer, introduced by the word DENN (because):

(3) MAGST DU DIESEN APFELSAFT GERNE?
Do you like this apple juice?

(4) JA, DENN EIN APFELSAFTGETRAENK IST OFT SUESS UND EIN APFELSAFTGETRAENK IST ALKOHOLFREI.
Yes, because apple juice is often sweet and apple juice is non-alcoholic.

(cf. the dialogue sequence reproduced in section 2.5.1.)

The dialogue partner can also influence this aspect of the system's behaviour directly through a specific request. Such requests are at present recognized through pattern matching during the handling of 'idioms' (see examples (6) and (7) in section 2.4.4).

Another type of question for which the appropriate length of the answer is largely determined by the interests of the questioner includes those in which the system is required to describe some part of the scene (see 2.13.4). The number of objects mentioned in the answer varies from one to three (see 2.5.2) and is determined by factors exactly analogous to those described above in connection with justifications.

This is clearly a simple approach to the problem of cooperatively adaptive dialogue behaviour. A more adequate treatment would require, among other things, the ability to represent explicitly the human dialogue partner's presumed intentions and the system's strategies for recognizing and adapting to them.

2.15 NP-GENERATION

The task of the NP-generation component in HAM-RPM is inverse to that of NP-resolution described in section 2.8. That means that internal object names contained in the semantic representation of the system's answer are to be transformed into definite descriptions. In HAM-RPM we view NP-generation as a cognitive decision process whose result - a definite description - should enable the human dialogue partner to uniquely identify an object intended by the system. HAM-RPM encodes one and the same object in different ways depending on the context of objects in the domain which may be confused with it.

NP-generation is a central problem in natural-language generation since definite NPs are not only contained in complete sentences but very often are the only element of an elliptical answer. In HAM-RPM the NP-generation component is also invoked in early processing phases, e.g. by the routines which answer follow-up questions (see 2.5) and by the NP-resolution component in case of clarification dialogues, in which the system proposes a possible referent to the human dialogue partner (see 2.8.7).

In the current version of HAM-RPM the output of the NP-generation component in general has the following syntactic structure:

$$\text{NP} ::= \underset{\text{(the)}}{\text{(D-)}} + \begin{pmatrix} \text{ADJ} \\ \{\text{ADJ}\}^{1-n} + \underset{\text{(and)}}{\text{UND}} + \text{ADJ} \\ \{\text{ADJ}\}^{1-n} + \underset{\text{(but not)}}{\text{ABER NICHT}} + \text{ADJ} \end{pmatrix} + \text{NOM} + \text{(RELCL)}$$

$$\text{RELCL} ::= \underset{\text{(which is)}}{\text{WELCH SICH}} + \text{PRP} + \text{NP} + \underset{\text{(located)}}{\text{BEFINDET}}$$

Let us illustrate this general structure by some examples:

(1)	TISCH1 table1	D- TISCH the table
(2)	STUHL1 chair1	D- ROT STUHL the red chair
(3)	SCHRANK4 cupboard4	D- ROT KAPUTT UND OFFEN SCHRANK the red damaged and open cupboard
(4)	SCHRANK6 cupboard6	D- WEISS KAPUTT ABER NICHT OFFEN SCHRANK the white damaged but not open cupboard
(5)	SESSEL4 armchair4	D- HINTER- BRAUN SESSEL WELCH SICH RECHTS/ NEBEN D- MITTLER ROT BILD BEFINDET the rear brown armchair which is located to the right of the red picture in the middle

The reader may have noticed that the expressions constructed by the NP-generator contain only stems of words. The output of the NP-generator undergoes several surface transformations, described in the next section (2.16), until it becomes morphologically and syntactically well formed.

The NP-generation process is governed by the principle of confusion-avoidance. In (1) the table is supposed to be the only one in this discourse world and hence is identified as 'the table'. When the object to be described is one of several belonging to the same conceptual class, the system looks among the properties of the object stored in the referential semantic net for one which distinguishes it from its cohyponyms as in example (2).

If there are several properties which refer only to the intended object and not to any of its cohyponyms, we have the case of multiple codability investigated by HERRMANN/LAUCHT 1976. In this situation the system applies the following algorithm to select one of these distinguishing properties. First it looks among the distinguishing properties for one whose z-value exceeds the z-values of the others markedly. When it finds one it encodes this property in the definite description. For example, suppose RED and OLD are the distinguishing properties of CHAIR1 and the referential net contains the assertions ((REF CHAIR1 RED) . 0.8) and ((REF CHAIR1 OLD) . 0.4). In that case the system selects the property RED and generates the NP 'the red chair'.

Second, when the first step does not succeed, i.e. the z-values of the distinguishing properties are approximately equal, the system encodes that property which it prefers according to a preference order of dimensions stored in the knowledge base. This preference order is interindividually relatively constant and in the present system it is represented simply as a list of dimensions, e.g. (colour, contrast, size, age ...).

For example, suppose that BROWN and BIG are the distinguishing properties of CHAIR2 and the assertions ((REF CHAIR2 BROWN) . 0.75) and ((REF CHAIR2 BIG) . 0.8) are contained in the referential semantic network. Then the system selects BROWN and generates the NP 'the brown chair' because it prefers colour to size. If the system does not find even one distinguishing property, it uses - in the current implementation - all of the properties of the intended object in the referential net, with no further attempt to find a minimal characterizing set. This means that the system uses redundant labels, which saves time both in generation and in the hearer's interpretation of definite descriptions. In that case the ordering of the adjectives in the generated NP reflects the preference order defined by the selection algorithm discussed above. Example (3) arose in this way.

If the characterizing properties of the intended object are a subset of those of a cohyponym, HAM-RPM uses negative characterizations, as illustrated in example (4) above.

The presence of several objects which are indistinguishable on the basis of their attributes alone is the worst case which can occur. The only way to distinguish such objects is by reference to spatial relations. Since objects chosen as spatial reference points in such a description must in turn be identified, the generation algorithm is applied recursively, as illustrated in example (5) above.

Perhaps the most difficult problem in NP-generation is the unique identification of an object when there are objects with exactly the same properties in its immediate neighbourhood. In the present version, the system then first describes the position of the intended object relative to the other objects in its group using the spatial attributes RECHT (right-hand), LINK (left-hand), VORDER (front), HINTER (rear) and MITTLER (middle). These complex relations are constructed from the elementary relations 'in front of', 'behind', 'to the left of' and 'to the right of', which are generated by the spatial-relations component (see 2.13).

Then the system identifies the group of which the intended object is a member within the scene as a whole by spatial relations which are always coded into a relative clause as illustrated in example (5).

Concluding this discussion of HAM-RPM's NP-generator, we would like to stress that our generator in contrast to those described in WOODS et al. 1976 and WALKER 1976 takes into consideration the communicative context of reference. A more complete discussion of this algorithm, which is distinguished from the related ones of WINOGRAD 1972 and WONG 1975 by its adaptation to results of psychological research on reference generation (HERRMANN/DEUTSCH 1976), is contained in Reports Nos. 5 and 7.

2.16 SURFACE TRANSFORMATIONS

The system's final task in answering a question posed by the natural partner is to generate a morphologically and syntactically well-formed output.

Regarding yes/no-questions, in most cases only punctuation marks have to be added to the deep structure of the answer (e.g. JA, NEIN or DOCH). If, however, an extensive clarification dialogue (see 2.8.7) has interrupted a single question-answer sequence, affirmation or negation explicitly refer to the initial question of the natural partner. This is achieved by filling out the one-word answer with a paraphrase of the initial question. The shallow structure as transformed by word-order rules (see 2.9.1) forms the basis of a paraphrase, which has to be retransformed into a natural utterance, as several processing steps had modified the shallow structure, including lexical analysis, modality and NP-resolution.

In the following example the natural language output (4) is obtained by transforming the deep structure of the answer (3) and the shallow structure of the question (2) by means of NP-generation (see 2.15) and surface transformations.

(1) STEHT DER STUHL NEBEN DEM TISCH?
Is the chair standing next to the table?

⋮

WELCHEN STUHL MEINST DU? WIESO FRAGST DU MICH DAS?
Which chair do you mean? Why do you ask me so?

WEIL ES FUENF DAVON GIBT!
Because there are five of them!

WELCHEN STUHL MEINTEST DU? DEN SCHWARZEN.
Which chair did you mean? The black one.

⋮

(2) ((NOM (STUHL5)) (VRB (STEH)) (PRP (NEBEN)) (NOM (TISCH1)))

⋮

(3) (NEIN)
(No)

(4) NEIN, DER SCHWARZE STUHL STEHT NICHT NEBEN DEM BRAUNEN TISCH.
No, the black chair is not standing next to the brown table.

The same difficulty arises with answers to wh-questions. The deep structure of the answer does not resemble natural language output. Conversational tactics have already determined some aspects of the answer (see 2.14.2) and internal names of objects have been replaced by noun phrases (see 2.15). But the answer still consists solely of canonical forms, i.e. only stems of words are used and punctuation marks are in general not present.

A different source of utterances of the system (see 3.2) are rejections, clarification dialogues and 'thinking aloud' (see 2.7, 2.8). These utterances, generated by different components of HAM-RPM, are composed of canonical forms with no explicit syntactic coherence whatsoever.

In the following the approach taken in HAM-RPM to transform these internal representations will be described. Any input to the surface transformations will be called the 'underlying utterance'. Their structure was introduced in the sections describing the components which generate them.

In a first step, each occurrence of 'D- MM' (the MM) is replaced by 'ICH' (I) as referential identity of this personal pronoun is unique for the system (see 2.6). The proper surface case for this pronoun is determined when inflectional suffixes are attached to nouns according to surface case. Numbers from 1 to 20 are replaced by the corresponding words at the same time.

The three basic grammatical categories for establishing the correct morphological forms of adjectives and nouns in sentences are gender, case, and number. For verbs the categories person and time replace case and gender. Having ascertained these three features any regularly inflected word can be generated correctly.

A prerequisite for detecting the relevant categories therefore is the construction of the preterminal string of the underlying utterance. The parts of speech of the known words are attached using procedures of the lexical-analysis component (see 2.4.3). The part of speech of an unknown word - which, of course represents an inconsistency in the knowledge base, since the system should have at least grammatical knowledge about any words it uses - is represented by a filler category called FUELLW (filler word) (cf. the class 'bogus' used by GERSHMAN 1977) in the preterminal string of the underlying utterance.

Together with parts of speech the gender of nouns is supplied by lexical analysis. Punctuation marks - if there are any, such as dots and blanks in the 'thinking aloud' utterances - are assigned to the category SATZZ (punctuation marks). An example of the lexical analysis employed in surface transformations (6) of an underlying utterance (5) is shown below.

(5) (. . . VOR D- TISCH . . . E- BRAUN STUHL . . .)

(6) ((SATZZ (.)) (SATZZ (.)) (SATZZ (.)) (PRP (VOR)) (DET (D-)) (NOM (TISCH)) (SATZZ (.)) (SATZZ (.)) (SATZZ (.)) (SATZZ ( )) (SATZZ ( )) (DET (E-)) (ADJ (BRAUN)) (NOM (STUHL)) (SATZZ ( )) (SATZZ ( )) (SATZZ ( )) (SATZZ (.)) (SATZZ (.)) (SATZZ (.)))

The category 'number' is at present restricted to singular in the generation component of HAM-RPM. The preterminal string of an underlying utterance having thus been generated, the only category still to be determined for nouns and adjectives is surface case.

In German there are two sources yielding information about surface case. Prepositions determine the case of the following noun phrase, although frequently not uniquely; syntactic dominance relations and/or specified verb frames such as those employed by GOLDMAN 1975 supply clues to the case of noun phrases. Syntactic information might be obtained by parsing the underlying utterance. This would, however, run into difficulties, as most of the system's utterances are not complete sentences, nor are they always grammatically well formed. A parser would, for example, have great trouble analysing 'thinking aloud' utterances.

In HAM-RPM a different method has therefore been developed which employs parts of speech in the delimitation of parts of sentences. Methodologically this heuristic approach resembles the rules introduced by GERSHMAN 1977 for identifying noun groups, especially in the respect that syntactically incorrect sentences should not necessarily be rejected.

The table below shows some rules based on parts of speech which introduce boundaries into underlying utterances. Square brackets in the examples indicate the boundaries between parts of sentences.

(7) The current word is a noun. A boundary is established behind it, if the word which follows is neither a verb, an interjection (ITJ) nor a filler word (FUELLW).

Examples:

```
( [ (DET (D-)) (ADJ (ROT)) (NOM (STUHL))] [(DET (D-))
    (ADJ (BRAUN)) (NOM (TISCH))] . . . )
      the red chair  the brown table . . .
( [ (DET (D-)) (ADJ (KLEIN)) (NOM (TISCH)) (ITJ (ALSO))] )
      the small table then
( [ (DET (E-)) (NOM (PARKZONE)) (VRB (SEIN))] [(DET (E-))
    (NOM (TEIL)) . . .] )
      a parking zone is a part . . .
```

(8) The current word is a verb. A boundary is set up if the word which follows is neither an adverb nor an adjective. If it is a pronoun the boundary is set up after this pronoun.

Examples:

```
( [. . . (PRP (AUF)) (DET (D-)) (NOM (TISCH)) (VRB (STEH))]
  [(DET (D-))  . . .] )
    . . . on the table is . . .
( [ (NOM (WASSER)) (VRB (SEIN)) (ADV (GRUNDSAETZLICH)) ...])
    water is by definition ...
( [ (PRP (VOR)) (DET (D-)) (NOM (HAUS)) (VRB (SEH))
    (PRN (ICH))][(NEG (KEIN)) (NOM (FRAU))] )
    in front of the house I do not see a woman
```

(9) Successive punctuation marks, such as the dots and blanks in (6), are grouped between boundaries.

As a result of the application of these rules to the underlying utterance from left to right, it is partitioned into smaller sections. Each of these sections is now subject to morphological transformation processes.

Depending on the parts of speech inflectional suffixes are added to the canonical forms. For nouns, adjectives and articles case information is supplied by examining the surroundings of the word, looking especially for prepositions, and the partitioning of the underlying utterance.

Rather simple rules describe the inflectional suffixes added to noun stems according to case and gender as shown in Fig. 13. The terminal symbol 'Ø' represents a zero morpheme. The 'E' of the genitive suffix is elided if the last letter of the stem is a vowel.

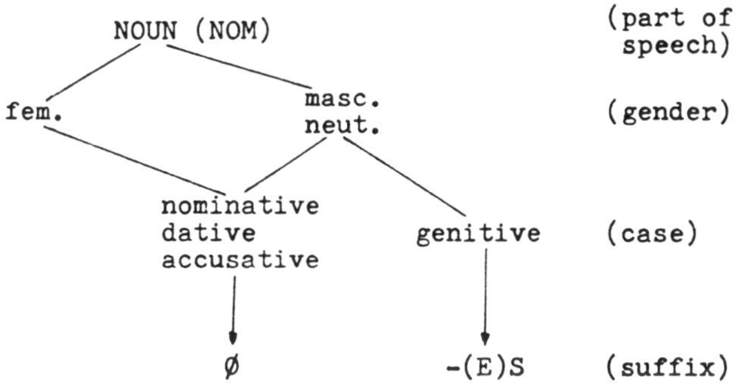

Fig. 13

In German the inflectional suffixes of adjectives also depend on the type of the article, i.e. definite or indefinite article. Fig. 14 represents the rules for generating inflected adjectives in HAM-RPM.

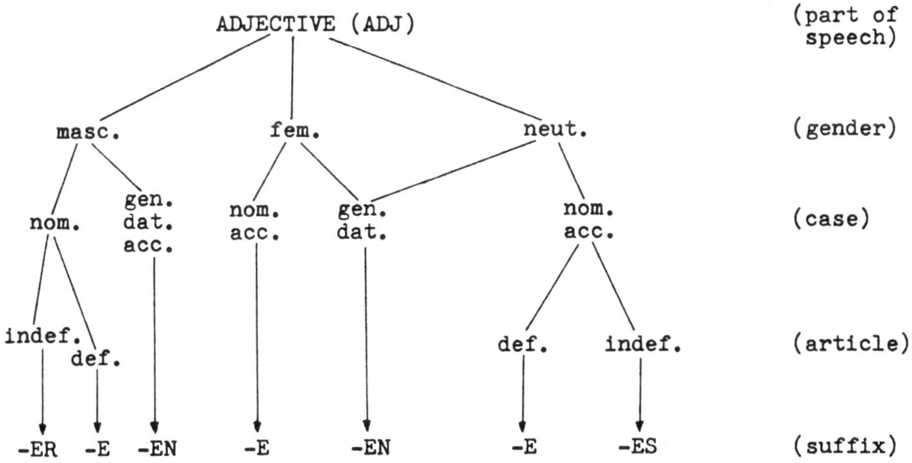

Fig. 14

Articles in German also vary according to gender and case. For the purpose of generating inflected words the canonical form of the definite article is 'D', for the indefinite article 'EIN' which are the maximal common letters of all article forms.

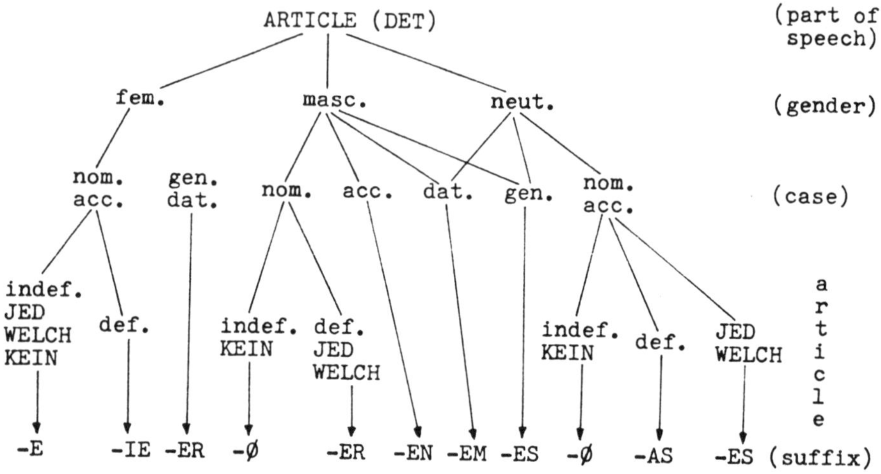

Fig. 15

As seen from Fig. 15 by the same rules suffixes are added to the canonical forms of the quantifiers KEIN (no) and JED (each) and to the relative or interrogative pronoun WELCH (which). In the case of relative pronouns the gender and the case of the preceding noun determines the choice of the inflectional suffix.

Preliminary rules supply verb forms with inflectional suffixes. Tense and number are at present restricted to present tense and singular. The category as far as surface transformations are concerned is therefore restricted to the three possibilities in the singular.

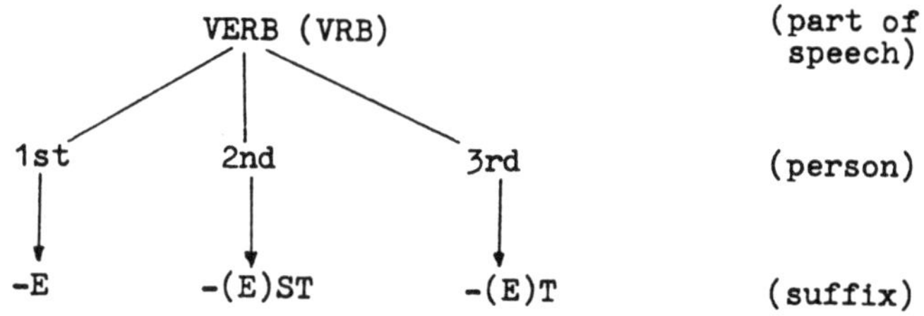

Fig. 16

The person is determined by looking for either ICH (I), DU (you) or something else in the part of the underlying utterance being investigated.

Generally speaking the rules described above only apply to regularly inflected words. Irregularities such as vowel mutation will not be treated correctly until lexical structures are developed to represent them.

Having transformed word stems into inflected words in all parts of the underlying utterance the last task of surface transformations is to introduce punctuation marks joining the parts together. This is achieved by classifying the single parts and establishing connection rules over these classes. Four classes of parts are defined:

- VST - The part is complete (VST: vollständig) if it consists of at least a verb and a noun group.
- UNV - The part is incomplete (UNV: unvollständig) if there is no verb.
- REL - The part is a relative clause (generated by NP-generation, see 2.15). Note that subclauses in German are normally delimited by commas.
- ZCH - The part consists solely of punctuation marks.

For combinations of these classes a decision is made as to whether a comma or an UND (and) is to be inserted between them. The following combinations are examined:

combination	comma ?	and ?
VST / UNV > VST	yes	yes
VST / UNV > REL	yes	no
REL < VST / UNV	yes	only if there are no further parts.
UNV — UNV — UNV	yes	no
UNV — UNV — VST	no	yes
UNV — UNV < REL / ZCH	yes	no
UNV — UNV	no	yes

After inserting commas and UND according to the rules above the complete underlying utterance has been transformed into a natural language utterance. The final punctuation mark is a full stop if no other mark, such as question mark or an exclamation mark, had terminated the underlying utterance.

Starting from the rather heuristic approach which is implemented at present to transform canonical utterances into surface structures a major task is to elaborate a complementary component of the lexical-analysis component (see 2.4). Note that the problems for surface transformations originate not only from the rich morphological structure of German but also from the limited capabilities of the current version of HAM-RPM in semantic and pragmatic processing.

Our system finally has to be able to analyse each of its own utterances by the same process as is already done for utterances of the natural partner. This postulate resembles the previously stated analogy between NP-resolution and NP-generation. In addition to eliminating restrictions already mentioned in this section important topics to be worked on are the use of idiomatic expressions and pronominalization in surface transformations and stylistic variation guided by conversational dynamics.

3 TRANSCRIPTS OF ACTUAL DIALOGUE SESSIONS

This section contains transcripts of actual dialogue sessions with HAM-RPM. The domain of discourse underlying the first session (see fig. 17) is WORLD2, the traffic scene (see 2.1.1). The last sentence in this session is traced, since the user has changed the output type via (IO-OPTIONS) (see 2.2.1).

In the second dialogue session (fig. 18) the domain of discourse is WORLD3 (see 2.1.1).

All system messages and the interaction with the user which follow the command DO WELT N until HAM-RPM signals that it is ready to begin the conversation by greeting the user have been removed from the actual protocol. Further annotated transcripts of actual dialogue sessions in which WORLD1 and WORLD2 are used as underlying discourse worlds are contained in Memo No. 4.

Fig. 19 summarizes all possible speech-act sequences which in the present version of HAM-RPM may occur in the communication with the system.

```
       .DO WELT 2
           :
       GUTEN MORGEN!
       Good morning!

(1)    ? WAS BEFINDET SICH IM MOMENT NEBEN DEM FACHBEREICH FUER
                                                     INFORMATIK?
         What's next to the Department of Computer Science at
                                                     the moment?
       DER KLEINE BAUM.
       The small tree.

(2)    ? SIEHST DU AUCH SIE?
         Do you see her too?
       AUF WAS BEZIEHT SICH 'SIE'?   AUF DIE FRAU.
       What does 'her' refer to?     To the woman.
       JA.
       Yes.

(3)    ? STEHT NEBEN DEM BAUM EIN ROTER WAGEN?
         Is there a red car standing next to the tree?
       NEIN.
       No.
```

Fig. 17a

(4) ? IST DENN EIN ROTER WAGEN VOR DER AMPEL RECHTS VORNE IM AUGENBLICK?
Is there a red car in front of the traffic light in front and to the left at the moment?

JA.
Yes.

(5) ? IST DER BAUM, WELCHER RECHTS NEBEN DER AMPEL STEHT,GROSS?
Is the tree which is next to the traffic light big?

. . . ES SOLL HIER RECHTS NEBEN EINER AMPEL EINEN BAUM GEBEN . . . DA MUSS ICH MAL GENAUER HINSEHN . . .
. . . behind a traffic light there's supposed to be a tree . . . I've got to take a closer look . . .

JA.
Yes.

(6) ? WELCHE FARBE HAT SIE MOMENTAN?
What colour is it (gender: feminine) at the moment?

GRUEN
Green.

(7) ? IST EINE PARKZONE GETEERT?
Is a parking zone tarred?

JA.
Yes.

!!! DIE AMPELN WURDEN UMGESCHALTET !!!
!!! The traffic lights have changed !!!

(8) ? WIE KOMMST DU DARAUF?
What makes you think so?

EINE PARKZONE IST MEIST EIN TEIL VON EINER STRASSE, UND EINE STRASSE IST OFT GETEERT.
A parking zone is usually a part of a street, and a street is often tarred.

(9) ? BEFINDET SICH IN DER NAEHE VOM HAUS HINTEN LINKS EIGENTLICH EINE PARKZONE?
Is there in fact a parking zone near the house in back and to the left?

JA.
Yes.

(10) ? WAS FUER EINE FARBE HAT DIE AMPEL VORNE RECHTS DENN JETZT?
What colour is the traffic light in front and to the right now?

ROT.
Red.

Fig. 17b

(11) ? DAS BLAUE AUTO, WELCHES IN DER NAEHE VOM HAUS HINTEN RECHTS PARKT, IST ALT?
The blue car that's parked near the house in back and to the right is old?

. . . EIN BLAUES AUTO . . . UND ZWAR IN DER NAEHE VOM HAUS HINTEN RECHTS . . .
. . . a blue car . . . next to the house in back and to the left . . .

IN DER NAEHE VON DEM HAUS RECHTS HINTEN SEHE ICH KEIN BLAUES AUTO.
I don't see any blue car near the house to the right and in back.

(12) ? WELCHE FAHRZEUGE SIND DENN UEBERHAUPT ALT?
Which vehicles are old then?

DER BLAUE PERSONENWAGEN, DER PARKENDE UND DUNKELE PERSONENWAGEN LINKS VORNE, DER PARKENDE UND WEISSE PERSONENWAGEN LINKS VORNE, DER PARKENDE UND GELBE PERSONENWAGEN RECHTS VORNE UND DER ROTE PERSONENWAGEN.
The blue car, the dark parked car in front and to the left, the white parked car in front and to the left, the yellow car in front and to the right and the red car.

? (IO-OPTIONS)

UEBLICHE IO-OPTIONS? NEIN
Standard IO-options? No

AUSGABE ALLER TEILERGEBNISSE? JA
Trace mode? Yes

STRUKTURBAUM AUCH? NEIN
Parse tree too? No

LINELENGTH ('J' = 72) : J

ZEITANGABE? NEIN
Time measurement? No

TTY-I-O? JA

(continued on next page)

Fig. 17c

```
(13)  ? WAS STEHT HINT%ER DER DAHME, WELCHE SICH NEBEN DEM
        GELBEN UND ALTEN AUTO BEFINDET?
        What's behi%nd the lahdy which is next to the yellow
        and old car?

      (IDIOMENBEHANDLUNG:)
      (WAS STEH HINTER D- DAHME WELCH NEBEN D- GELB UND ALT
       AUTO STEHT)

      WAS HEISST 'DAHME'?   ICH MEINTE DAME

      (L VERBESSERUNG DAHME (DAME))

      WAS HEISST 'DAME'?   DASSELBE WIE FRAU

      (L SYNONYM DAME (FRAU))

      (WAS STEH HINTER D- FRAU WELCH NEBEN D- GELB UND ALT
       PERSONENWAGEN STEH)

      (W-FRAGE)

      . . . NEBEN DEM GELBEN UND ALTEN PERSONENWAGEN . . .
      EINE FRAU . . .
      . . . next to the yellow and old car . . .   a woman . . .

      ((IPRN (WAS)) (VRB (STEH)) (PRP (HINTER)) (NOM (FRAU1)))

      (KEINE PRAETRANSFORMATION MOEGLICH)

      (SATZ AKZEPTIERT :)

      (S (NP (IPRN (WAS))) (VP (VRB (STEH)) (PP (PRP (HINTER))
       (NOM (FRAU1)))))

      (NIL (FRAU1) (HINTER))
                 (PERSONENWAGEN6)   0.875

                 (AMPEL1)   0.35

      DER BRAUNE PERSONENWAGEN.
      The brown car.

(14)  ? TSCHUESS.
        Good bye.

      DIE NEU GELERNTEN WOERTER:
      New words:

      (DAME (SYNONYM (FRAU) ))    NEIN

      DAS WAREN ALLE.

      KEINE NEUEN WOERTER.

      TSCHUESS BIS ZUM NAECHSTEN MAL!
      See you later!

      *
```

Fig. 17d

.DO WELT 3

⋮

GUTEN ABEND!
Good evening!

(1) ? KANNST DU MIR BITTE MAL SAGEN, WO SICH HIER EIN GETRAENK BEFINDET?
Could you please tell me where there's a drink?

AUF DEM COUCHTISCH.
On the couch table.
(8.9 SEC)

(2) ? KANNST DU DEN WHISKY TRINKEN?
Can you drink the whisky?

ES GIBT HIER KEINEN WHISKY.
There's no whisky here.
(2.7 SEC)

(3) ? WAS IST DENN IM GLAS?
What's in the glass then?

DAS APFELSAFTGETRAENK.
The apple juice.
(6.1 SEC)

(4) ? MAGST DU DEN APFELSAFT GERNE?
Do you like the apple juice?

ICH GLAUBE JA.
I think so.
(7.6 SEC)

(5) ? WIESO DENN?
Why?

EIN APFELSAFTGETRAENK IST OFT SUESS UND EIN APFELSAFTGE-TRAENK IST ALKOHOLFREI.
Apple juice is often sweet and apple juice is non-alcoholic.
(0.9 SEC)

(6) ? WAS IST AUF DEM ROTEN BILD?
What's in the red picture?

DIE MARILYIN MONROE.
Marilyn Monroe.
(10.2 SEC)

(7) ? FINDEST DU SIE SCHOEN?
Do you find her pretty?

JA.
Yes.
(3.8 SEC)

Fig. 18a

(8) ? WARUM DENN EIGENTLICH?
Really, why?

IST DOCH KLAR!
It's obvious!

(0.9 SEC)

(9) ? WELCHE HAARFARBE HAT SIE DENN?
What colour hair has she got?

BLOND.

(1.5 SEC)

(10) ? WELCHE FARBE HAT EIN KLAVIER?
What colour is a piano?

MEISTENS SCHWARZ.
Usually black.

(2.3 SEC)

(11) ? SIEHST DU EIGENTLICH EIN PIANO HIER?
Do you actually see a pianoforte here?

WAS HEISST 'PIANO'? DAS IST DASSELBE WIE KLAVIER.
What's the meaning of 'pianoforte'? The same as piano.

JA.
Yes.

(6.9 SEC)

(12) ? WELCHE FARBE HAT DIESES KLAVIER?
What colour is this piano?

WEISS.
White.

(2.9 SEC)

(13) ? IST DER TISCH GROSS?
Is the table big?

MEINST DU DEN COUCHTISCH? WIESO WILLST DU DAS WISSEN?
Do you mean the couch table? Why do you want to know?

WEIL ES ZWEI GIBT!
Because there are two!

MEINTEST DU DEN COUCHTISCH? NEE.
Did you mean the couch table? Nope.

DEN ESSTISCH ALSO.
The dining table then.

JA, DER ESSTISCH IST GROSS.
Yes, the dining table is big.

(6.3 SEC)

(14) ? TSCHUESS.
Good bye.

⋮

*

Fig. 18b

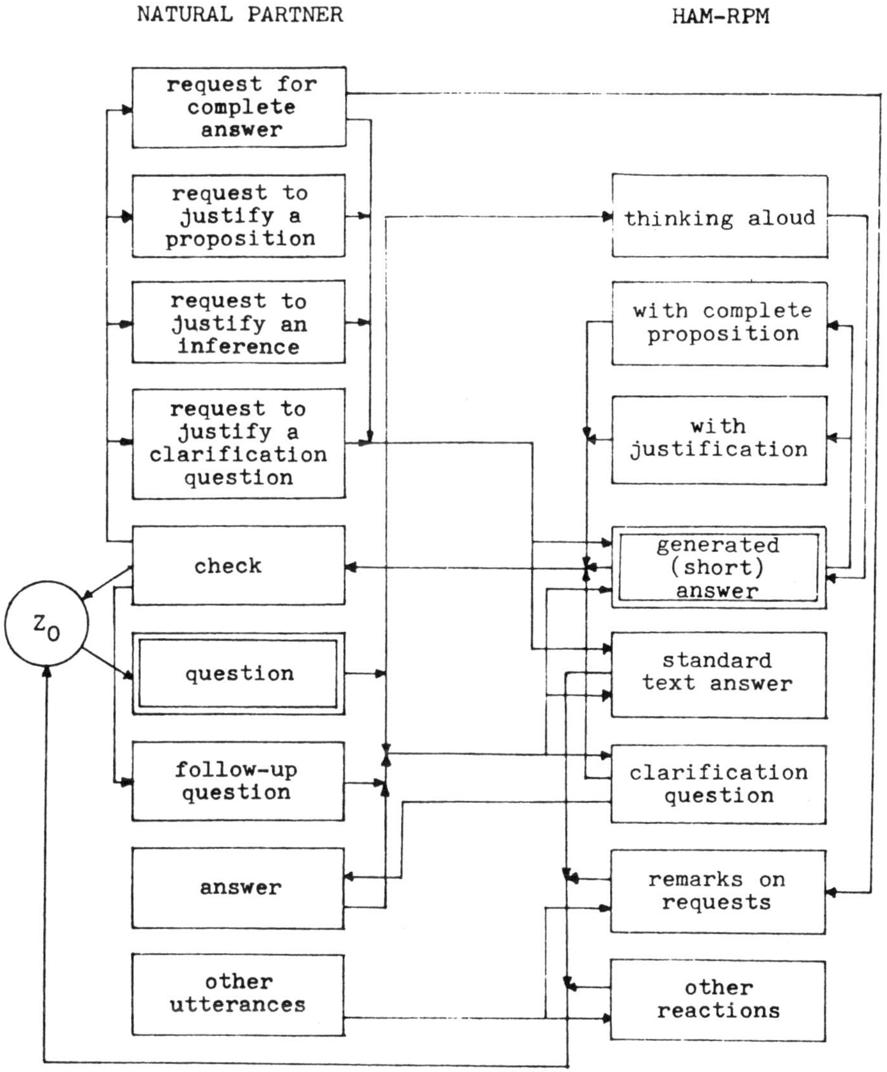
NATURAL PARTNER
HAM-RPM
request for complete answer
request to justify a proposition
request to justify an inference
request to justify a clarification question
check
Z_0
question
follow-up question
answer
other utterances
thinking aloud
with complete proposition
with justification
generated (short) answer
standard text answer
clarification question
remarks on requests
other reactions

Fig. 19

4 HAM-RPM'S PROGRAMMING ENVIRONMENT

4.1 Technical data

A non-compiled version of HAM-RPM is running on the DECsystem 1070 (PDP-10) of the Fachbereich für Informatik of the University of Hamburg under the TOPS10 Operating System. Comprising approximately 400 LISP/FUZZY procedures, the current version occupies 150K of 36-bit words and requires from one to fifteen seconds for a response.

4.2 Auxiliary software

Although Rutgers-UCI-LISP represents one of the most advanced interactive programming systems available, we have found it worthwhile to develop additional auxiliary software to help to overcome the problems which arise when several designers work together on a large system like HAM-RPM. In such a situation the designers, as well as the users, must constantly deal with procedures and data whose design they have not directly participated in.

Complete documentation and manuals could, in principle, provide the necessary information, and in fact reference material does exist for most parts of the system. But on the one hand, the experimental nature of HAM-RPM limits the value of such documents, as it means that any particular version of the system is likely to be used for only a relatively short time. On the other hand, the fact that HAM-RPM is implemented in an interactive programming language makes available other means of making the system understandable and manageable. These fall mainly into two categories:

- techniques which make parts of the system largely self-explanatory, so that the use of reference material is in general unnecessary.
- software which makes possible efficient, semi-automatic communication among the designers of the system, so as to help them to keep abreast of new developments both on a large and on a small scale.

A technique which falls into the first category is a simple but effective abbreviation system for LISP. This has increased greatly the readibility of the code of HAM-RPM. It is always useful to be able to assign long, self-explanatory names to procedures and variables, such as INFERENZ-REGELN-NACH-PRAEFERENZEN-ORDNEN (order inference rules according to preferences). The use of such names often makes it possible, for example, to understand a call to a procedure within another procedure without looking at either the definition of the called procedure or its documentation. Self-explanatory names are in this respect even better than comments within a procedure's definition which explain its function. The use of such names on a large scale is only practical, however, if the designer can, while the procedure is being modified and tested, type in an abbreviation which is immediately expanded by the system into the full form.

At a number of points the system must request some sort of input from the user, e.g. when the system is being started (see 2.2.1). The user must know what inputs are admissible and what consequences they will have. Such sets of possible inputs and their respective consequences are represented within HAM-RPM's programming environment as production systems which are handled by an interpreter with the following special properties, among others:

- It doesn't accept any input which doesn't match any of the patterns provided.
- If the user types HELP, the production system is printed in an easily readable form which in most cases permits it to be understood adequately even by a naive user.

The second category of techniques mentioned above comprises several packages of LISP procedures which allow the user to write messages of various sorts onto files directly from the LISP system. These packages make it possible for him to transmit useful information quickly without interrupting his work with the system. The efficiency of this type of communication is largely due to the fact that all of the facilities of the LISP system are available to facilitate the preparation of the message. Such things as formatting and the printing of the date and the user's name are done automatically. More important, data structures of interest can be printed and examples of interactions with the simulated dialogue partner can form part of the message.

One of these packages is used for writing short notes to a text file which is consulted regularly by all of the system's designers. This package is also used to generate semi-automatic protocols of faulty system performance during dialogues.

Another package in this category is a documentation system which elicits a standardized description of a procedure from its designer in prompting mode.

The very number of auxiliary procedures used in HAM-RPM's programming environment at first created a problem: on the one hand such procedures should be readily available when needed, but on the other hand it would be impractical to load them all every time the system was used. This problem was solved through the creation of a library system for LISP: Most of the auxiliary procedures are not loaded when the LISP system is initialized; instead, a catalogue is loaded which contains the names of the files on which they can be found. A special definition is assigned to all of the library procedures when the system is initialized. When a library procedure is called, this definition in effect tells the interpreter to load the true definition of the procedure from the file listed in the catalogue before evaluating the call.

The usefulness of these techniques so far in keeping HAM-RPM manageable and modifiable suggests that they will be adequate to support the extensive development which is planned for the system in the future.

ACKNOWLEDGEMENT

This research is currently being supported by the Deutsche Forschungsgemeinschaft.

HAM-RPM PUBLICATIONS

Reports

1 v. Hahn, Walther, Henskes, Dieter, Hoeppner, Wolfgang, Wahlster, Wolfgang: HAM-RPM: Ein Redepartnermodell als Simulationsprogramm. In: Braunmüller, K., Kürschner, W. (eds.): Grammatik. Akten des 10. Linguistischen Kolloquiums Tübingen 1975. Band II. Tübingen: Niemeyer 1976. 337-357

2 Wahlster, Wolfgang, v. Hahn, Walther: Einige Erweiterungen des natürlichsprachlichen AI-Systems HAM-RPM. In: Laubsch, J., Schneider, H.-J. (eds.): Dialoge in natürlicher Sprache und Darstellung von Wissen. Arbeitstagung der Fachgruppe 'Künstliche Intelligenz' der Gesellschaft für Informatik. Freudenstadt 1976. 204-225

3 v. Hahn, Walther, Hoeppner, Wolfgang, Jameson, Anthony, Wahlster, Wolfgang: HAM-RPM: Natural Dialogues with an Artficial Partner. In: Proceedings of the AISB/GI Conference on Artificial Intelligence. Hamburg 1978. 122-131

4 v. Hahn, Walther: Überlegungen zum kommunikativen Status und der Testbarkeit von natürlichsprachlichen Artificial-Intelligence-Systemen. In: Sprache und Datenverarbeitung 1, 1978, 145-169

5 Wahlster, Wolfgang: Die Simulation vager Inferenzen auf unscharfem Wissen: Eine Anwendung der mehrwertigen Programmiersprache FUZZY. In: Ueckert, H., Rhenius, D. (eds.): Komplexe menschliche Informationsverarbeitung. Bern: Huber 1979. 249-259

6 v. Hahn, Walther: Probleme der Simulationstheorie und Fragepragmatik bei der Simulation natürlichsprachlicher Dialoge. In: Ueckert, H., Rhenius, D. (eds.): Komplexe menschliche Informationsverarbeitung. Bern: Huber 1979. 260-269

7 Wahlster, Wolfgang, Jameson, Anthony, Hoeppner, Wolfgang: Glancing, Referring and Explaining in the Dialogue System HAM-RPM. In: American Journal of Computational Linguistics, 1979

8 v. Hahn, Walther: Dialogkohärenz in natürlichsprachlichen AI-Systemen. Dezember 1978

9 Wahlster, Wolfgang: Algorithmen zur Beantwortung von 'Warum'-Fragen in Dialogsystemen. Januar 1979

10 v. Hahn, Walther: Überlegungen zum Handlungsrahmen von Fragen in Artificial-Intelligence-Systemen. Januar 1979

11 Wahlster, Wolfgang: ATNs und die semantisch-pragmatische Steuerung der Analyse und Generierung natürlicher Sprache. März 1979

Memos

0 Jameson, Anthony: Eine Einführung in die interaktive Arbeit und die Programmierung mit FUZZY. 1978

1 Wahlster, Wolfgang: Eine kurze Einführung in die Organisation der assoziativen Netze in der Programmiersprache FUZZY. Februar 1978

2 Hoeppner, Wolfgang: Nominalgruppen mit unbestimmtem Artikel. Februar 1978

3 Wahlster, Wolfgang: Zur Überführung eines Konstituentenstrukturbaums in eine semantische Repräsentationskonstruktion mit Hilfe von Pattern-Matching-Operationen. Mai 1978

4 Hoeppner, Wolfgang, Wahlster, Wolfgang: Die Performanz von HAM-RPM: Zwei kommentierte Beispieldialoge und ein Interaktionsbeispiel. Juni 1978

5 Hoeppner, Wolfgang: NP-Referenzanalyse in HAM-RPM: Kommentierte Performanzbeispiele. Juli 1978

6 Demnick, Gudrun, Marburger, Heinz: Benutzeranleitung für das System HAM-RPM. Februar 1979

REFERENCES

Bates, M. (1978): The theory and practice of augmented transition network grammars. In: Bolc, L. (ed.): Natural language communication with computers. Berlin: Springer, 191-259

Bobrow, D.G., Kaplan, R.M., Kay, M., Norman, D.A., Thompson, H., Winograd, T. (1977): GUS - A frame-driven dialog system. In: Artificial Intelligence, 8, 1, 155-173

Bobrow, D.G., Winograd, T. (1977): An overview of KRL - a knowledge representation language. In: Cognitive Science, 1, 1, 3-46

Borgida, A.T. (1975): Topics in the understanding of English sentences by computer. Univ. of Toronto, Dept. of Computer Science, Technical Report No. 78

Charniak, E. (1973): Context and the reference problem. In: Rustin, R. (ed.) Natural language processing. Englewood Cliffs: Prentice-Hall, 311-329

Charniak, E. (1976): Inference and knowledge I, II. In: Charniak, E., Wilks, Y. (eds.): Computational Semantics. Amsterdam: Noth-Holland, 1-21, 129-154

Deutsch, W., Clausing, H. (1979): Das Problem der Eindeutigkeit sprachlicher Referenz. In: Ueckert, H., Rhenius, D. (eds.): Komplexe menschliche Informationsverarbeitung. Bern: Huber, 369-377

Gershman, A.V. (1977): Analysing English noun groups for their conceptual content. Yale Univ., Dept. of Computer Science, Research Report No. 110

Goldman, N.M. (1975): Conceptual generation. In: Schank, R.C. (ed.): Conceptual information processing. Amsterdam: North-Holland, 289-371

Grice, H.P. (1975): Logic and conversation. In: Cole, P., Morgan, J.L. (eds.): Syntax and semantics, Vol. 3: Speech acts, N.Y.: Academic, 41-58

Grosz, B.J. (1976a): Discourse analysis. In: Walker, D.E. (ed.): Speech understanding research. Final Technical Report, Stanford Research Institute, Chapter VIII

Grosz, B.J. (1976b): Resolving definite noun phrases. In: Walker, D.E. (ed.): Speech understanding research. Final Technical Report. Stanford Research Institute, Chapter IX

Grosz, B.J. (1976c): Ellipsis. In: Walker, D.E. (ed.): Speech understanding research, Final Technical Report, Stanford Research Institute, Chapter X

Hayes, P.J., Rosner, M.A. (1976): ULLY: A program for handling conversations. In: Proc. of the AISB Summer Conference, Edinburgh, 137-147

Hendrix, G.G. (1977): Human engineering for applied natural language processing. In: Fifth International Joint Conference on Artificial Intelligence, 183-191

Herrmann, T., Deutsch, W. (1976): Psychologie der Objektbenennung. Bern: Huber

Herrmann, T., Laucht, M. (1976): On multiple verbal codability of objects. In: Psychological Research, 38, 355-368

Hobbs, J.R. (1976): Pronoun resolution. City Univ. of New York, Dept. of Computer Science, Research Report No. 76-1

Lakoff, G. (1975): Hedges: A study in meaning criteria and the logic of fuzzy concepts. In: Hockney, D., Harper, W., Freed, B. (eds.): Contemporary research in philosophical logic and linguistic semantics. Dordrecht: Reidel, 221-272

LeFaivre, R.A. (1977): FUZZY reference manual. Rutgers Univ., Dept. of Computer Science, March 1977

LeFaivre, R.A. (1978): Rutgers/UCI LISP manual. Rutgers Univ., Dept. of Computer Science, June 1978

McDermott, D. (1978): The last survey of representation of knowledge. In: Proc. of the AISB/GI Conference on Artificial Intelligence, Hamburg, 206-221

Morton, J. (1976): On recursive reference. In: Cognition, 4, IV, 309

Norman, D.A., Rumelhart, D.E. (1975): Explorations in cognition. San Francisco: Freeman

Oomen, I. (1977): Determination bei generischen, definiten und indefiniten Beschreibungen. Tübingen: Niemeyer

Ritchie, G.D. (1977): Computer modelling of English grammar. Univ. of Edinburgh, Dept. of Computer Science, Report CST-1-77

Schank, R.C. (ed.) (1975): Conceptual information processing. Amsterdam: North-Holland

Siklóssy, L. (1976): Let's talk LISP. Englewood Cliffs: Prentice-Hall

Sridharan, N.S. (ed): AIMDS - User manual. Version 2. Rutgers Univ., Dept. of Computer Science, June 1978

Wahlster, W. (1977): Die Repräsentation von vagem Wissen in natürlichsprachlichen Systemen der Künstlichen Intelligenz. Univ. Hamburg, Fachbereich Informatik, Report IfI-HH-B-38/77

Waltz, D.L. (ed.) (1977): Natural language interfaces. In: SIGART Newsletter, 61, 16-65

Waltz, D.L. (1978): An English language question answering system for a large relational database. In: CACM, 21, 7, 526-539

Winograd, T. (1972): Understanding natural language. N.Y.: Academic

Winograd, T. (1977): A framework for understanding discourse. Stanford Univ., Memo-AIM-297

Winston, P.H. (1977): Artificial Intelligence. Reading: Addison-Wesley

Wong, H.K.T. (1975): Generating English sentences from semantic network structures. Univ. of Toronto, Dept. of Computer Science, Technical Report No. 84

Woods, W.A. et al. (1976): Speech understanding systems. Final Report, Vol. V, BBN Report No. 3438, Cambridge: Bolt, Beranek & Newman

Zadeh, L.A. (1974): The concept of a linguistic variable and its application to approximate reasoning. San Jose: IBM Research Report RJ1355

Zadeh, L.A. (1978): Fuzzy sets as a basis for a theory of possibility. In: Fuzzy Sets and Systems, 1, 3-28

USL - AN EXPERIMENTAL INFORMATION SYSTEM BASED ON NATURAL LANGUAGE

by

Nikolaus Ott, Magdalena Zoeppritz

IBM Germany
Heidelberg Scientific Center
Tiergartenstrasse 15
D-6900 Heidelberg

Abstract: An information system based on natural language is introduced which operates on a relational data base. The paper outlines the representation of language concepts in the data base, followed by a detailed description of the methods of language processing employed in USL. The language facilities implemented are listed as indication of the scope of the system and a brief account of its use is given.

CONTENTS

1 INTRODUCTION

The USL (User Specialty Languages) System is an experimental information system developed at the Heidelberg Scientific Center of IBM Germany as an interface to a relational data base. It is designed as a tool mainly for users without education in data processing to make it possible for them to query and manipulate data in a subset of the German language.

The present report is an introduction to the way the system works and the facilities it offers. The reader is not expected to be familiar with linguistic terminology, only terms that are used in high-school, as e.g. 'subject', 'object', 'predicate', 'noun', etc. will be used. Knowledge of the terms 'structure variable' and 'pointer' as used with the programming language PL/I, as well as the term 'tree structure' from computer science is assumed. Details on the system that are not presented here can be found in the references [5 to 11, 14].

What is reported here is the result of the joint efforts of our colleague Hubert Lehmann and ourselves. In addition we would like to thank H. Lehmann for many suggestions for improvement of the report.
Thanks are also due to the students K. Horlaender and W. Sauermann for their valuable contributions to the USL project.

2 MAIN COMPONENTS OF THE USL-SYSTEM

The USL-System consists mainly of three parts:

1. A grammar for that part of the German language which is needed for interaction with a data base, consisting of about 800 rules and a parser for this grammar.
2. About 70 interpretation routines, representing the semantics of the system, whose function is to map the natural language input sentence into an expression of a formal data manipulation language, and the function processor for these routines.
3. An independent relational data base management system with its own formal data manipulation language.

Accordingly, the processing of an input sentence proceeds in three steps:

```
Input sentence ——> syntactic tree ——> expression in   ——> answer
                |                  |     formal lang.  |
                |                  |                   |
   step one:                 step two:                step three:
     Syntact. analysis         semant. analysis         processing of the
     through grammar           through interpre-        formal expression
     and parser                tation routines          in the data base
                               and                      and generation
                               function processor       of the answer
```

In most cases the answer is simply formatted output from the data base. There is no generation of natural language sentences. For some queries the result is translated into 'yes' or 'no', or additional operations are performed on the result before printing.

3 STRUCTURE AND STORAGE OF LANGUAGE CONCEPTS IN THE DATA BASE

In addition to the grammar, there is a lexicon in the USL-system with a fixed basic vocabulary containing 'have', 'be', possessive pronouns, prepositions, etc., words that are needed in all application contexts and the meaning of which does not change with the application. The lexicon also contains the terms necessary for a particular application - the verbs, nouns, and adjectives used to talk about the concepts in the application.

But how are these terms and the relationships between them represented in the data base (DB)?

In a question answering system based on natural language, the power of the system is largely dependent on the structuring of these terms. Therefore this question is central for the USL-System; it must be considered first when implementing an application and is therefore the first to be discussed in this paper.

Much has been written on the representation in a DB of human knowledge contained in natural language text. The problem of the most suitable DB model has no easy and certainly no single solution, even if the problem is restricted to a limited factual context (universe of discourse). Despite certain equivalences between the different models proposed [2], a solution will probably depend in each case on the specific purpose that the DB model is to serve. We make the following assumptions:

Meaningful sentences of a natural language consist of words and the semantic relationships between them. Words can refer to individuals or to relationships between individuals, e. g. in the sentence

Braun is the manager of Schmidt

the relationship 'manager of' is asserted of the individuals Braun and Schmidt. These relationships are representable as relations in the sense of the relational data base model. From this point of view it at least seems as if the relational model were especially suited for representing natural language concepts. Whether the relational DB models developed so far fully meet the requirements of such representation, shall not be discussed here.

The term 'store', applied to relations in the following sections, does not refer to p h y s i c a l storage, but to l o g i c a l representation. The relations described can therefore be regarded as 'virtual relations' in the sense that the logical representation is the one operated on by USL. The way these relations are defined for physical representation can, but need not, coincide with their logical form.

This section discusses the following 3 questions:

1. Which language concepts are represented as relations (tables)?
2. What is stored, i.e. what are the entries in the tables?
3. In what form are relations stored, i.e. what is the structure of the tables?

Ad 1.: Elements from the three main categories in the language #) are represented as tables:

[VERB]	e.g. 'live' Exceptions: 'have','be' (see below)
[NOUN]	e.g. 'employee'
[ADJECTIVE]	e.g. 'married'

Ad 2.: Numbers or proper names of objects are stored: they are entries in the columns of the relations.

Ad 3.: The tables have as column headings so-called role-names. They are abbreviations for the linguistic terms that characterize the role in the relation (subject: nominative case, object, genetive-attribute, locative or temporal adverbial, etc.) played by the corresponding entries in these columns.
The role-names are standardized in USL; that means that in all relations in the DB, the same names are used for the same roles, whereby the columns can be arranged in any order. Such role-names are: NOM (nominative), ACC (accusative), VON (of, genetive-attribute), LA (local adverbial), TA (temporal adverbial), etc.

Example 1:

Which employee of the manager Schmidt lives in Heidelberg?

Ad 1.: Tables are the following:

EMPLOYEE, MANAGER	(nouns)
LIVE	(verb)

#) Note: The linguistic categories, e. g. NOUN, VERB, SENTENCE, ADJECTIVE etc., are also called constructs in this report, to emphasize their function in the grammar rules as 'nodes constructed by rule'. The meaning of these constructs is defined by their function in the grammar; most of the construct names are familiar terms in linguistics, but others have meaning only with respect to the implementation in USL. Also, use of a particular term in USL does not necessarily imply adoption of the theory in which the term was coined.

Ad 2.: Entries in these tables are:

Schmidt, Heidelberg (proper names of objects)

Ad 3.: Structure of the tables:

'Which employee' is subject (case: nominative) of the sentence and is related to the local adverbial 'Heidelberg' by the (at least) two-place relation 'live' as follows:

'x lives in y'

As a consequence, the table LIVE should have at least #) two columns:

LIVE

NOM	LA
.	.
Braun	Heidelberg
.	.

NOM = nominative

LA = locative adverbial

'Schmidt' is the name of a manager.

The table MANAGER, then, must have at least one column:

MANAGER

NOM
.
Schmidt
.

'manager' is genetive-attribute to 'employee'; consequently there exists a two-place relationship between 'employee' and 'manager':

'x is employee of manager y'

#) Note: If example 1 contained the phrase 'live in Heidelberg in the year 1977', LIVE would have to have a third, temporal, column.

Therefore, the table EMPLOYEE should have two columns:

EMPLOYEE

NOM	VON(MANAGER)
.	.
Braun	Schmidt
.	.

Example 2:

What salaries do married employees have?

Ad 1.: Names of tables:

SALARY, EMPLOYEE (nouns)
MARRIED (adjective)

The verb 'have' is n o t represented as a table, since 'have' can be used to express many different relationships (possession, part-of, or other). It can be said, that 'have' asserts the existence of a relationship, without expressing what that relationship is [14].

Ad 2.: Since there are no proper names or numbers in the sentence, no specific entry in a table is addressed.

Ad 3.: Structure of the tables:

Since the verb 'have' does not exist as a table, the information must be stored in a different way.
The salaries are salaries o f the persons (here: 'married employees') who 'have' them; i.e. the (at least) two-place predicate holds:

'x is salary of (person) y'

As a consequence, SALARY should have at least two columns:

SALARY

NOM	VON(PERSON)
.	.
3000	Braun
.	.

In the case of the verb 'to have', the role of the subject of sentence is taken over by the VON-column of a noun.
Similarly, in the case of the verb 'be', the role of subject is represented by the NOM-column of a noun or adjective.

'Married' is adjective attribute to 'employee'; the one-place predicate must hold:

'(person) x is married'

As a consequence, MARRIED has one column:

```
MARRIED
-----------
   NOM
-----------
    .
  Schulz
    .
```

The relation EMPLOYEE can be structured as in example 1.

The fact that most of the vocabulary needed in an application and the corresponding relations in the DB have to be defined and structured before the application can be run does not mean that these definitions and structures cannot be changed later on by the user. If the user realizes during a session that the system cannot answer specific questions, because the definition of individual words or their representation in the DB is not suited to these questions, or if definitions are missing altogether, these definitions and the corresponding DB representations can be changed or added at any time. The task is facilitated by prompting routines to assist the user with the lexicon and DB formats.
For example, the system cannot answer a question like

When did Braun live in Heidelberg?

if the verb 'live' has been defined as above, with nominative and locative columns only. If the application requires that questions on dates can be put, the definitions of the corresponding words must contain temporal columns.

4 ISBL - THE FORMAL DATA BASE LANGUAGE OF PRTV

The data base management system used in USL is the Peterlee Relational Test Vehicle PRTV [13].
Data analysis and manipulation in PRTV is done via the formal language ISBL (Information System Base Language), based on relational algebra. Each natural language query is translated by USL into an expression in this language. For better understanding the possibilities and restrictions in USL that result from the target language of the translation, a brief overview of ISBL is included here.

The most important operators of ISBL are:

+ union	set operators
- difference	
. intersection	

* join-operator. This operator corresponds to forming the Cartesian product of set theory.

; select-operator. This operator precedes a role-name (also called selector name) or the corresponding column number indicated by the letter 'c' - and a condition for selection. The operator has the effect of selecting those rows in a table, for which the condition for selection holds in the column indicated.

% projection-operator. This operator precedes a list of role-names or column numbers and projects these columns out of the corresponding relation. If there are multiple rows with the same contents, they are reduced to one in the result, as for sets.

This shall be illustrated by three sample queries with the corresponding expressions in ISBL - the ISBL-strings. The relations addressed are restricted to three rows each, so that the results of the operations triggered by the ISBL-strings can be verified, as shown for the first example.

Relations in PRTV are represented in lexicographic order, i. e. tuples are sorted according to the entries in the first column. Where they are the same, the sequence is determined by the entries in the second column etc.

The relations used in the examples are:

LIVE

NOM	LA
Bauer	Wiesloch
Braun	Heidelberg
Schmidt	Mannheim

EARN

NOM	ACC
Bauer	4000
Braun	3000
Schmidt	3500

NEED

NOM	ACC
Braun	Mueller
Krause	Braun
Mueller	Braun

EMPLOYEE

NOM	VON(MANAG)
Braun	Schmidt
Schmidt	Bauer
Schulz	Schmidt

MANAGER #)

NOM	VON(EMP)
Bauer	Schmidt
Schmidt	Braun
Schmidt	Schulz

SECRETARY

NOM	VON(MANAG)
Graf	Schmidt
Krause	Meier
Mueller	Bauer

The three sample sentences and the corresponding ISBL-strings are the following (HD in the ISBL-strings stands for Heidelberg):

(1a) Which employee of the manager Schmidt lives in Heidelberg?

(2a) Who earns more than his manager?

(3a) Which employee do the secretaries of Meier and of Bauer need?

(1b)

((LIVE;c2='HD')*(EMPLOYEE*(MANAGER;c1='SCHMIDT');c2=c3);c1=c3)%c1

(2b) ((EARN*(EARN*MANAGER;c1=c3);c2 c4);c1=c6)%c1

(3b) (((NEED*(SECRETARY;c2='MEIER');c1=c3)*EMPLOYEE;c2=c5)%c2).
(((NEED*(SECRETARY;c2='BAUER');c1=c3)*EMPLOYEE;c2=c5)%c2)

#) Note that the relation MANAGER here has two columns, as opposed to one in section 3. In the examples, this relation can be thought of as the inverse of the relation EMPLOYEE.

The resolution of an ISBL-string shall be illustrated for example (1b):

```
((LIVE;c2='HD')*(EMPLOYEE*(MANAGER;c1='SCHMIDT');c2=c3);c1=c3)%c1
||I_________I  |            I________________I    |             |  |
|| Selection of|            Selection of those    |             |  |
|| those rows  |            rows from the         |             |  |
|| from the rel.            relation MANAGER,     |             |  |
|| LIVE, where |            where the 1st column  |             |  |
|| the 2nd column           (NOM-column)          |             |  |
|| (LA-column) |            contains the entry    |             |  |
|| contains the|            'Schmidt'.            |             |  |
|| entry 'HD'. |            Result:               |             |  |
|| Result:     |               Schmidt | Braun    |             |  |
||   Braun | HD|               Schmidt | Schulz   |             |  |
||             |------------------------------------             |  |
||              Join of the result above with the               |  |
||              relation EMPLOYEE and selection of              |  |
||              the rows where the VON-column of                |  |
||              EMPLOYEE contains the same individuals          |  |
||              (managers) as the NOM-column of MANAGER         |  |
||              (in this case the individual 'Schmidt').        |  |
||                                                              |  |
||              Result of the join-operation:                   |  |
||      Result | Braun   | Schmidt | Schmidt | Braun  |         |  |
||      c2=c3  | Braun   | Schmidt | Schmidt | Schulz |         |  |
||               Schmidt | Bauer   | Schmidt | Braun            |  |
||               Schmidt | Bauer   | Schmidt | Schulz           |  |
||      Result | Schulz  | Schmidt | Schmidt | Braun  |         |  |
||      c2=c3  | Schulz  | Schmidt | Schmidt | Schulz |         |  |
|---------------------------------------------------------------   |
| Join of the two results above and selection of the rows          |
| where the entries in the NOM-columns of LIVE and EMPLOYEE        |
| are the same (so-called equi-join).                              |
|                                                                  |
|    Result of the join-operation:                                 |
|  | Braun | HD | Braun   | Schmidt | Schmidt | Braun | Result     |
|  | Braun | HD | Braun   | Schmidt | Schmidt | Schulz|  c1=c3     |
|    Braun | HD | Schulz  | Schmidt | Schmidt | Braun              |
|    Braun | HD | Schulz  | Schmidt | Schmidt | Schulz             |
--------------------------------------------------------------------
 The NOM-column of the above result is projected out.

    Result:
            Braun
```

The strings (2b) and (3b) are resolved in the same way as shown for (1b). An additional operation in the case of (3b) is the intersection of the results of the two substrings. The results are:

for (2b): Nobody

for (3b): Braun

As can be seen from the examples above, parentheses are used freely in ISBL to establish precedence among the operations to be performed. The order of execution is from the innermost parentheses out. The columns are numbered from left to right with a new start for each pair of parentheses.

5 OPERATION OF THE PARSER

The parser is a program for syntactic analysis of input sentences or strings. Various parsing algorithms have been proposed, some working top-down, others bottom-up. The parsing algorithm used in USL was originally developed by Kay [4], it works bottom up. It was used together with a function processor in the REL system (Rapidly Extensible Language) [12]. The parser and function processor have been considerably altered and extended to serve as a tool for language development under the name of USAGE (User Application Generator) [1]. USL uses the parser and function processor of USAGE.

The parser works from left to right character by character through the input string and compares the words and substrings in the input with entries in the lexicon. Where a match is found, the parser creates the constructs assigned to the strings by the lexical rules. If more than one rule is found for a given string or overlapping strings, all rules found are applied. The resulting ambiguities are resolved later in the parsing process. If there is a word (substring between blanks or delimiters) for which there is no construct, the parser assumes that the string represents the proper name of an object in the DB and creates from it a construct [NAME].

After the first pass through the sentence and the creation of the constructs corresponding to words and affixes, the parser continues with the grammar rules proper. The parser tries to match adjacent word-constructs of the input against the right hand sides of grammar rules in order to combine the constructs found to a single new construct of the type indicated by the left hand side of the corresponding grammar rule. In addition to testing the construct names, a number of syntactic and semantic features are checked also to avoid creating constructs from incompatible representatives of certain categories. These features contain information on case, number, and gender of nouns, transitive and intransitive use of verbs, verbal complements, etc. If, e. g., there is a verb followed by a noun, and there is a rule to build a construct [VC] out of [VERB][NOMEN], the rule is applied only if the complement feature of the verb matches the case feature of the noun.

There is a large number of such features serving to subcategorize the constructs. Their use makes it possible to avoid unnecessarily many 'mismatches' without having to increase the number of different constructs intolerably and still conver a relatively large subset of the language as described by the about 800 rules.

An essential part of each lexical and grammar rule is the name of the interpretation routine (IPR) associated with it. This name tells the function processor - after the parser has built a complete syntactic tree over the entire input - , which semantic routine must be called to establish the semantic relations corresponding to the syntactic node in the tree. The functioning of some of the IPRs shall be described in detail in the next section.

The parser in USL provides all syntactic ambiguities inherent in the input by constructing a different tree for each of the different readings. Sometimes these different readings correspond to different meaningful semantic interpretations. Where this is not so, it is the task of the semantic component (IPRs), to eliminate the ones that are not meaningful (see tree No. 2 of example 2 below). If the parser does not find a complete tree, i. e. a tree that spans the entire input and leads to one single root, the system sends a message of 'not understood' to the user. The user then has various possibilities of finding out why the input was not understood - typing error, missing word in the lexicon, or use of a defined word in a way incompatible with the definition. Error messages are described in [8].

The following section shows the complete syntactic trees for two sample sentences. The first example, used already twice above, is syntactically unambiguous, the second example is two-way ambiguous.

The names in square brackets are the names of linguistic constructs, their meaning is as follows:

[NOMEN] = noun	[QU] = article or quantifier
[NAME] = proper name	[VERB] = verb
[PREP] = preposition	[VC] = verbcomplex verb and one or more complements
[SK] = sentence kernel verb and all complements	[SENT] = sentence
[NP] = noun phrase	[ABL] = locative adverbial

The names in parentheses are the names of the semantic interpretation routines (IPRs) belonging to the nodes. The numbers below the IPRs indicate the sequence in which they are called by the function processor.

Example 1:

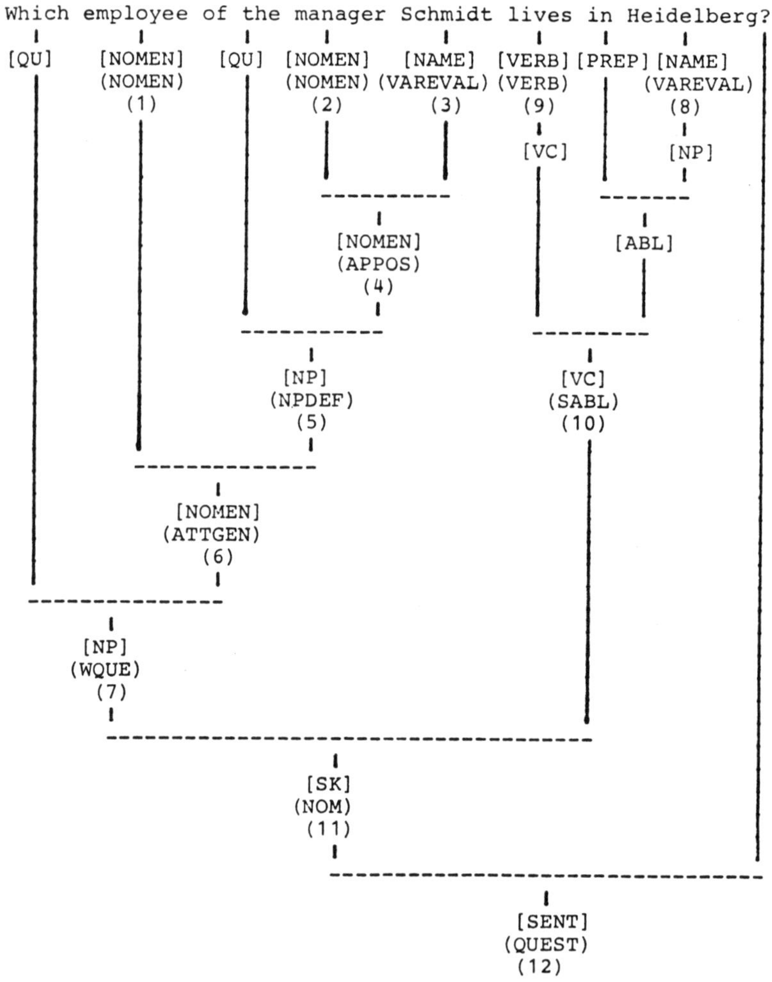

Figure 1

Example 2:

Welche Gehaelter haben die Mitarbeiter?

This sentence is syntactically ambiguous in German, because either noun phrase can be both subject and object. In English the two meanings are differentiated syntactically by the auxiliary verb 'to do':

What salaries do employees have?
What salaries have employees?

The first translation corresponds to the analysis in tree No. 1, the second to the one in tree No. 2.

Tree 1:

What salaries do the employees have?
Welche Gehaelter haben die Mitarbeiter?

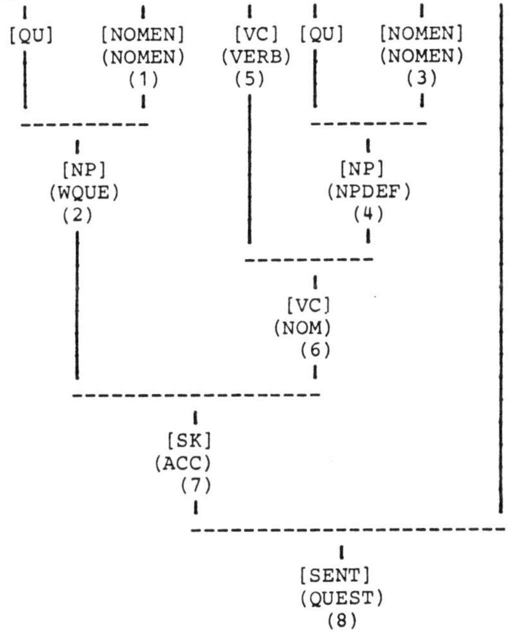

Figure 2a

Tree 2:

```
What salaries have the employees?
Welche Gehaelter haben die Mitarbeiter?
  |        |         |    |       |       |
 [QU]   [NOMEN]    [VC] [QU]  [NOMEN]     |
  |     (NOMEN)   (VERB) |    (NOMEN)     |
  |       (1)      (5)   |      (3)       |
  |        |        |    |       |        |
  ----------        |    ---------        |
      |             |        |            |
     [NP]           |       [NP]          |
    (WQUE)          |     (NPDEF)         |
     (2)            |       (4)           |
      |             |        |            |
      |             ----------            |
      |                 |                 |
      |                [VC]               |
      |               (ACC)               |
      |                (6)                |
      |                 |                 |
      -------------------                 |
               |                          |
              [SK]                        |
             (NOM)                        |
              (7)                         |
               |                          |
               ----------------------------
                            |
                          [SENT]
                         (QUEST)
                           (8)
```

Figure 2b

The only difference between trees 1 and 2 of example 2 is that the calls to the semantic routines in the [VC] and [SK] nodes are reversed. That means that in the second tree the salaries play the role of subject,which is semantically anomalous. (The second tree is abandoned in the course of the interpretation).

As mentioned above, such syntactic trees are constructed by the parser according to the rules of the lexicon and grammar. To illustrate this point, some of the rules applied to construct the trees above are now described in more detail. They are given in a modified version of the BNF (Backus Normal Form) format:

(R1) [NOMEN:+MAS:IPR-NOMEN('EMPLOYEE')]<='EMPLOYEE';

(R2) [NOMEN:1,CMP=1:IPR-APPOS(1,2)]
<-[NOMEN:CMP=0,-CNT,SYST=0][NAME];

```
(R3) [SK:2,+WPRO,+CN:IPR-NOM(1,2)]
     <-[NP:+NOM,-NEU,SG=SG(2),PL=PL(2),+WPRO][VC:TYP=NI,-PPE];

(R4) [SENT:+WPRO:IPR-QUEST(1)]<-[SK:+WPRO,-NS]'?';
```

Rule (R1) is a so-called fixed token rule, i. e. this rule is an entry in the lexicon and serves to create basic or word constructs (leaves of the tree) from the character string enclosed in single quotes to the right of the double arrow '<='. The same character string also occurs as the parameter of the IPR NOMEN. That means that the corresponding relation in the DB in this case can also be found under this name. This is not necessarily so, as the relation name in the DB may be the word used to address the relation, but any other name can be chosen as well.

The remaining three rules are grammar rules. They are used - together with other grammar rules - to build the syntactic tree step by step from the leaves down to the root by combining each time the constructs to the right of the arrow (<-) to form the new construct to the left.

The strings +MAS, +CN, -PPE, etc., found in the rules are the so-called logical features. They only take the values plus or minus. In addition, there are integer features and case features. Case features take their values from a set of values specified for each case feature (E. g. TYP=NI, indicating the intransitive use of a verb as required for rule (R3) to be applicable, and set for the verb 'to live' above. The value NI is taken from the set of values for the case feature TYP).
The integer features (e. g.: CMP=1, set for 'complex noun or verb phrase') take natural numbers as their values.

The remaining numbers found in the rules refer to the sequence of constructs on the right hand side. They are used in place of features to transfer some or all features of one of the input constructs to the resulting construct, and they are used to pass the interpretation routines of input constructs as parameters to the IPR of the resulting construct.

More detail can be found reference [9].

6 OPERATION OF THE INTERPRETATION ROUTINES

As has been mentioned already in the previous section, an essential part of almost all rules of the lexicon and grammar is the name of a routine for the semantic interpretation. That means that for nearly each node in the syntactic tree there is a call to a routine that establishes the semantic relationships corresponding to the syntactic construction. These semantic relationships are also represented as a tree, the nodes of which are formed by essentially two different PL/I structures, which are chained by pointer. After the semantic tree is completed, it is processed recursively, starting from the root node, by a special program (named ASSARG). There the tree is converted into an ISBL string which represents the semantic content of the input sentence and starts the DB query. Because of the necessary automatism in creating the ISBL strings, it is clear that these strings cannot be formulated optimally for each individual sentence, optimal in the sense, that the number of data accesses is minimized or the operator used is the one best suited in each individual case.

The manner of operation of the IPRs shall be illustrated briefly using the syntax tree in Fig. 1 as an example. Fig. 1 shows the sequence in which the IPRs are called. It can be seen that the function processor walks down the left branch of the tree till a routine is reached which needs as input a construct from the right branch of the tree. At this point, the processor walks up to the leaves of the right branch and continues downward, as long as there is no branch. The semantic tree is constructed in such a way that the main verb becomes the root of the tree. The verb is considered to play a central role in the sentence, all other parts of the sentence are attached to the verb as 'arguments'.

The two basic PL/I structures - called here RELATION and ARGUMENT - contain several variables, the structures are shown below with the most important variables used in the example:

```
  RELATION
----------
| ISBL    |  - character variable for the ISBL-string
----------                          (often name of relation)
| ARGOFF  |  - pointer to the first argument
----------
| LASTARG |  - pointer to the last argument
----------
| WHICH   |  - information on occurrence of the
----------                            interrogative 'which'
|  ...    |
----------

  ARGUMENT
----------
| TYPE    |  - code for the argument type (type 1: character
----------             string or number, type 6: relation)
| ROLN    |  - information on the role of the argument in the
----------                                          sentence
| ARGNAMP |  - pointer to the value of the argument
----------
| NEXTARG |  - pointer to the next argument
----------
|  ...    |
----------
```

For the example in Fig. 1, the semantic tree is built and processed in the following manner:

1. IPR-NOMEN: processing of 'employee'

   Input: character string 'employee'

   Allocation of (reserving storage for) the argument structure. Since 'employee' addresses a relation in the DB, a relation structure is allocated as well. The following entries and pointer chains are established:

```
ARGUMENT          |-> RELATION
----------        |   ----------
| TYPE=6  |       |   | ISBL = EMPLOYEE
----------        |   ----------
| ROLN=''|        |   | ARGOFF  |->|   (NULL-pointer)
----------        |   ----------
| ARGNAMP|--------    | LASTARG|->|
----------            ----------
| NEXTARG|->|         | WHICH=F|
----------            ----------
```

   Output: pointer to the argument structure 'employee'

2. IPR-NOMEN: processing of 'manager'

   The operations are the same as for 'employee' above.

3. IPR-VAREVAL: processing of 'Schmidt'

   Input: character string 'Schmidt'

   An argument structure and a string-variable are allocated and the two are chained by pointer.

```
ARGUMENT
----------
| TYPE=1  |
----------
| ROLN=''|
----------         --------------------
| ARGNAMP|------->| STR = 'SCHMIDT' |
----------         --------------------
| NEXTARG|->|
----------
```

   Output: pointer to the argument structure 'Schmidt'

4. IPR-APPOS:

   Input: 1st parameter: pointer to argument 'manager'
          2nd parameter: pointer to argument 'Schmidt'

   Chaining of the arguments 'manager' und 'Schmidt'. Since appositions specify the noun to which they belong, the name in the apposition must be found in the NOM-column of the relation corresponding to the noun, therefore, the ROLN-variable of the argument 'Schmidt' is set to NOM. 'Schmidt' is a manager, so he should occur in the NOM-column of MANAGER.

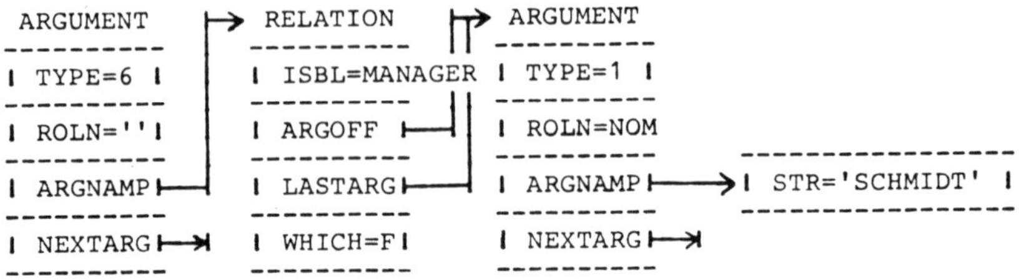

Output: pointer to the argument 'manager'

5. IPR-NPDEF:

Input: 1st parameter: character string 'of the' ('des' in German),
2nd parameter: pointer to the argument 'manager'

In this routine, information on gender and number of the article is read from the corresponding node in the syntactic tree and stored in one of the additional variables of the argument structure 'manager'. This information is recorded in case further processing shows that the input contains coordination or possessive pronouns. It is then used to find the referent of possessive pronouns and to select the appropriate coordination operation (not used in this example).

Output: pointer to the argument structure 'manager'

6. IPR-ATTGEN:

Input: 1st parameter: pointer to the argument 'employee'
2nd parameter: pointer to the argument 'manager'

Chaining of the arguments 'employee' and 'manager'. In addition, since 'manager' plays the role of genetive attribute to 'employee', the ROLN-variable of the argument 'manager' is set to VON.

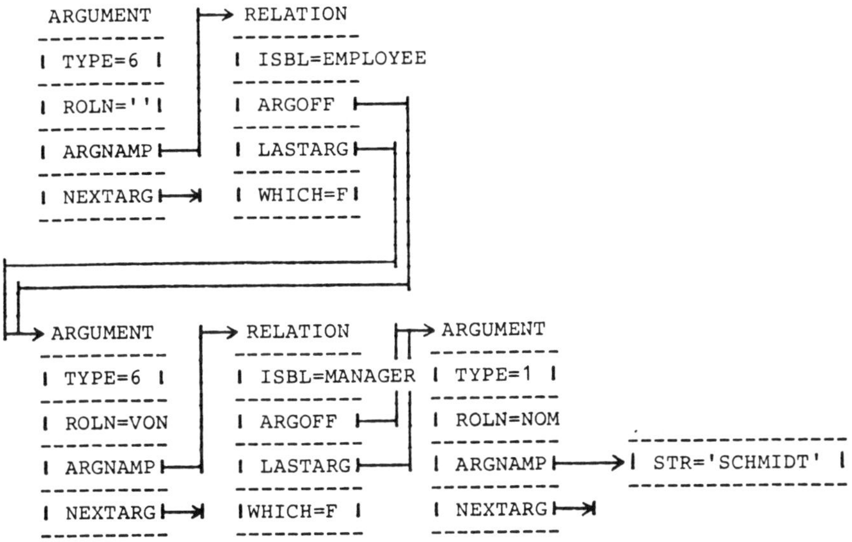

Output: pointer to the argument structure 'employee'

7. IPR-WQUE:

Input: 1st parameter: character string 'which'
2nd. parameter: pointer to the argument 'employee'

In this routine again, gender and number of the interrogative pronoun are stored in case they are needed later for reference purposes. In addition, the Boolean variable WHICH of the relation structure 'employee' is set to 'true', to indicate that this relation has been requested as part of the answer by the phrase 'which employee'.

Output: pointer to the argument structure 'employee'

8. IPR-VAREVAL: processing of 'Heidelberg'

The routine VAREVAL performs the same operations on 'Heidelberg' as in 3. above on 'Schmidt'.

9. IPR-VERB: processing of 'lives'

Input: character string 'live'

Since the verb shall constitute the root of the semantic tree, this IPR only allocates a relation structure and no argument structure. The variable ISBL is set to LIVE.

Output: pointer to the relation structure 'live'

10.IPR-SABL:

Input: 1st parameter: pointer to the relation 'live'
2nd parameter: pointer to the argument 'Heidelberg'

This routine first checks in the data base whether the relation of the verb contains a locative column. If not, there is an error message, but if it is there, this locative column is assigned as value to the ROLN-variable of the argument 'Heidelberg'. This means that 'Heidelberg' is to be found in the locative column of the verb relation.
The argument 'Heidelberg' is then chained to the relation 'live':

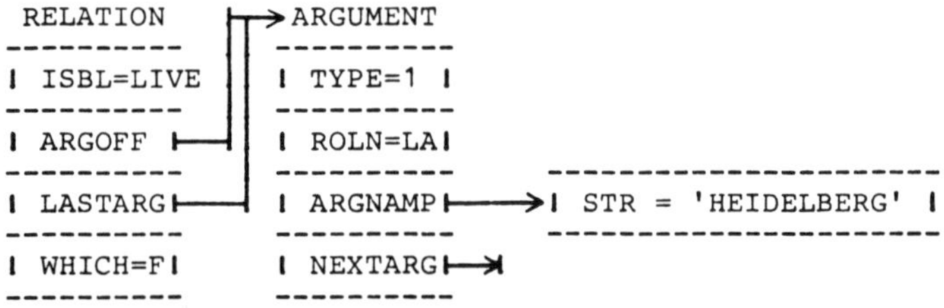

Output: pointer to the relation structure 'live'

11.IPR-NOM:

Input: 1st parameter: pointer to the argument 'employee'
2nd parameter: pointer to the relation 'live'

Here the ROLN-variable of the argument 'employee' is set to NOM, since 'employee' has the role of subject in the input sentence. Then the remaining arguments are chained together so that the semantic tree is now complete.

Semantic tree for
'which employee of the manager Schmidt lives in Heidelberg?':

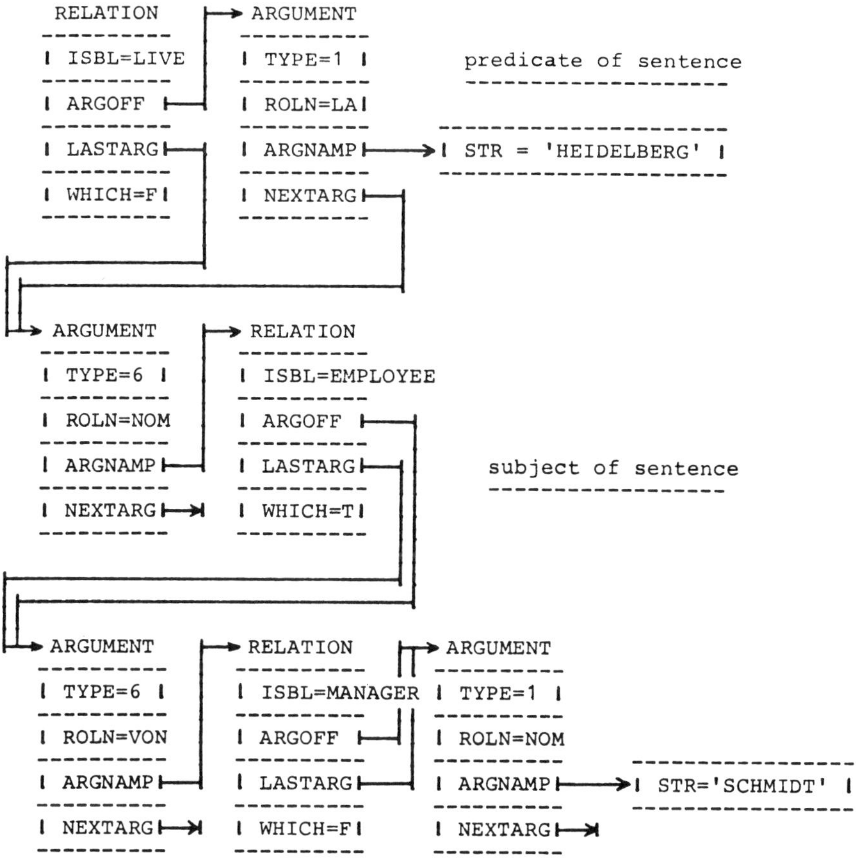

A simplified representation makes the tree structure easier to see. This leads to the following tree, with the root at the top:

```
             ------------------------------
             |     verb relation 'live'   |
             ------------------------------
                |                       |
                |  locative adverbial   |  subject
                v                       v
   --------------------     --------------------
   | argument, type=1 |     | argument, type=6 |
   |   'Heidelberg'   |     |    'employee'    |
   --------------------     --------------------
                                    |
                                    |  genetive-attribute
                                    v
                            --------------------
                            | argument, type=6 |
                            |    'manager'     |
                            --------------------
                                    |
                                    |  apposition
                                    v
                            --------------------
                            | argument, type=1 |
                            |    'Schmidt'     |
                            --------------------
```

Output: pointer to the relation structure 'live'

12.IPR-QUEST:

Input: pointer to the relation structure 'live'

This routine calls the program ASSARG, which processes the semantic tree recursively, starting from the root. As it walks through the tree, the program successively builds up the ISBL string for the input sentence. Arguments of argument type 1 are represented as filters, i. e. a selection operator followed by a condition for selection. Arguments of argument type 6 are respresented by a join operation, here the information stored in the variable ROLN indicates which columns must be tested for equi-join. The variable WHICH serves to build the projection list, NOM-columns of those relations are projected for which the variable is true.
The tree above yields the following intermediate results:

```
(LIVE;c2='HEIDELBERG')                       predicate
and
(EMPLOYEE*(MANAGER;c1='SCHMIDT');c2=c3)      subject
```

The intermediate strings are joined, then the NOM-column of 'employee' is projected, resulting in the string (1b) of section 4 above:

```
(1b)    ((LIVE;c2='HEIDELBERG')*(EMPLOYEE*(MANAGER;
                          c1='SCHMIDT');c2=c3);c1=c3)%c1
```

The sample sentence was very simple and its analysis and interpretation therefore were equally simple and straightforward. Needless to say, processing gets more complicated for sentences with AND or OR coordination, quantifiers, and possessive pronouns.

Since the ISBL language does not have an operator which would allow it to handle universal quantifiers or number quantifiers (like Codd's division-operator for handling universal quantifiers [3]), a special program was written for this purpose [11], which is called by the program ASSARG.

In the case of coordination, whole subtrees are copied after syntactic analysis for the semantic interpretation, for it is clear that for example the sentence

Who lives in Heidelberg or Munich?

can be interpreted as:

Who lives in Heidelberg or who lives in Munich?

(See in this context also example (3a) and the corresponding ISBL-string (3b.))

Where possessive pronouns occur in coordinated sentences, the ISBL-strings can become very complicated, depending on the noun to which the possessive pronoun refers. Thus e. g. the sentence

Who needs the manager Schmidt or his secretary?

leads to the following ISBL-string if 'his' refers to 'manager Schmidt':

```
(((NEED*(MANAGER;C1='SCHMIDT');C2=C3)%C1)+
   ((((MANAGER;C1='SCHMIDT')*(NEED*SECRETARY;C2=C3);C1=C6)%C3))
```

This string is much more complicated than the string resulting from the same sentence, if 'his' has the same referent as 'who':

```
(((NEED*(MANAGER;C1='SCHMIDT');C2=C3)%C1)+
   (((NEED*SECRETARY;C2=C3);C1=C4)%C1))
```

There are many other examples which are difficult to handle semantically. E. g. the sentence

Who earns more than a (nominative) manager?

requires a totally different processing than the sentence

Who needs more than one (accusative) manager?

'Earn' and 'need' are verbs of the same syntactic type and therefore cannot be distinguished syntactically. The difference lies in the objects of the sentences. In the first case, the object contains a reduced clause, the subject of which is 'a manager', this sentence must be interpreted as

Who earns more than a manager earns?

In the second sentence, 'a manager' is in fact the accusative object of the verb 'need'.

Because many nouns in German do not show the difference between nominative and accusative, these sentences are not distinguished in the syntax. Which of the two interpretation applies in a given case is decided on the semantic level.

7 LANGUAGE FACILITIES OF USL

The applications independent subset of the German language contained in USL includes among others the following linguistic constructions:

1. Complement questions (Wh-questions)

   W h o lives in Heidelberg?
   W h i c h employee lives in Heidelberg?
   H o w m a n y employees live in Heidelberg?

2. Decision questions (yes/no questions)

   D o e s Braun l i v e in Heidelberg?

3. Commands

   L i s t the employees of Schmidt!

4. Negated questions

   Which employee does n o t live in Heidelberg?
   Does Braun have n o manager?

5. Relative clauses

Who are the employees, w h o l i v e i n H e i d e l b e r g ?
List the employees, w h o d o n o t l i v e i n H e i d e l b e r g

6. Adjectives

Who is m a r r i e d ?
Who are the m a r r i e d employees?
Which employees l i v i n g i n H e i d e l b e r g are married?

7. Constructions with genetive attributes

Which employee o f S c h m i d t lives in Heidelberg?
Is Braun the employee o f a m a n a g e r ?

8. Appositions

Which employee of the m a n a g e r S c h m i d t is married?

9. Noun complements

Where does the employee w i t h salary 3500 live?

10.AND-Coordination

What s a l a r y a n d a g e do the employees have that live in Heidelberg?
Which employee has a manager b u t no secretary?

11.OR-Coordination

Who lives in H e i d e l b e r g o r M a n n h e i m?

12.Quantifiers

Do a l l managers have a t l e a s t 5 employees?
H o w m a n y employees do not live in Heidelberg?

13.Comparison

Whose salary is g r e a t e r (l e s s) t h a n 3000?
Who earns m o r e t h a n Braun?
H o w m u c h does Meier earn m o r e t h a n Braun?

14.Possessive pronouns

Which employee earns more than h i s manager?

15.Locative adverbials

Who drives *from* Heidelberg *to* Munich?

16.Time adverbials

Who *came* to Munich *before May 1970*?
Whose birthdate is *February 5, 1936*?
How many *days* does the trip take?
From when to when does the trip take?
How long does the trip take?

17.Sum, average, maximum, and minimum

What is the *average* (*maximum, minimum*) salary?

What is the *sum* of the salaries?

18.Subtotals

What is the *sum* (*average, maximum, minimum*) of the salaries of the employees of *each* manager?

19.Ordinal numbers

Who has the *highest* (*lowest*) salary?
Who has the *3rd highest* (*lowest*) salary?
Which employees have the *5 highest* (*lowest*) salaries?

20.Arithmetic expressions

```
What is ( 2 * 27 ) + 16?
List 2 * * 4
```

21.Definition of variables

```
x = 1.1
y = the salary of the employees of Schmidt
What is x*y?
```

22.Definition of arithmetic functions

```
f ( x ) = x * x
g ( x , y ) = ( f ( x ) + f ( y ) ) * * 0.5
What is g(3,4)?
```

23.Declarative sentences

Declarative sentences are interpreted in USL as on-line updates of relations in the DB. At this time only those relations can be updated that already exist in the DB e.g. in the following manner:

Maier is an employee of the manager Schmidt.
Maier lives in Heidelberg.
etc.

8 USE OF USL

The USL-system is now being evaluated in various institutions with real applications. As was said in the introduction, it was developed with the aim of providing users not trained in data processing with an instrument to get desired information quickly out of a data base prepared for the application. USL is not designed for routine queries or reports, its main concern are questions that are 'ad hoc' and unanticipated and therefore little suited for programming. In these application contexts, the relative freedom of formulating questions is needed most. The results of the various application studies that are underway will show whether USL can meet these requirements.

9 REFERENCES

[1] Bertrand,O., Daudennarde,J.J.: USAGE - Processing and Natural Languages. IBM Paris Scientific Center, mimeo.

[2] Blaser,A., Schmutz,H.: Data Base Research : A Survey IBM Heidelberg Scientific Center, TR 75.10.009, 1975

[3] Codd,E.F.: Relational Completeness of Data Base Sublanguages. IBM Research Report RJ 987, 1972

[4] Kay,M.: Experiments with a Powerful Parser. Second International Conference on Computational Linguistics, Grenoble, August 1967

[5] Kogon,R.et al.: The User Specialty Languages System. Proc. 6th Annual Meeting of Gesellschaft fuer Informatik, Stuttgart, Springer 1976

[6] Lehmann,H.: Aspects of the Interpretation of Natural Language in an Information System. IBM Heidelberg Scientific Center, TR 77.11.006, 1977

[7] Lehmann,H.: The USL System - its Objectives and Status. Proc. IBM Int. Technical Conf. on Relational Data Base Systems, Bari, 1976

[8] Lehmann,H.: Hinweise fuer die Benutzung von USL. IBM Heidelberg Scientific Center, TN 76.01, 1976

[9] Lehmann,H., Ott,N., Zoeppritz,M.: Language Facilities of USL/German. Version III, IBM Heidelberg Scientific Center, TN 77.04, 1977

[10] Lehmann,H., Ott,N.: Interpretation Routines for German Grammar Rules. IBM Heidelberg Scientific Center, TN 75.03, 1975

[11] Ott,N.: Interpretation Of Questions with Quantifiers and Negation in the USL System. IBM Heidelberg Scientific Center, TR 77.10.005, 1977

[12] Thompson, F. B., Lockemann, P. C., Dostert, B. H., Deverill, R. S.: 'REL: A rapidly extensible language system', Proc. 24th National ACM Conference, New York, August 1969.

[13] Todd,S.J.P.: The Peterlee Relational Test Vehicle - A System Overview. IBM Systems Journal, Vol. 15, No. 4, 1976

[14] Zoeppritz,M.: The Meaning of OF and HAVE in the USL system. forthcoming

ROBOT:
A HIGH PERFORMANCE NATURAL LANGUAGE INTERFACE FOR DATA BASE QUERY

by

Larry R. Harris

Mathematics Department
Dartmouth College
Hanover, New Hampshire 03755

Abstract

This paper describes the structure and the capabilities of the ROBOT natural language interface for data base query. The ROBOT system translates English questions about the contents of a data base into the formal retrieval language used by the data base management system (DBMS). The subset of English understood by the system ranges from compound-complex sentences to sentence fragments. As such the system provides a sophisticated man-machine interface for querying the contents of large data bases.

Introduction

Natural language access to a computerized data base has long been recognized as a useful application of computational linguistic techniques. Since the pioneer systems of Winograd[1] and Woods[2] it has been clear that the state of the art in natural language processing was capable of providing a sufficiently usable interface for certain "micro-world" applications. However, several problems prevent the direct application of these techniques to a real world environment. These problems range from the important, but theoretically uninteresting problems of resource requirements, to more profound questions of moving the natural language processor from one micro-world to another.

The ROBOT project is an attempt to solve this full range of problems in an attempt to provide a high performance natural language facility for data base query. Specifically the goals of the project are to refine the natural language processing capability to the point whereby only small dictionary changes would be necessary to move from one area of discourse to another. Furthermore, the resource demands of the system, in terms of both time and space, should fit well within the capabilities of existing medium to large computers. The ROBOT project has already been successful in solving these problems in as much as it is already in use in over a dozen applications in four commercial environments.

This paper gives an overview of the structure of the ROBOT system and discusses how several important problems are solved within this structure. In order to demonstrate the current level of competence of the system, this discussion is preceeded by a sample dialog exhibiting the capabilities discussed later in the text.

Sample Dialog

This section is meant to aquaint the reader with the current level of performance of the ROBOT system. The data base used for this dialog is a personnel file for a fictitious company. The first question requests a description of the contents of the file.

The dialog that follows makes use of the proprietary software of Artificial Intelligence Corporation, and Software Ag of North America. The author gratefully acknowledges the contributions made by these companies.

The questions are broken into sections that correspond to the discussion in the text. The information typed by the user has been underlined for clarity. All other printing is generated by the program, except for the explanatory text that preceeds each section.

The total processing time of ROBOT for this session was 30 cpu seconds, not including the cost incurred by the DBMS. The average response time for all questions was less than 10 seconds on an IBM 370/155 in a TSO environment. The file contains just over 60,000 records. The program requires 250k bytes.

WHAT FIELDS ARE IN THE EMPLOYEE FILE?

The first question is typical of the first question asked by many end users. It is a meta question that refers to a higher lever description of the data, rather than the data itself.

FIELDS OF THE EMPLOYEE FILE

NAME	SEARCHABLE	SORTABLE	FORMAT	LENGTH
NAME	YES	YES	ALPHANUMERIC	20
CITY	YES	YES	ALPHANUMERIC	15
STATE	YES	YES	ALPHANUMERIC	2
JOB	YES	YES	ALPHANUMERIC	20
PHONE	YES	YES	ALPHANUMERIC	8
SALARY	YES	YES	NUMERIC	6
SEX	YES	YES	ALPHANUMERIC	1
AGE	YES	YES	NUMERIC	2
FAMILY STATUS	YES	YES	ALPHANUMERIC	10

Range of Expression

The following four questions ask for the same information, but do so with widely varying syntactic forms. The first question is an imformation rich compound-complex sentence. Contrast this with the other less verbose wordings. Increasingly in these latter examples the syntax provides fewer clues, forcing ROBOT to use the data base itself as an aid in understanding the questions.

GIVE ME THE NAMES OF ALL EMPLOYEES WHO HAVE JOBS WORKING AS A SECRETARY IN CHICAGO.

PRINT THE NAME OF ANY EMPLOYEE WITH CITY=CHICAGO AND JOB=SECRETARY.

THE NUMBER OF RECORDS TO RETRIEVE IS 30

REINSTEDT

LAWLER

MOOERS

SORIANO

LORIE

PRINT THE NAMES OF ALL CHICAGO EMPLOYEES WORKING AS SECRETARIES.

PRINT THE NAME OF ANY EMPLOYEE WITH CITY=CHICAGO AND JOB=SECRETARY.

THE NUMBER OF RECORDS TO RETRIEVE IS 30

REINSTEDT

LAWLER

MOOERS

SORIANO

LORIE

WHO ARE THE CHICAGO SECRETARIES?

PRINT THE NAME OF ANY EMPLOYEE WITH CITY=CHICAGO AND JOB=SECRETARY.

THE NUMBER OF RECORDS TO RETRIEVE IS 30

REINSTEDT

LAWLER

MOOERS

SORIANO

LORIE

SECRETARIES IN CHICAGO.

PRINT THE NAME OF ANY EMPLOYEE WITH CITY=CHICAGO AND JOB=SECRETARY.

THE NUMBER OF RECORDS TO RETRIEVE IS 30

REINSTEDT

LAWLER

MOOERS

SORIANO

LORIE

Lexical Ambiguity

The following sentences exhibit ROBOT's capability in dealing with lexical and word sense ambiguity. The word "and" is used in four distinctly different ways in the following sentences.

PRINT THE SALARY OF SMITH AND LAWLER.

In this request "and" really means "logical or". Notice how the canonical English rephrasing of the request reflects this interpretation. Note that the system does not take the request too literally. The request only asked for the Salary field to be printed, but with this type of search logic it is important to see the names as well. It is a good example of the system giving you what you want, not what you asked for.

PRINT THE SALARY, AND NAME OF ANY EMPLOYEE WITH NAME = SMITH OR LAWLER.

THE NUMBER OF RECORDS TO RETRIEVE IS 269

$7,500	LAWLER
$9,600	SMITH
$10,800	LAWLER
$5,100	LAWLER
$12,000	SMITH

WHO EARNS BETWEEN 20,000 AND $30,000?

In this case "and" calls for a range search. Once again the English rephrasing reflects the interpreted meaning.

PRINT THE NAME OF ANY EMPLOYEE WITH SALARY BETWEEN 20000 THRU 30000.

THE NUMBER OF RECORDS TO RETRIEVE IS 730

SAMUELSON

MELKANOFF

DUYVERMAN

SHURTLIFF

FLETCHER

FOR OHIO AND IOWA EMPLOYEES, PRINT THE NAME, JOB AND SALARY OF ANYONE WHO IS EARNING BETWEEN $3,000 AND $8,000 AND IS MARRIED.

Here "and" is used four times in different ways. Notice how the English rephrasing shows how each was interpreted. The response time for this request is not perceptably longer than for any other request, even in this nearly worst-case of lexical ambiguity.

PRINT THE NAME, JOB, AND SALARY OF ANY EMPLOYEE WITH STATE = OHIO OR IOWA AND SALARY BETWEEN 3000 THRU 8000 AND FAMILY STATUS = MARRIED.

THE NUMBER OF RECORDS TO RETRIEVE IS 209

FORREST	CLAIMS ADJUSTER	$7,500
TELL	CLAIMS TYPIST	$3,010
MIKHAILOV	CLAIMS EXAMINIER	$5,150
REINSTEDT	SECRETARY	$3,800
PEITSCH	BOOKKEEPER	$6,300

The lexical ambiguity of the word "and" is not unique. Any word in the system is allowed to have any number of meanings. The parser determines which meaning is most appropriate in a given instance. Usually this is done, as exemplified here, without requiring user clarification.

Abbreviation

This section demonstrates how much the automatic abbreviation facility aids in making the dialog more natural. In the sample data base the sex field is coded either M or F, and the state field uses the standard two letter abbreviation. The first sentence shows how stilted the dialog would be if users were forced to refer to the data exactly as it appears in the data base. The remaining questions show the effects of defining words like "men", "women" or "New York" to abbreviate to M, F or NY respectively. The net impact of this capability is that data bases can be compressed efficiently without impacting the user's access to the data. In this way the coding scheme is made transparent to the user. In cases where the codes are in common usage and can reduce typing the codes themselves can be defined as legal words in the dictionary.

ARE ANY F PEOPLE IN MA?

> The direct use of encoded data in allowed since it often minimizes typing. However, confusion may also result since the end user would not typically be aware of the entire coding scheme.

IS THERE ANY EMPLOYEE WITH STATE = MASSACHUSETTS AND SEX = FEMALE.

YES

GIVE ME A LIST OF NAMES AND PH^NE NUMBERS OF ALL THE WOMEN IN NY.

> By informing ROBOT of the coding scheme by putting it into its dictionary, end users can refer to the data in a more natural way, without worrying about how things are actually stored. In this case the user chose to have ROBOT find the coding for "women" but give the abbreviation for "New York".

PRINT THE NAME AND PHONE OF ANY EMPLOYEE WITH STATE = NEW YORK AND SEX = FEMALE.

THE NUMBER OF RECORDS TO RETRIEVE IS 690

FRONTERA	547-8803
FARRIS	389-1258
OFER	131-9782
RUBIN	228-1158
BONNER	908-5498

PRINT THE NAME, PHONE, AND FAMILY STATUS OF ALL THE NEW YORK STATE GIRLS.

This example illustrates the case of an ambiguous coding. "New York" can refer either to the city of the state in which case it is abbreviated NY. If the word "state" were not used in this request the system would have required clarification. However, in this case the parser determined from the sentence itself that the state interpretation was intended, and thus no clarification was required.

PRINT THE NAME, PHONE, AND FAMILY STATUS OF ANY EMPLOYEE WITH SEX = FEMALE AND STATE = NEW YORK.

THE NUMBER OF RECORDS TO RETRIEVE IS 690

FRONTERA	547-8803	MARRIED
FARRIS	389-1258	MARRIED
OFER	131-9782	MARRIED
RUBIN	228-1158	MARRIED
BONNER	908-5498	MARRIED

Phrases

A phrase is a group of words that relate to a single concept, such as "Los Angeles" or "area manager". The following questions illustrate how ROBOT determines which words constitute a phrase without requiring the use of delimiters. Virtually all other query facilities would require the use of quotation marks in the examples that follow. This form of "computereze" often confuses naive users since it is not clear to them when they must be used.

WHO ARE THE VICE PRESIDENTS?

In this request the phrase "vice president" must be formed by looking up its singular form in the data base.

PRINT THE NAME OF ANY EMPLOYEE WITH JOB = VICE PRESIDENT.

THE NUMBER OF RECORDS TO RETRIEVE IS 718

TANIMOTO

FLETCHER

STOGNIY

SPARCK JONES

ALEXANDER

WHAT IS THE FAMILY STATUS OF THE AREA MANAGERS THAT LIVE IN NEW YORK?

REQUEST AMBIGUOUS, IS IT:

NUMBER 1

PRINT THE FAMILY STATUS OF ANY EMPLOYEE WITH STATE = NEW YORK AND JOB = AREA MANAGER.

NUMBER 2

PRINT THE FAMILY STATUS OF ANY EMPLOYEE WITH CITY = NEW YORK AND JOB = AREA MANAGER.

PLEASE TYPE THE NUMBER 1 OR THE NUMBER 2.

1.

THE NUMBER OF RECORDS TO RETRIEVE IS 120

MARRIED

MARRIED

DIVORCED

MARRIED

SINGLE

LOS ANGELES AREA MANAGERS?

This request consists of nothing but words that must be formed into phrases.

PRINT THE NAME OF ANY EMPLOYEE WITH JOB = AREA MANGER AND CITY = LOS ANGELES.

THE NUMBER OF RECORDS TO RETRIEVE IS 14

ATHERTON

HOLZBAUR

HERZOG

Spelling Checker

In order to avoid requiring the user to retype entire requests because of simple spelling errors, a spelling checker can be invoked. The spelling checker will not allow words it does not recognize to get past the initial scan. The user can then retype the misspelled word without having to retype the entire request. The impact of this is illustrated in the following questions.

TURN SPELLING CHECKER ON.

This activates the spelling checker.

SPELLING CHECKER IS NOW ON.

WHAT IS THE SALAY OF THE PEOPLE NAMED CHOMSKY?

In this example the word "salary" is purposely misspelled. The system detects this and allows the user a chance to correct it.

I'M NOT FAMILIAR WITH THE WORD "SALAY".

IF MISSPELLED PLEASE CORRECT IT, OTHERWISE TYPE A SYNONYM FOR IT.

SALARY.

PRINT THE SALARY OF ANY EMPLOYEE WITH NAME = CHOMSKY.

THE NUMBER OF RECORDS TO RETRIEVE IS 114

$3,900

$3,900

$36,000

$8,800

$5,500

Fragments

The following sentence fragments contain enough information for ROBOT to piece together a complete query. The method for loosening the syntax -equirements is discussed in the text. Fragments allow users to choose from the tersest possible expressions of their questions.

SINGLE IN CHICAGO.

This request is phrased about as concisely as possible to convey the desired meaning. English need not be a verbose form of communication.

PRINT THE NAME OF ANY EMPLOYEE WITH CITY = CHICAGO AND FAMILY STATUS = SINGLE.

THE NUMBER OF RECORDS TO RETRIEVE IS 61

MIKHAILOV

REINSTEDT

GENTLEMAN

MOOERS

OLLE

<u>THEIR</u> <u>SALARIES</u>.

Here again we see how concise English can be, in this case through the use of a pronoun. Notice how ROBOT knew to print the names again even though they were not explicitly requested. The system is geared to giving the user what he wants, instead of exactly what he asks for.

PRINT THE NAME AND SALARY OF ANY EMPLOYEE WITH CITY = CHICAGO AND FAMILY STATUS = SINGLE.

THE NUMBER OF RECORDS TO RETRIEVE IS 61

MIKHAILOV	$5,150
REINSTEDT	$3,800
GENTLEMAN	$6,300
MOOERS	$3,800
OLLE	$9,300

<u>NAME</u> <u>JOB</u> <u>PHONE</u> <u>OF</u> <u>THOSE</u> <u>MEN</u>.

This is an extremely concise form for such a complex query. Notice the length of the canonical English reformulation.

PRINT THE NAME, SALARY, JOB, AND PHONE OF ANY EMPLOYEE WITH SEX = MALE AND CITY = CHICAGO AND FAMILY STATUS = SINGLE.

THE NUMBER OF RECORDS TO RETRIEVE IS 3

MIKHAILOV	$5,150	SECRETARY	653-4677
REINSTEDT	$3,800	BOOKKEEPER	116-2971
REINSTEDT	$3,800	BOOKKEEPER	116-2971

Processes

ROBOT hosts a generalized interface to data processing routines, so that the data retrieved by the user's request can be processed in an arbitrary way. The interface supports programs written in PL/I, COBOL, FORTRAN, or ASSEMBLER. The following sentences illustrate a few of the builtin processing routines.

GIVE ME A SALARY HISTOGRAM FOR THE PEOPLE IN NH AND MO.

```
PRINT A HISTOGRAM OF SALARY SORTED BY SALARY OF ANY EMPLOYEE WITH
STATE = NEW HAMPSHIRE OR MISSOURI.
THE NUMBER OF RECORDS TO RETRIEVE IS   76
 SALARY
 $2,700   29 *****************************
 $3,010   13 *************
 $3,080   13 *************
 $3,100   14 **************
 $3,200    7 *******
```

WHAT IS THE PERCENTAGE BREAKDOWN OF SALARY BY SEX FOR THOSE PEOPLE.

```
PRINT A PERCENTAGE BREAKDOWN OF SEX AND SALARY SORTED BY SALARY
FOR ANY EMPLOYEE WITH STATE=NEW HAMPSHIRE OR MISSOURI.

THE NUMBER OF RECORDS TO RETRIEVE IS   76
SEX        SALARY   PERCENT
FEMALE  $105,840     47.40
MALE    $117,430     52.60
TOTAL   $223,270    100.00
```

BROKEN DOWN BY STATE AND CITY, PRINT A SALARY REPORT FOR THE SINGLE NEW HAMPSHIRE AND CONNECTICUT PEOPLE, INCLUDING THEIR NAME AND AGE.

This request interfaces to a report generation process that produces a logically indented report with subtotals on all numeric items.

PRINT A REPORT OF STATE, CITY, SALARY, NAME, AND AGE SORTED BY STATE, F AND CITY OF ANY EMPLOYEE WITH STATE = NEW HAMPSHIRE OR CONNECTICUT AND FAMILY STATUS = SINGLE.

STATE	CITY	SALARY	NAME	AGE
CT	STAMFORD	$48,000	VAN CUYN	69
		$3,500	CLEVERDON	61
		$3,010	SALTON	57
		$3,100	ROMERIO	47
		$6,000	MORRISON	57
		$3,200	FREEMAN	41
CT	STAMFORD	$66,810 *		332 *
CT	TOTAL	$66,810 *		332 *
NH	HANOVER	$2,700	CHERNYI	69
		$24,000	SAMUELSON	35
		$4,200	RUSSEL	66
		$5,500	SCHRIBER	38
NH	TOTAL	$36,400 *		208 *
GRAND	TOTAL	$103,210 *		540 *

WHAT JOBS ARE THERE IN NH?

This request will print the job of every New Hampshire employee.

PRINT THE JOB OF ANY EMPLOYEE WITH STATE = NH.

THE NUMBER OF RECORDS TO RETRIEVE IS 232

RECEPTIONIST

RECEPTIONIST

SECRETARY-TREASURER

CLERK TYPIST

SECRETARY

PRINT A UNIQUE LIST OF THOSE JOBS.

This request will print each of the jobs only once.

PRINT EACH UNIQUE JOB SORTED BY JOB OF ANY EMPLOYEE WITH STATE = NH.

THE NUMBER OF RECORDS TO RETRIEVE IS 232

ACTUARY

ADMIN ASSISTANT

AREA MANAGER

BOOKKEEPER

CLAIMS ADJUSTER

Pronoun Reference

The use of pronouns has already been demonstrated in several previous sentences. In this section a more complex discourse context is created to further illustrate the pronoun capabilities of ROBOT. In each case below ROBOT must determine exactly what each pronoun refers to. The dialog builds up several possibilities but ROBOT only asks the user for clarification when absolutely necessary.

WHO ARE THE SECRETARIES?

This question establishes the context for the remaining discourse.

PRINT THE NAME OF ANY EMPLOYEE WITH JOB = SECRETARY.

THE NUMBER OF RECORDS TO RETRIEVE IS 3523

BENNY

CHOMSKY

SPIEGEL

RAEBIGER

WALLACE

WHICH OF THEM LIVE IN CHICAGO?

The pronoun "them" in this question clearly refers to the secretaries in the previous question.

PRINT THE NAME OF ANY EMPLOYEE WITH CITY = CHICAGO AND JOB = SECRETARY.

THE NUMBER OF RECORDS TO RETRIEVE IS 30

REINSTEDT

LAWLER

MOOERS

SORIANO

LORIE

WHICH OF THEM LIVE IN DETROIT?

The referent of "them" in this case is more difficult. It does not refer to the Chicago secretaries above, but to the group of all secretaries. ROBOT figures this out without requiring clarification from the user.

PRINT THE NAME OF ANY EMPLOYEE WITH CITY = DETROIT AND JOB = SECRETARY.

THE NUMBER OF RECORDS TO RETRIEVE IS 32

KUNEY

ZINN

STERLING

ALLEN

SMITH

<u>WHICH ONES ARE NOT MARRIED?</u>

The pronoun "ones" in this case is truly ambiguous since it could refer to any of the contexts established above. ROBOT detects this ambiguity and asks the user for clarification by listing the choices that it determined were reasonable.

REQUEST AMBIGUOUS: IS IT

NUMBER 1

PRINT THE NAME OF ANY EMPLOYEE WITH FAMILY STATUS NOT MARRIED AND JOB = SECRETARY.

NUMBER 2

PRINT THE NAME OF ANY EMPLOYEE WITH FAMILY STATUS NOT MARRIED AND CITY = DETROIT AND JOB = SECRETARY.

PLEASE TYPE THE NUMBER 1 OR THE NUMBER 2.

<u>2</u>.

THEN NUMBER OF RECORDS TO RETRIEVE IS 3.

ZINN

ALLEN

SMITH

Basic Structure

The ROBOT system is an example of a transform centered design (Yourdon[3]). The structure chart below indicates the high level modular structure of the system. The high-level input is provided by the scanner. The transform center, consisting of the PARSER, WEED, and DECIDE modules, generates the high level representation of the intended meaning. This is passed to the RETRIEVE module for generating the desired output.

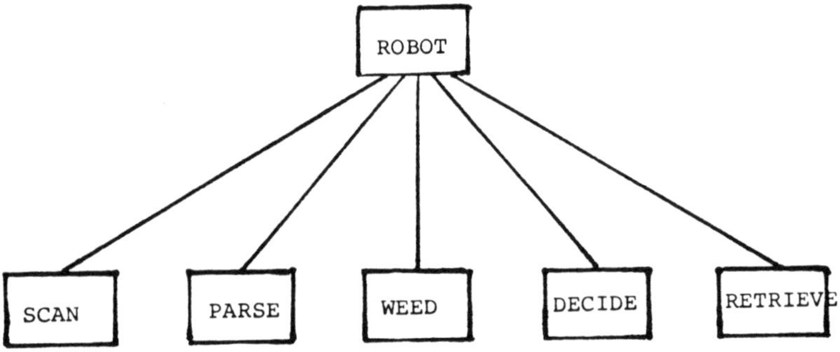

The SCAN module changes the card image input into a list structure of the words of the sentence. This abstraction of the input is accomplished by standard techniques for stripping tokens. The only complicating factor is that many "words" in the data base are really phrases (e.g., they contain blanks, such as "New York"). We wish the scanner to treat these as a single word, but want to avoid forcing the user to use quotes as delimiters. Resolving this issue requires interacting with the DBMS. We will discuss this issue in more detail later.

The PARSE module is an augmented transition network (ATN) that is fully recursive with automatic backup at all levels. As such it always generates every possible parse of the sentence. All such parses, which we will refer to as interpretations, are given a preference rating based on how well the constituents of the sentence fit together. In order to allow the parser to generate this complete list of possible interpretations in a reasonable period of time we disallow any use of the DBMS during the parsing process. Instead we employ the philosophy of letting the parser run, providing a fast syntactic analysis, and ask questions about semantics later. In this way we avoid asking questions needed by interpretations that will eventually fail syntactically anyway. Also, since each question asked of the DBMS later will be from an already completed parse, we can generate more complete and meaningful questions. The only disadvantage of this philosophy is that in the case where one question is common to several interpretations, we would have to ask that same question several times. We solve this problem by distributing the answers to all such questions among the various interpretations. Thus the information gained by asking one question is automatically dispersed to all other interpretations requiring it. Given this philosophy it is best to think of the parser as generating a potentially long list of interpretations, many of which are incomplete or semantically inaccurate, but all of which are syntactically acceptable.

The WEED module has the responsibility for isolating the semantically valid interpretations from the rest. This is done by interacting with the DBMS to fill in all the holes of each interpretation. Interpretations with semantic discrepancies are deleted. The result is a list of fully specified interpretations all of which could make sense with respect to the data base. All of interpretations with preference rating close to the maximum preference interpretation are retained.

The DECIDE module takes this list of plausible interpretations and has the responsibility for choosing the one intended by the user. This selection is made by consulting the DBMS as to the likelihood of a given question with respect to the current state of the data base. In extreme cases where no clear choice exists, as in the case of a truly ambiguous question, the user is asked to choose which of the interpretations he meant.

Once the intended interpretation is found it is passed to the RETRIEVE routine where the final answers that satisfy the user's original question are pulled from the data base. This information is given to the PROCESS module to format or compute the final answers given to the user.

Dictionary

In order for the scanner to recognize words and for the parser to make use of them, an in-core dictionary is employed. Since the DBMS can look up the contents of its indexed fields, there is no need to include the words of the data base in the dictionary (Harris[4]). Thus the dictionary consists mostly of linguistic terms, "who", "what", "is", "are", etc., and meta-terms for the data base such as file and field names.

The structure of the dictionary is the same as in our earlier works (Harris[5]), based on the notion of concepts. The ROBOT system is built with a limited number of basic concepts. Therefore, to define a word we merely associate it with a set of concepts. Thus, the dictionary consists of a symbol table and an associated concept list for each word. We will see that this very simple mechanism provides some very elegant solutions to some of the problems we will be discussing.

Lexical Disambiguation

The dictionary represents the multiple meanings of a given word by associating the word to more than one concept. We wish to manifest this lexical ambiguity by having the parser generate a different interpretation for each meaning of the word, assuming of course, that each of the meanings is syntactically appropriate.

This is accomplished by the ATN parser simply iteratively trying all the meanings of each word when a given arc in the network is taken. Since the ATN interpreter is fully recursive this is easily accomplished.

During the parsing process no attempt, other than syntactic checks, is made to select the appropriate meaning of an individual word. The full set of interpretations is automatically generated and the question of choosing the right meaning of a word is postponed until later when each completed interpretation can be examined.

Abbreviation

One of the goals of accessing a data base via natural language is to minimize, if not eliminate, the need for the user to know exactly the structure and form of the data. One required facility in achieving this end is the automatic abbreviation of words to their form in the data base. Consider the question "Who lives in New Hampshire?" The search term "New Hampshire" might actually appear in the data base in the standard two digit abbreviation "NH". If the natural language system is to process such a query without burdening the user with this fact it must have some way of automatically translating the search term.

Normally this translation process converts the user's long form to an abbreviated form that appears in the data base.

However, the reverse operation may also apply. For example, the user may type "VP" when referring to "Vice President" in the data base.

The word to concept mapping mechanism we developed for representing lexical ambiguity also provides this abbreviation mechanism. For each such abbreviation a concept is created that maps to the actual character string that appears in the data base. This being done we can create as many "synonyms" as desired for this concept. We need only remember to communicate with the DBMS using the defining string no matter what representation the user employs.

The impact of the automatic abbreviation facility is actually quite profound, since it introduces a formal mapping between the language of the user and the language of the DBMS. This means that there is no particular reason to store the data in a human oriented fashion, since the human orientation can be provided by the abbreviation facility. This allows the actual format of the data to be defined in the most efficient form possible, without impacting the user's view of the data. A few bytes of storage in the dictionary used to define this mapping can save several megabytes in the actual data base, since the field values can be coded or otherwise abbreviated.

The use of phrases within data bases causes a very special problem in natural language processing. We wish to avoid the situation where the user must employ computereze to specify some queries. For example "Who works as a secretary?" might be all right, but "Who works as an executive secretary?" might require the use of single quotes around "executive secretary".

The problem arises because the phrase "executive secretary" is a single data item with respect to the DBMS. That is, the DBMS can talk about the phrase "executive secretary", but possibly not the word "executive" itself. In contrast, the natural language system would view this phrase as a sequence of individual words, with some structure in its own right. Our approach resolves this conflict by attempting to detect the phrase as such as early as possible (in the SCAN module) and treating it logically, as a single data item, just as the DBMS does.

The problems that may arise here, are mainly knowing when the user has entered a phrase, and the exact extent of the phrase. These answers are found either in the dictionary or the indices of the data base. The dictionary may store some specific phrases used in the data base. Failing the recognition of any phrase in the dictionary, an attempt is made to find a phrase within any sequence of unrecognized single words. The DBMS helps tremendously in quickly responding to questions like "Does this character string appear anywhere in the data base?" In this way most phrases can be recognized without imposing the use of quotes on the user. This capability contributes significantly to the freeness of expression allowed by the system.

Spelling Checker

Given this ability to query the DBMS about its use of individual words or phrases, it is possible to view the entire data base as an extension of the dictionary. Each word entered by the user must be found either in the dictionary or the data base or in a phrase that itself appears in either the dictionary or the data base. Words that cannot be so located are considered in error since the system has no knowledge about them and cannot deal with them. In this way a spelling checker is implemented, which allows the user to retype or replace unrecognized words, without requiring him to retype the entire question.

Structural Ambiguity

Structural ambiguity arises when the words of a sentence, even without lexical variation, can be parsed by the ATN network in more than one way. Since the ATN parser is fully recursive with backup, all of the structural interpretations will be investigated. The process is handled in a fashion identical to that of lexical ambiguity. That is, any ambiguity, whether lexical or structural, manifests itself in the same way, namely by the parser generating multiple interpretations. The WEED routine will eliminate some, and the DECIDE routine eventually choose the intended interpretation.

It is worth contrasting one point with other natural language systems. Since all parses of the sentence are going to be attempted, there is no particular benefit in attempting to impose any order to the ATN network. No additional credence is given to parses that follow along ordinary paths as opposed to the more obscure parses. The preference rating are based on the coherence of the interpretation being built, not on the particular arcs taken to build the structure.

One additional form of ambiguity arises from search terms of the questions. For example, in the question "Tell me about Green", under the conditions that green does not appear in the dictionary, but does appear in 2 places in the data base, i.e., the name of someone and the color of something. Since green is not in the dictionary we can't determine its syntactic category, but by querying the data base we can determine its semantic use in the data base. Since the word relates to two semantic senses its use in the question is ambigious.

In cases such as these only one interpretation is generated, since the structure of the semantic interpretations is independent of the usage of this word. The search term is actually only a parameter of the semantic interpretation, which can be filled in later. Of course, other information in the query, or the discourse may be brought to bear on finally making the choice of the sense of "green". In the exact example given it is likely that any such additional context would be insufficient to eliminate either meaning, so the user would have to be asked which sense of green he had intended. These are the two ways in which all ambiguities are resolved.

Fragments

In early sessions with naive users one fact became apparent. Users don't always speak in full sentences. In fact as users became more and more familiar with the system their use of full sentences deminished as they tried to achieve some level of discourse that minimized typing yet achieved the desired results.

Since it was determined that the goal of this project was not to teach people English grammar, but to act as a useful tool for the user, the need to deal with fragments became clear. At first, attempts were made to loosen the grammar by adding additional arcs to the ATN. However, doing this severely degraded the performance of the system on grammatically correct sentences, since there were so many additional parse paths available. For this reason a few key syntactic bottlenecks were left in the grammar to restrict the number of valid parses of full sentences.

For example, the use of conjuctions is taxing on the ATN so that their elision was not allowed. Thus the query "Give me the name, city, sex and salary of all blonde, blue eyed secretaries." was okay but not "Give me the name city sex salary of all blonde, blue eyed secretaries."

Unfortunately people began tripping up continually on this rather minimal syntax requirement. As people began to use fragments more and more, the appearance of small syntactic annoyances became more and more noticeable.

For this reason a new approach had to be formulated that would allow for arbitrary semantically correct fragments but without degrading the overall efficiency on full sentences. The choice was made that two ATNs were necessary, one for full sentences, and one for fragments. The two are used in sequence unless the full sentence ATN provides a parse. Thus no overhead at all is imposed on full sentences and since fragments often fail the full ATN rather quickly, little additional cost is incurred when processing fragments. The real cost of this approach arises when the sentence is syntactically incorrect in the first place. In these cases we will put it through both ATNs. However, if one views the fragment ATN as a last ditch effort to parse something known to be difficult to understand, it is just these sentences on which we want to try harder.

This two parse approach has worked out quite satisfactorily in terms of the trade off of efficiency for user convenience. It is clear from looking at logs of user sessions that the fragment capability is heavily used. Furthermore, the fragment capability satisfies the people who believe that natural language is too verbose for a query facility. They feel that formal query languages will always be preferred for this reason. Actually given the fragment capability and the powerful knowledge structure use of the data base itself, along with the expectations and defaults that must be included in a natural language system for other reasons, I believe that any query can be expressed more succinctly in "natural language". For example the question "Give me the names of all the people working as secretaries that live in New York." could be expressed as succinctly as "New York secretaries". Any formal query language will require at least these words, since they are search terms, as well as a few keywords and computereze such as equal signs and quote marks, e.g., "FIND: EMPLOYEE JOB='SECRETARY' AND CITY='NEW YORK'".

Print Determination

The semantics of data base retrieval require ascertaining which entity and what attributes of those entities will provide the the desired answer to the user's questions. In this section we discuss how the appropriate attribute fields are chosen that will provide the answer the user's questions.

We partition all questions into 4 types. These four categories are: explicit, implicit, everything, and nothing.

Explicit sentences are the easiest to deal with since they tell exactly what to retrieve. For example: "Print the name, job and salary of all Vice Presidents." Explicit references may be specified in many ways in English. For example, in a sentence such as "What does Smith earn?" it appears in the predicate. The parser extracts the print specification in all such explicitly stated cases.

A queston is said to implicitly state the print specification when it has a WH word qualifier but not an explicit list of fields to print. For example "Who works as a secretary", "Where are they?", or "Why are they there?". Hopefully, the answers to such questions must be in the data base and we must determine what fields to retrieve to provide these answers. As a general solution to this problem, for each file and for each WH word we define a list of fields that can answer that type of question.

For example "who" questions might imply the retrieval of the name field, "where" questions the city and state fields and so on. In some cases the answer to a given type of question may not be contained within the file. The "why" question above would be of that type unless some sort of reason field existed in the file. These implicit print specifications are defined when ROBOT is first applied to a file.

The third class of questions, the "everything" class, are those questions that request the printing of all the attributes of an entity, such as "Tell me everything about people earning $12,000 or more." Such requests can come about in other ways. For example "Who is Smith" should generate more of an answer than his name, which would be retrieved if we used the implicit print specification for "who" without thinking. In cases like this where the search term is an element of the print specification, we print everything about the entities.

But is "everything" to be taken literally? Many real files contain over a hundred fields, many of which are cryptically coded. To print all of these in an on line mode is probably not what the user really wanted. For this reason "everything" is given some possibly limited definition of what fields should be printed in these cases.

Finally, there are questions that contain no print specification, the "nothing" class. For example, "Print the area managers in California." tells nothing about what fields are to be printed. We must have some indication as to what fields will be most meaningful to the user in response to such questions. This determination is made just once when ROBOT is first applied to the file.

It may seem that such static associations are risky since we may not retrieve exactly what the user wants. However, our experience has shown that it is easy to give a list of fields that will answer almost all "who" questions from a given file. These lists are usually made generous since the printing of an extra field or two will not bother most users. But even in the cases where we miss completely, the user need only respond with "Print their ..." to retrieve the fields he wishes. With pronoun reference allowed within the discourse, the burden added upon the user in cases where the correct fields are not printed, is slight indeed.

Processes

Another aspect of data base query that our early user sessions detected was the need for more than pure retrieval. That is, they need to have the retrieved data processed in some way. This may range from numeric functions applied to the data, such as minimum, maximum, or summation, to formating the output into reports.

To provide for this capability required extensions throughout the system. The syntax had to be capable of allowing the specification of how the data is to be processed. The semantics had to be extended to cope with what was meant, and of course the actual programs had to be provided to do all the processing.

One nice aspect of this is that the data processing routines could be added external to the natural language system itself so that they could be added at any time with only dictionary changes to tell the parser about the process name. The parser has the duty of determining the relationship between the process routine name and the fields to be retrieved. Once the scoping of process routines is determined the data can be eventually retrieved,and the process applied to the appropriate data.

In essence this facility puts in the hands of the application programmer the ability to hook up any data processing program without requiring any knowledge of the inside of the parser. In this way users can activate a wide range of programs using natural language.

Pronoun Reference

The use of pronouns in a natural language dialog provides one of the most useful mechanisms for making use of the discourse to minimize the number of words required to convey an idea. As such, the use of pronouns in a data base query dialog is of critical importance in making the dialog flow easily and naturally.

The ROBOT system maintains a separate storage area in which the semantic structures of past queries are kept. Parts of these structures are eligible referents for pronouns that appear in the dialog. In this way the context of the dialog is maintained, and biases the interpretation of future sentences. Once the proper referent is determined, the relevant substructure is actually copied into the interpretation being built for the current sentence. The basic difficulties that occur in this regard are determining what queries could possibly contribute to the context of the current question, and of course, which specific substructure of the overall context is actually being referred to by a particular pronoun.

The first problem is resolved by keeping all queries that contributed to the context of the previous question. In some cases this could include questions from several queries back in the dialog, if they were recently referred to.

The second problem is resolved in the classic automatic backup approach. A separate interpretation is generated for each possible pronoun referent. No attempt is made to restrict the choices when the pronoun is first encountered. Rather, we choose to wait until the sentence is fully parsed to employ our standard heuristics of reasonableness within the current state of the discourse and the data base. This approach is taken because the unparsed part of the sentence will often impact the viability of a particular referent. In these cases it is better to evaluate a particular choice after the entire sentence has been parsed, rather that attempting to do so with incomplete information.

The sample dialog illustrated several uses of pronouns, including a case where there were two viable pronoun referents. In this case the two interpretations that were generated both survived and eventually required an interaction with the user to determine exactly what was meant. This disambiguation dialog is the same mechanism used for lexical or structural ambiguity. In fact, once the interpretations are generated the source of the ambiguity is lost, only its effects remain. In this sense pronoun reference ambiguity is just another kind of semantic ambiguity that is handled in a uniform manner within the system.

Conclusion

We have discussed how the ROBOT system deals with many of the problems encountered in natural language data base query. In particular we have focused on the aspects of data base query that many earlier natural language systems have not addressed. The result is a high performance natural language interface capable of working with the existing technology of DBMS. This marriage of these two very important technologies promises a great future for man-machine communications.

References

1. Winograd, T., Understanding Natural Language, Academic Press

2. Woods, W.A. et al, "The Lunar Sciences Natural Language Information System", Bolt Beranek and Newman Report 2378, June 1972

3. Yourdon, E., Constantine, L.L., Structured Design, Yourdon Press

4. Harris, L.R., "Using the Data Base Itself as a Semantic Compenent to Aid in the Parsing of Natural Language Data Base Queries", Technical Report 78-1, Mathematics Dept, Dartmouth College

5. Harris, L.R., "A Model for Adaptive Problem Solving Applied to Natural Language Acquisition", Technical Report 72-133, Cornell University

6. Harris, L.R., "User Oriented data base query with the ROBOT natural language query system", International Journal of Man-Machine Studies(1977) 9,pp 697-713

7. Waltz, D.L., "An English Language Question Answering System for a Large Relational Data Base", Communications of the ACM, July 1978, vol 21, no 7, p 526

8. Hendrix, G. et al, "Developing a natural language interface to complex data", Proceedings of the Third International Conference on Very Large Data Bases, Oct 1977

THE HEX-SYSTEM:
EXPERIENCES WITH AN EXPECTATION-BASED PARSER

by
G. Goerz

University Erlangen-Nuernberg
RRZE
Martensstr. 1
D-8520 Erlangen

1 Introduction

Within the framework of computer-aided instruction (CAI) we were faced with the problem of natural-language communication with a machine. We thought that this would be the most general approach to the task of analyzing "free" inputs of the user to overcome the rigid restrictions on the user's possibilities of interaction within most CAI-Systems. The work presented in this article was done in 1976 and 1977 and shows our first try to become acquainted with some conceptions of processing natural language within the "Artificial Intelligence Paradigm" (Wilks (1977)). Our main interest was to understand specific techniques by means of realizing an example.

As the domain we chose the game "Hex". The system allows the user to formulate propositions, questions and instructions referring to specific situations during the course of a game which are translated to disambiguated conceptual structures by means of a parser which in turn are executed over a data base by an interpreter.

The programme described in this article represents the first complete step of the project. Because a strategy module has not yet been implemented (see section 6.2) the system cannot be looked at as a game playing one; from this point of view its contributions are rather trivial. Nevertheless we decided to choose this domain because its semantics is definite, the administration of the data base is not too simple and the strategy is very interesting from the viewpoint of game theory.

Schank's "conceptual information processing" approach (Schank (1975)) seemed promising to us to realize a system for understanding natural language - even when restricted to a well-defined small subset of everyday German. It is based on a set of basic elements of a conceptual representation of sentences: "The elements must be defined on a level deeper than a semantic level that relates words to each other. We call this the <u>conceptual level</u>. The conceptual level is really not the same thing as the semantic level, since it has nothing whatsoever to do with a particular language."

Thanks go to A. v. Loehneysen and R. Mueller who did most of the implementation work and to Prof. G. Nees for his cooperation in this project.

2 System Overview

The Hex-system's capabilities include executing instructions in the model world, i.e. to transform one situation of the game to another by putting pieces on the dress-board, answering questions about situations and checking propositions. We planned to extend it to an active partner which is able to play real games and to answer questions after each move about its reasons to do so.

Within the system three levels of representation of information can be distinguished:

- surface structure (representation by a string)

- conceptual structure (interpretable expressions of an 'intermediate language')

- data-base representation (MICRO-PLANNER assertions and theorems)

Fig. 1 shows an overview of the system's structure.

The scanner analyzes the input sentences. It's present capabilities do not include morphological analysis; different word forms are explicitly included in the dictionary. At the present time the dictionary is fairly small (about 100 words); for future extensions morphological analysis should be considered.

Our parser is a modified version of an analyzer designed by C. Riesbeck (1975). It generates conceptual structures in a fairly simple 'intermediate language' from the input sentences.

The interpreter analyzes these conceptual structures, generates MICRO-PLANNER-programs from it and controls their execution over a database. Besides some geometrical properties of the board the database contains the actual game situation in the form of

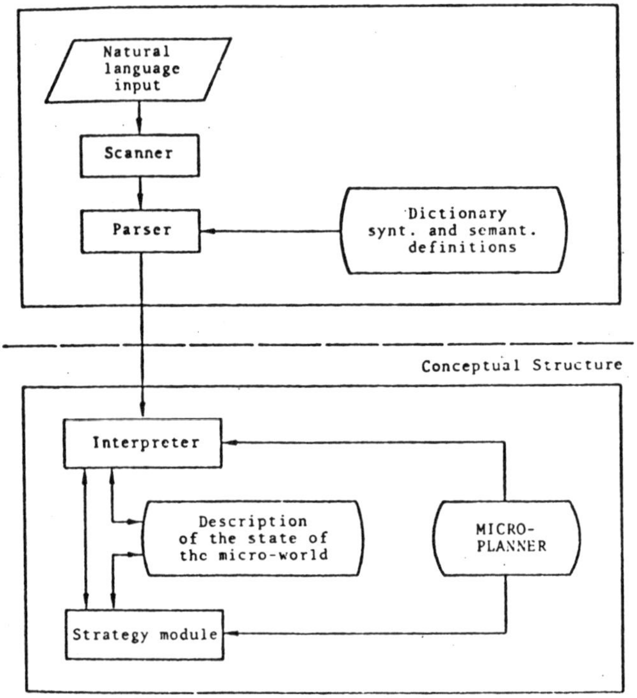

Fig.1: The Hex-System

assertions and some complex sentences, which are universally quantified expressions ("theorems") about connectivity relations.

The strategy module which is necessary for the system to be able to play games has not yet been implemented. Only a general tree-pruning procedure is available; a static evaluation function for game situations has not yet been developped.

According to Wilks' (1977) classification the Hex system is a 'first generation language understanding system' with a slight touch of systems of the 'second generation' as far as the analyzer is concerned. Indeed the analyzer is able to manipulate complex linguistic objects, but the system as a whole cannot guide mixed initiative dialogues. The semantic structures are not used to "attempt to specify in advance what is going to be said, and how the world encountered is going to be structured" in future dialogue steps. This criterion applies in a very restricted sense only to the parser when analyzing a single sentence.

From the language processing point of view the system is operable. It has been completely implemented in MACLISP.

In the following sections after a description of the model world the components of the system are presented together with some experiences we made. Finally there are some considerations on extending systems of this kind to larger domains of discorse.

3 The Model-World: Hex

The game Hex was chosen as the domain of our system because it offers interesting problems from the point of view of geometry as well as of game theory. Until now only a classical proof of the existence of a winning strategy for the player who has the first move is known. But only a constructive proof could show the winning strategy explicitly (Gardner (1968), Pierce (1969)).

3.1 The Dress-Board

The Hex-board is a section of the plane, parquetted with regular hexagons. Usually a parallelogram-shaped area containing 11x11 hexagons is taken; this is also the commercial version of the game.

In a plane with hexagonal "squares" every square has six immediately adjacent neighbours, i.e. squares, which have a common edge. To identify the neighbours exactly the six directions in which a neighbour square can be found are numbered (see Nees (1973)). Fig. 2 shows the shows the definition of the directions of the square marked "x". The coordinate system shown in this figure is the one which will be referred to in the following sections.

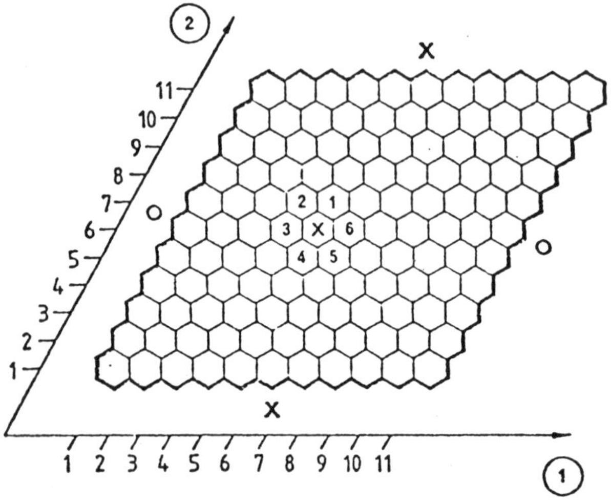

Fig.2: The six directions of a square

For strategical considerations a larger environment of a square than the immediate neighbourhood is needed. Therefore we introduce the degree of connectivity. Fig. 3 shows the neighbours of the square marked "x" of degrees 1, 2, and 3. Neighbourhood-relations of a higher degree will not be considered in the sequel. (Another possibility to define the degree of connectivity can be found in Golay (1969). He considers the distances between the centres of the squares. If the distance between the centres of two adjacent squares is taken as the unit, neighbours of second degree have the distance 3 and neighbours or third degree the distance 2.)

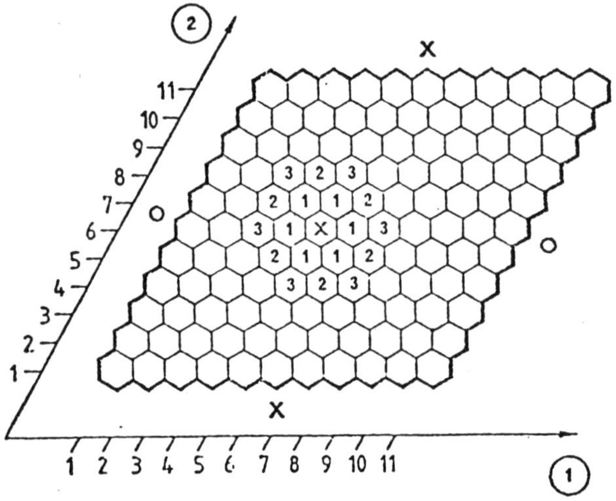

Fig.3: Neighbour squares with different degrees of connectivity

The notions of "neighbour", "direction" and "degree of connectivity" are introduced as fundamental notions at the conceptual level.

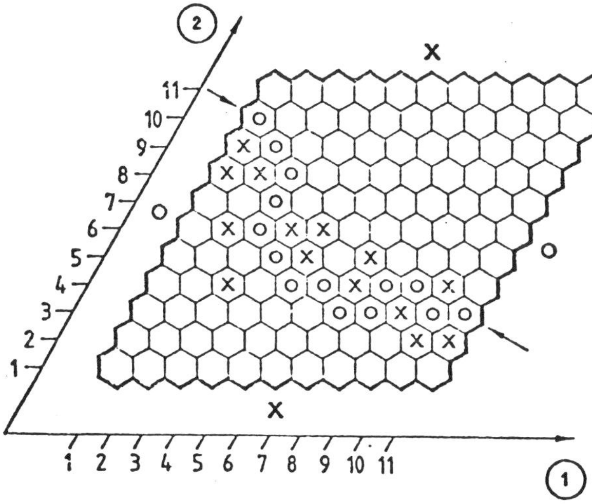

Fig.4: A winning position for White

3.2 Rules of the Game

At the beginning the two players decide which of them will take the white and which the black pieces. Usually "White" starts the game. White pieces will be symbolized by "o", black ones by "x".

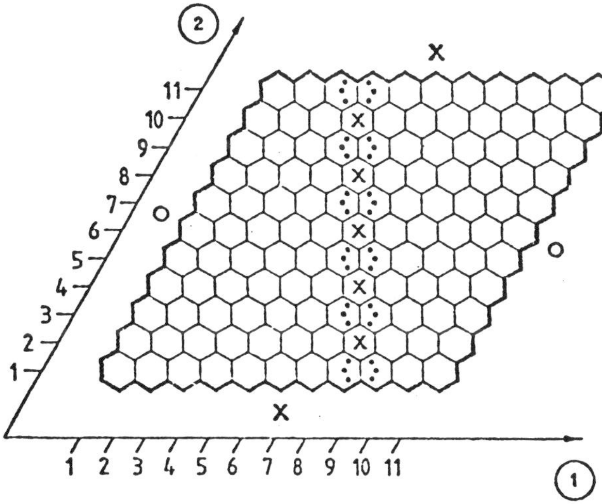

Fig.5: A chain of second degree

The goal of each player is to build a closed chain of pieces between the opposite borders marked with his color. The pieces are put on arbitrarily chosen squares by turns until one of the players has reached a closed chain.

In the game of Hex there is no draw. One player can block the other one completely only by constructing a closed chain. An example of a winning situation is shown in fig. 4.

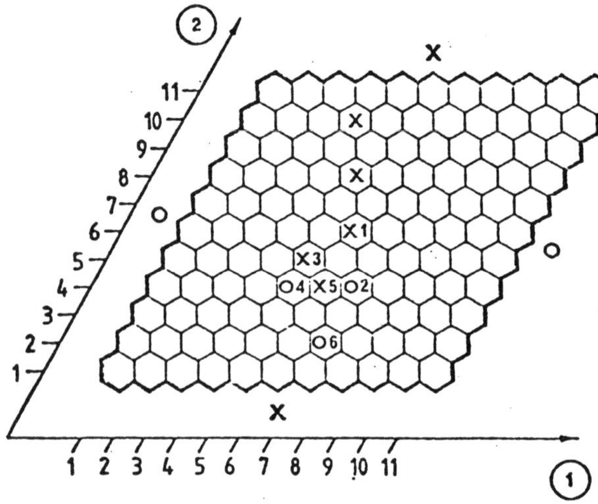

Fig.6: A defensive position of White

Chains of second degree , i.e. chains, the neighbours of which have a degree of connectivity of 2, are important for strategical considerations; fig. 5 shows such a chain. Between two neighbouring pieces of second degree there are two possibilities to place a piece in order to construct a closed chain. These pieces must be put on the board only if the opponent seizes one of the two alternative squares.

One possibility of defence is demonstrated in fig. 6. The figures attached to the pieces give the order of the moves. The white pieces there have the degree of connectivity 3. (See Gardner (1968), Pierce (1969) and Taernlund (1974)).

Important notions to be represented at the conceptual level are here "piece" and "chain", and, as an important property of them, their "color". Squares are identified by their coordinates.

4 The Parser

4.1 Expectation-Based Parsing

The parsing algorithm implemented by our group relies heavily on an implementation by Riesbeck which in turn is strongly influenced by Schank's hypothesis of understandig language by expectations. By "understanding" here we only mean a translation - justified by a problem-analysis - from a surface structure into a conceptual structure, which in turn can be interpreted by further processes. By explicitly defining a definite domain of discourse we do not face the problematic encounter to introduce a generally valid system of semantic primitives (Schank's "primitive acts", which are not founded in a theory of action). The primitive functions defined in our system have intentionally been chosen as domain-dependent. Taking just this parser had mainly pragmatic reasons, because we are sceptic about the hypothesis of understanding it is based on.

Our main interest was to investigate specific techniques of analyzing natural language input, some of which are present also in different approaches to parsing. From the technical point of view Woods' ATN parser has some similarities (e.g. depth-first search) with the one described here.

Riesbeck (1975) describes the properties of his parser as follows:

"(1) Its object is not to parse a sentence into a syntactic structure, be it surface or deep. Its goal is to discover the meaning of the sentence, in the context in which it occurred.

(2) Even as a tool, syntax plays a small role in the analysis. Of greater importance to the program are the partial meanings that are found during the processing. These provide much of the information necessary for continuing the analysis.

(3) There is not a clear division between linguistic and non-linguistic knowledge. Beliefs and inferences play an important part in the determination of meaning. The representation used allows the analyzer to interact with a memory model. ..."

In analyzing German sentences syntax plays a much more important role. For this reason we had to introduce some modifications which will be described in a later paragraph. The memory model quoted is in our case a database-system with inferencing capabilities.

The main principle of the parser is its control by expectations. Riesbeck (1975):

> "Expectations are the basic mechanisms of comprehension used by the program. An expectation is a description of a situation that is recognized as likely to become true in the next future. Further, associated with any expectation is a set of actions to perform, actions that are appropriate in the expected situation. The importance of an expectation is not just that it prepares a set of actions for use if needed, but also that it narrows how future situations are perceived. If certain features are enough to satisfy an expectation, its actions are performed. In language processing, for example, expectations are used to predict what concepts and words may occur and thus ambiguity is not normally noticed. Of concern are those expectations that are closely related to language comprehension, what their sources and effects are."

Expectations can be obtained:

(1) From single words and their grammatical properties: so, e.g., after an indefinite article a noun phrase is expected.

(2) From the concepts associated with the particular words: so, e.g., a primitive function tries to fill "slots" in their descriptions.

(3) From the "configuration" (conceptual structure) constructed so far: so, e.g., transformations of this structure may be necessary.

(4) From the general context and the objects which is talked about.

Expectations can be made:

(1) On the meaning of words which could poosibly found as the next ones.

(2) On the place of a concept within a configuration: so, e.g., primitive functions wait for concepts with specific properties for their slots.

(3) On the relations between concepts: e.g. in the case of relative clauses.

To each expectation there are attached specific actions, e.g.:

(1) Realization of expectations: construction of conceptual structures.

(2) Attaching new expectations and changing already existing ones.

(3) Modification of already existing actions which are waiting for execution.

4.2 The 'Intermediate Language' for Formulating Conceptual Structures

The conceptual structures are formulated in an 'intermediate language' in which all words relevant to the model-world are defined.

P.J. Hayes has called such a language a "schema"; a schema can be considered as a formal language the sentences of which we call configurations (after Krause (1975)). The 'intermediate language' is constituted by primitive functions which are defined by the construction of the model, and descriptions of objects which can instantiate the variables of the primitive functions. Obviously there is some similarity to frames (Minsky (1975)).

A necessary condition is that every natural language sentence - restricted to the model-world - can be translated into a configuration. Sentences with the same meaning should be mapped into the same configuration. Ambiguous sentences should be associated to more than one configuration according to their meanings, unique sentences to exactly one configuration. ("Small" differences in meaning should be reflected by small differences in the configurations.)

Furthermore a configuration should contain the whole information of its corresponding sentence, also the one implicitly contained in it (cf. Schank (1975), p.12). In this case the interpreter module can operate upon the configuration alone. Access to past events is made easier: Past states of the model world can be reconstructed from the recorded configurations and the present state of the model.

Fig. 7 shows the semantic relations of the Hex-World

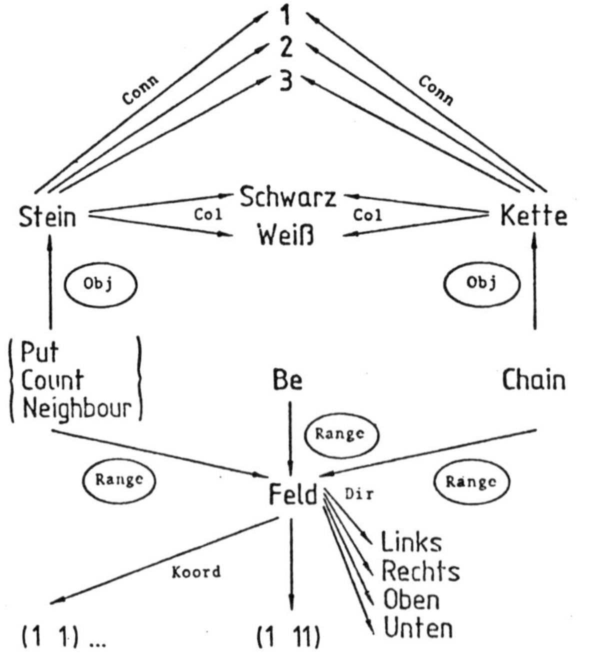

Fig.7: 'Semantic Network' of the Hex-World

After defining the syntax of our scheme in a modified Backus-Naur-Form we describe how objects, specifications and primitive functions are defined.

```
<Configuration> ::= (CON <Mode> ( <Function> <Case> ...))
<Mode> ::= (MODUS <Kind> )
<Kind> ::= IMP | DECL | WQ | JNQ
<Function> ::= PUT | COUNT | BE | NEIGHBOUR | CHAIN
<Case> ::= ( <Slot> <ObjectDescription> )
<Slot> ::= OBJ | RANGE
<ObjectDescription> ::= <Objet> | <Configuration>
<Object> ::= ( <Type> <Spec> ... )
<Type> ::= STEIN | KETTE | FELD        (i.e.: Piece, Chain, Square)
<Spec> ::= ( <SpecType> <Val> )
<SpecType> ::= NUM | ORD | COL | KOORD | CONN | DIR
<Val> ::=
      <SpecType> = NUM   ->   ALL | EX | 1 | 2 | 3 | 4 | ...
                 = ORD   ->    1 | 2 | 3 |   | ...
                 = COL   ->   Ø | 1 | 2 | ALL | *
                 = KOORD ->   (1 1) | (1 2) | ... | (11 11) |
                              ALL | *
                 = CONN  ->   1 | 2 | 3
                 = DIR   ->   1 | 2 | ... | 6 | (1 2) |
                              (3 2 4) | (4 5) | (6 1 5)
```

4.2.1 Configurations

Configurations are the sentences of the 'intermediate language'. The mode specifies whether there was an imperative sentence (IMP), a proposition (declarative, DECL), a wh-question (WQ) or a yes-no-question (JNQ). An imperative is interpreted as a request to execute an action which can modify the current state of the model world. Propositions demand for verification, while in this case the state of the model world, i.e. the data base, remains unchanged. Yes-no-questions yield simply the words "Ja" or "Nein" as an answer, wh-questions ask for objects or numbers. There is no module for generating natural answers; the answers are simple instantiated pre-formed patterns.

Furthermore a configuration contains a function with its slots. Object descriptions may be configurations themselves. At the OBJ-slot only objects of type STEIN or KETTE are allowed, at the RANGE-slot only those of type FELD.

4.2.2 Objects

Objects in the Hex-world are pieces, chains, and squares. They are marked by their types (STEIN, KETTE, FELD). The types are used as semantic markers by the parser to decide the compatibility with the slots of the primitive functions.

The objects are specified precisely by <Spec>. So STEIN has as a necessary specification its color (SpecType = COL) with two possibilities of instantiation: black and white. A chain is defined as a sequence of pieces of the same color with a given degree of connectivity which leads from one border of the board to the opposite one. The type KETTE has as a necessary specification the color of its pieces. Pieces and chains are the only objects in the model-world which can be manipulated, therefore they occur in the OBJ-slot of the primitive functions. The second possible slot of primitive functions describes the RANGE on which the functions operate. Only the type FELD can occur in this slot. FELD describes - dependent on specifications - a single square (if a coordinate is given), a couple of squares ("... links von ...", i.e. "... left of ...") or the whole board ("... auf dem Spielfeld ...", i.e. "... on the board ..."). FELD has as a necessary specification KOORD.

4.2.3 Specifications

COL and KOORD are necessary specifications which are always attached to their corresponding objects (STEIN, KETTE, FELD resp.). Possible values (val) for COL are Ø for "free", 1 for "white" , 2 for "black", ALL for "white" or "black" and * for a reference to a color still to be determined. A reference can occur in noun phrases like "den Stein" ("the piece") or "diesen Stein" ("this piece") which refer to the preceding sentence.

The specification KOORD has single coordinate pairs like (1 1) or ALL as values. The latter means the whole board.

The specifications CON and DIR will occur in a configuration only if a corresponding phrase can be found in its natural language sentence. Otherwise for CON the value 1 is assumed which means immediate neighbourhood. Besides the value 1 the system can handle the degrees of connectivity 2 and 3. The specification DIR ("direction") can take the values 1 to 6 for the six different directions. The corresponding natural language expressions are:

1	"rechts oben"	("right above")
2	"links oben"	("left above")
3	"genau links"	("exactly to the left of")
4	"links unten"	("left below")
5	"rechts unten"	("right below")
6	"genau rechts"	("exactly to the right of").

4.2.4 Primitive Functions

Five basic functions constitute the Hex-world:

In order to play Hex one must be able to put pieces on the board. This is provided by the function PUT.

The function COUNT is useful for counting the pieces in a part of the board.

The function BE checks whether a square is occupied.

By means of the function NEIGHBOUR neighbourhood relations of a square can be checked.

CHAIN, the last function, deals with questions on chains.

4.3 The Analyzer

The analyzer's main task is sophisticated word recognition. Riesbeck (1975): "The first things recognized in a sentence are its words. ... Associated with words are not only the concepts that the words refer to, but also the expectations that predict what words and concepts might co-occur and how these words and concepts are realted to the total meaning being communicated." The words play the central role: "... Words and not syntactic structures are the source of expectations in a sentence. This is because syntactic structures, insofar as they can be said to exist in this analyzer, are themselves predictions." The last point had to be relativized in our case of analyzing German sentences.

4.3.1 Control Structure

Basic elements of the parser's control structure are units called actors. Actors consist of a test and actions, which are executed if the test is successful, and a status which denotes the state of activity. There are three different states of activity: inactive, passive, and active. Inactive are those actors which have not yet been activated or still have executed their actions. Inactive actors can be activated by the control function or by different active actors.

Actors are bundled up in groups on only one of which the control function operates. This group of actors is called the actual one. Within the actual group of actors there may be active and inactive actors. New actors entering the actual group are always active; they become inactive if they have executed their actions.

All actors contained in groups which are currently not the active one are passive; they keep their previous status.

The control function always operates on the actual group of actors. Doing this the control function eventually activates new actors and evaluates the tests of the active actors what may happen in parallel. The actions of those actors whose tests were successful are executed. The result of the tests may depend from the contents of global registers by means of which the actors exchange information. After having executed its actions an actor is becoming inactive.

Actors can execute the following kinds of actions:

(1) Change the contents of global registers,

(2) Add new actors to the actual group, i.e. activate them.

(3) Passivate the actual group of actors and establish a new one. Actors cannot activate or passivate single actors, but only groups of them. An actor activating a group and passivating another one does not know which actors in detail with which actions are contained in this group.

(4) Let the control function operate recursively on the actual group of actors, i.e. call the control function itself.

If the possibility to execute actors in parallel is disclaimed, the control structure is similar to production systems (Newell (1973)). There are also some similarities with the control structure of Woods' (1970) ATN-parser.

To summarize in Riesbeck's words:

"The analysis of a sentence is driven by the execution of programs attached to each of the words that occur in this sentence. But the programs associated with a word are not executed immediately upon the discovery of the word. Instead, to each program is attached a condition which the state of the analysis must fulfill before that program is executed. This pair, of condition and program, is a request, and the two parts are called test and action, respectively. The whole package of requests which is attached to a word is called the sense of that word. Also part of the sense of a word is a set of features that describes various passive aspects of the word or the concept to which it refers.

The analysis of a sentence consists of two activities:

(1) The requests attached to a word are added to the list of requests active, i.e. those requests that have previously been added, but whose conditions have not yet been fulfilled.

(2) The list of requests is rechecked whenever new words or concepts occur to see if any of the conditions of the requests have become satisfied. If so, the actions associated with these satisfied conditions are executed, and then the list is rechecked to see if any more conditions have become fulfilled.

These two steps make up the monitoring control program of the analyzer. This program looks for knowledge about the language relevant to the text being analyzed and applies the information that is found."

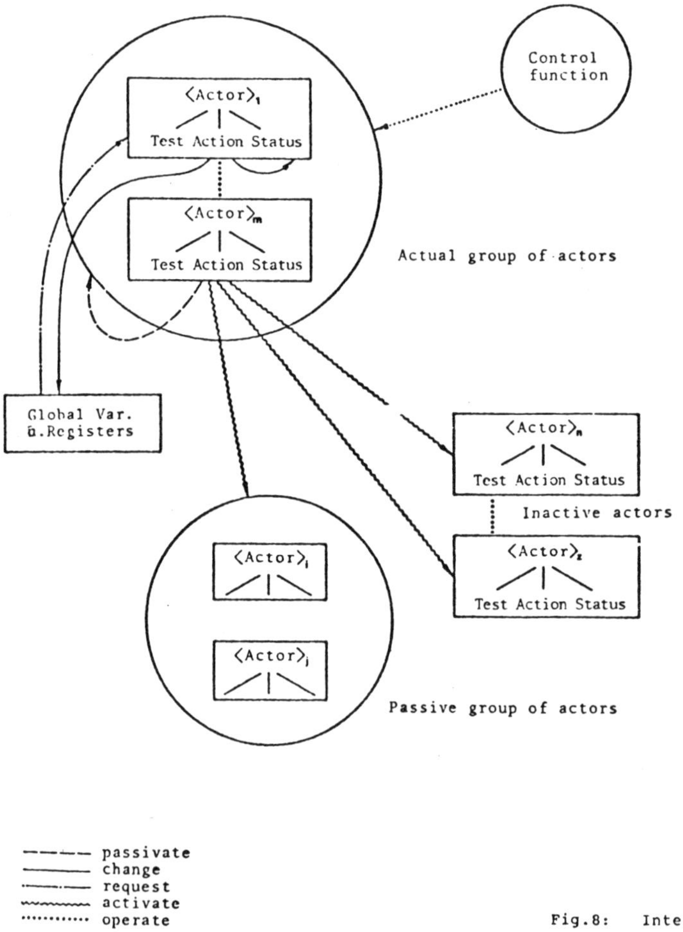

Fig.8: Interaction of the actors

4.3.2 On the Implementation of the Parser

The parser can be subdivided into five modules (groups of LISP-functions):

(1) Functions to prepare the input sentence,

(2) Functions for syntactic analysis,

(3) Functions for searching word features,

(4) Functions to manipulate configurations,

(5) Control functions.

4.4 Dictionary and Grammar

4.4.1 Structure of Dictionary Entries

The dictionary contains the known words together with its syntactic and semantic definitions.

We must distinguish between dictionary entries of words and concepts. Concept entries contain the semantic definition ('sense') of words attached to them; concepts are represented by special symbols consisting of a "word" and a number. So e.g. STEIN1 is the concept for "Stein", "Steine" ("piece", "pieces") and its synonyma. The definition of words and concepts is done by means of features which are stored as property-value pairs on the property list of the word or concept respectively.

The following properties can be assigned to the dictionary entry of a word:

<word>	REQUESTS	(set of requests, i.e. actors)
	SYNT	(word class, e.g. verb)
	COMMON	(pointer to corresponding concept)
	ETYP	(set of global registers for noun phrases)

The properties REQUESTS and COMMON are optional, ETYP is only used with nouns and determiners.

Dictionary entries of concepts have these properties:

```
           ,REQUESTS
          /
<concept>——MARKTYP     (set of semantic markers,
          \             e.g. STEIN, KETTE)
           \
            CTYP        (concept type, e.g. PP for
                         "picture producer")
```

Additionally the properties COL, DIR, CONN, KOORD, and VAL may occur according to the concept type. KOORD is generated at execution time, VAL is generated by the concept types NUM and ORD during the parsing.

"The term 'sense'", Riesbeck (1975) writes, "has a very specialized meaning for the analyzer. It is the label for a package of requests and features that together describe how a word with that sense interacts with other words in a text. A sense, therefore, is not directly equivalent to the meaning of a word, i.e., to a conceptual representation. It differs in two ways from the idea of meaning:
(1) The same sense of a word in two different contexts may produce two different meanings. ...
(2) ... A sense is distinguished from the idea of meaning in that the task of a sense is to contribute to the interpretation of the text as a whole, and not of the word alone. ..."

4.5 Properties of the Dictionary Entries

In the simplest case only their classes are attached to words. This is the case for fillers which contribute nothing to the meaning of the sentence. The parser recognizes words as known if they have a non-empty property list. Meaningful words have a COMMON-property which points to the concept representing the meaning or they have requests themselves under the corresponding indicator.

Concepts are provided for the representation of meaning. Originally there were only "nominals", actions and modifiers. A word to which a nominal is associated is said to "produce a picture of the object" in the listener. Therefore it gets the concept type PP for "picture producer". The only actions within the system are the primitive functions; their concept type is ACT. Modifiers are concepts which are only meaningful in relation to a nominal or an action. They may have the concept type PA ("picture aider") or AA ("action aider"), respectively.

Further concept types which are necessary depending on the construction of the model world have the CTYP COL, CONN, DIR, KOORD, NUM, or ORD. An indicator out of the set COL, CONN, DIR, KOORD or VAL is assigned to these concepts under which their values can be found. So, e.g., the concept WEISS1 (for "white") has the property-value pairs CTYP:COL, COL:1.

To control the parser a further concept type FW was introduced to indicate that a noun phrase has to be completed. The concept type REF is assigned by the parser in the case of noun phrase references, e.g. (REF DIE).

The ETYP-property is necessary to classify noun and prepositional phrases. According to Heringer (1970) we introduced five registers E1 to E5 to record noun groups of different syntactical cases and prepositional groups. The registers are used in the following way:

E1 nominative-NPs
E2 accusative-NPs
E3 genitive-NPs
E4 dative-NPs
E5 prepositional phrases.

Special functions for syntactic tasks analyze these noun and prepositional phrases and assign them in the form of object descriptions to the corresponding registers. An assignment to a register is made if its name occurs under the ETYP property of the determiner and of the noun. Setting the variable PREP causes an access to E5.

The MARKTYP-property is a means to check the semantic compatibility between the slots of the functions and the object descriptions in the E-registers. In our case, markers are STEIN, KETTE, and FELD.

The entry REQUEST in fact controls the whole analysis. A request is a conditional term in the form

(TEST ACTION STATUS),

where e.g.

TEST may be "concept empty?" or "check register Ei: obj. descr. ?",

ACTION may be "load obj. descr. from register to slot",

STATUS may be "executed?".

The analyzer builds up a queue of requests. If, e.g., a noun phrase NP is expected, by means of the trivial test TRUE an interrupt may occur and the action "Parse NP" can be executed. The requests are just the actors mentioned above.

The experimental grammar we implemented is a grammar for atomic sentences. It has been strongly influenced by Fillmore's case grammar in the sense that the verb plays the central role and so usually does most of the work in giving an expected meaning. If the vocabulary should be extended by logical operators and quantifiers this extension would heavily rely on the analyzer's interrupt mechanism. So, for example, in case of a conjunction after parsing a noun phrase and finding the word "and" the normal parsing process ought to be interrupted and a phrase similar to the one just analyzed would be expected. The problem of similarity in this case is not easy to solve; what in fact is needed is a matching algorithm for phrases.

5 Interpreting the Conceptual Structure

MICRO-PLANNER (Sussman et al. (1971)) is the "problem solver" framework of the Hex system. It is necessary to construct and maintain a database which contains all the knowledge on the model world - i.e. the state of the model - achieved so far in the form of elementary propositions and universally quantified theorems. The kind of representation (extensional or intensional) has an enormous influence on the efficiency of the system.

First of all the database must contain the coordinates of the border sqıares of the board and general information on neighbourhood relations. The form for the data mentioned first are elementary sentences shaped (EDGE x y denotation-of-border), the information on neighbourhood relations is represented for reasons of complexity by universally quantified conditional sentences the right hand side of which has the pattern (CONN x1 y1 x2 y2 degree).

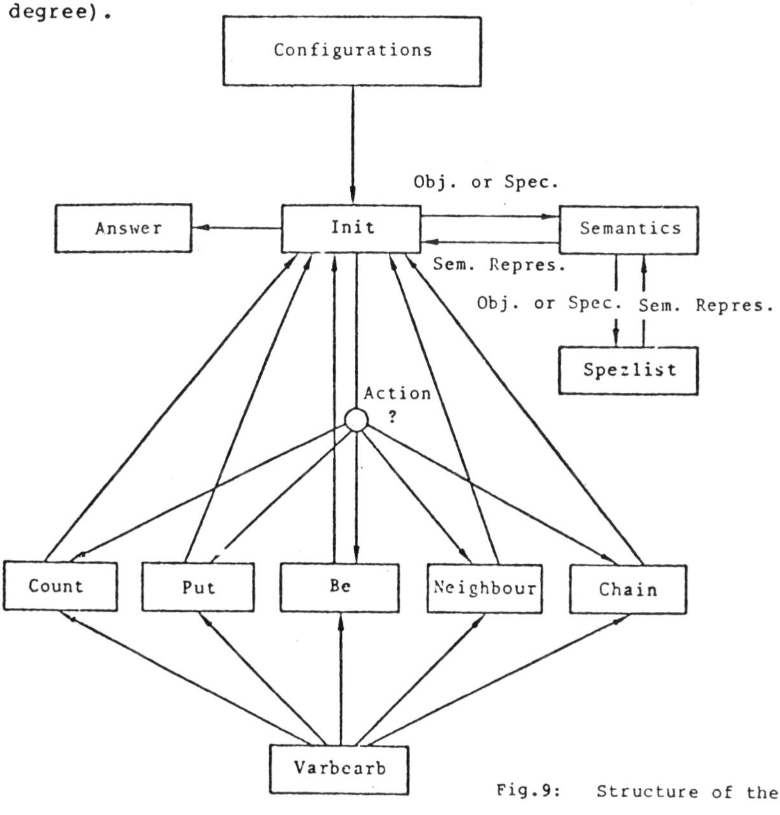

Fig.9: Structure of the Interpreter

At the beginning of a dialogue all squares are initialized which can later on be occupied by a piece. For each square there is an elementary sentence of the form (ON x y color), where color=Ø means free, =1 means occupied by a white and =2 means occupied by a black piece.

The interpreter the control function of which is named INIT accepts a conceptual structure, i.e. a configuration, as it is produced by the analyzer. Fig. 9 presents an overview over the main functions of the interpreter. An arrow signals parameter passing.

5.1 Interpretation of Objects and Specifications and Variable Binding

In the 'intermediate language' there are three objects: STEIN (piece), KETTE (chain), and FELD (square). Because FELD is the only object which can be associated with RANGE and the RANGE-slot must be present, the word FELD is redundant in configurations. The same argument applies to the word STEIN. It is sufficient to know that the object considered is not a KETTE.

The word KETTE is translated into (CHAIN *X1 *Y1 *C *Z). The objects - in our case only KETTE - are translated into lists which correspond to elementary sentences. In the case of KETTE the sentence means that we are looking for a chain which the square (*X *Y) is an element of, which has the color *C and the degree of connectivity *Z. The values of the variables prefixed by * have to be inserted later on.

The processing of objects and specifications is done by the function SEMANTIK. It fetches the patterns of the corresponding elementary sentences from a list called SPEZLIST (see Table 1). The specification DIR is treated in a special way: to process it another function and a list containing the conditions for the different directions is required.

object/spec.	PLANNER/LISP	sentence pattern/statement
STEIN	L	NIL
KETTE	P	(CHAIN *X1 *Y1 *C *Z)
FELD	L	NIL
COL	P	(ON *X1 *Y1 *WERT)
KOORD	L	(COND ((NUMBERP (CAR WERT)) (SETQ X (CAR WERT)) (SETQ Y (CADR WERT))))
DIR	L	(DIRBEARB WERT)
NUM	L	(SETQ ANZ *WERT)
CONN	P	(CONN *X *Y *U *V *WERT)

Table 1: SPEZLIST

5.2 Interpretation of the Functions

5.2.1 PUT

The task of the function PUT is to put a piece on a square. Therefore the PLANNER-expression will always contain an instruction
(THASSERT (ON <var. or number> <var. or number> <color>) $T).
In the simplest case when coordinates and color are known only a check whether the square was empty is necessary in advance. If the color is not specified the system assumes white as default value. References are resolved in advance by a little PLANNER-program.

It is also possible to use sentences where the coordinates have still to be computed like
"Setze einen weissen Stein links von (4 5)!"
("Set a white piece left of (4 5)!")
In this case the following sequence of PLANNER-expressions is generated:

```
(THVSETQ $?GESKOORD
         (THFIND (AS-MAY-AS 1) ($?U $?V) (U V)
                 (ON $?U $?V Ø)
                 <proposition augmented by THGOAL and THV>))
(THVSETQ $?GESX (CAAR $?GESKOORD))
(THVSETQ $?GESY (CADAR $?GESKOORD))
```

Then the variables GESX and GESY contain the components of the respective coordinate. For the sake of conformity also in the case of already known coordinates these variables are assigned by

```
(THVSETQ $?GESX <x-coordinate>)
(THVSETQ $?GESY <y-coordinate>).
```

The whole PLANNER-expression then looks like:

```
(THPROG (GESKOORD GESX GESY)
        <preparations as shown above>
        (THCOND ((THGOAL (ON $?GESX $?GESY) $T)
                 (THFAIL THPROG))
                (T
                 (THASSERT (ON $?GESX $?GESY <color>) $T)
                 (THRETURN (LIST $?GESX $?GESY)))))
```

5.2.2 COUNT

The function COUNT counts pieces in an area of the board. Therefore the PLANNER-function THFIND is used. As usually all pieces in the specified area shall be counted the value ALL is assumed for the missing specification NUM. The result is a PLANNER-expression like:

```
(THFIND ALL <variable list augmented by $?> <variable list>
           <proposition augmented by THGOAL and THV>)
```

The value of this expression is the length of the retrieved list of items.

5.2.3 BE

In the case of BE it is possible that the proposition to be dealt with is empty, i.e. a proposition of the form
(ON <x-coordinate> <y-coordinate> <color>)
is missing, because the color was requested which did not occur in the configuration. Then a special completion device is requested. BE is also computed by means of a THFIND-expression.

```
(THFIND <how many> <sentence pattern for result> <var. list>
      <proposition augmented by THGOAL and THV>).
```

The <sentence pattern for result> is choosen depending on the type of the surface sentence.

5.2.4 NEIGHBOUR

When the function NEIGHBOUR is involved possibly references can occur. They are resolved by a special device: A special elementary proposition (SC *U *V *X *Y) is appended to the original proposition which invokes a check to insure that the requested square has the same color as the given one. In this manner a list of patterns for elementary propositions is constructed out of the OBJ- and RANGE-slots of the configuration which is a skeleton for the desired PLANNER-program.

Example:

The question

"Hat (4 3) zwei weisse Nachbarn zweiten Grades?"
("Does (4 3) have two white neighbours of degree two?")

is represented by the configuration

```
(CON (MODUS JNQ)
     (NEIGHBOUR (OBJ (STEIN1 (COL 1) (CONN 2) (NUM 2)))
                (RANGE (FELD1 (KOORD (4 5))))))).
```

Processing OBJ and RANGE results in the following steps:

STEIN1	has in SPEZLIST a dummy expression, is therefore discarded,
(COL 1)	is substituted by the pattern (ON *X1 *Y1 1),
(CONN 2)	is substituted by the pattern (CONN *X *Y *U *V 2),
(NUM 2)	ANZ is set to 2,
FELD1	like STEIN1,
(KOORD (4 3))	X is set to 4, Y is set to 3.

Then the list ((ON *X1 *Y1 1) (CONN *X *Y *U *V 2)) is passed to NEIGHBOUR. Now the *-variables have to be assigned: The list is passed to the function VARBEARB, which substitutes *X1 by *U, *Y1 by *V, as *U and *V are already given and the color shall refer to the neighbours, i.e. the coordinates in question. For *X and *Y the values of X and Y, 3 and 4, are substituted. The stars prefixing U and V are deleted and U and V are inserted into the variable list. NEIGHBOUR gets back the list
((ON U V 1) (CONN 4 3 U V 2))
The corresponding PLANNER-expressions are:

```
(THGOAL (ON $?U $?V 1) $T)
(THGOAL (CONN 4 3 $?U $?V 2) $T).
```

NEIGHBOUR is also computed by means of THFIND; the generated PLANNER-expression is similar to that of COUNT.

5.2.5 CHAIN

Processing the function COUNT is a little bit more complicated than the previous functions. First the color and the degree of connectivity have to be extracted from the corresponding elementary propositions. The default value for the degree of connectivity is 1. Then the propositions for ON and CONN are erased. If no square is specified to be contained in the chain all border squares of the color in question are checked whether they are contained in a chain. The resulting PLANNER-expression has the form

```
(THFIND <how many> ($?CHN) <variable list + CHN + R>
        (THSETQ $?R <color>)
        (THGOAL (EDGE <x-coordinate> <y-coordinate> $?R))
        (THSETQ $?CHN <list augmented by THGOAL and THV>)).
```

In the last line the theorem CHAIN is called. If a chain is found, it is returned as the value of the expression.

6 On Extending the Hex-System

6.1 Problems with the Analyzer

The system could be extended in various ways: The natural language part urgently needs to be extended, mainly the processing of wh-questions. The capability to treat modalities would be convenient (Joshi et al. (1976)).

An interesting task would be the implementation of an "expert module" which is able to comment game situations and to advise a human player in choosing an optimal move (cf. Goldstein (1976)). Such a module should also be able to explain the system's moves and strategy (cf. Miller (1975)).

The most important experience we made was the inflexibility of Riesbeck's approach to parsing. An analyzer which tries to avoid syntactic analysis as far as possible is not as well suited for German as for English. For this reason some modifications had to be introduced into the parser during the implementation. Extensions of the grammar, even extending the dictionary by new words - with the exception of synonyma - is rather clumsy because of the complexity of the dictionary entries. Another critique is concerned with the overall depth-first strategy of the analyzer with does not seem to be appropriate for the analysis of natural language (cf. Kaplan (1973)). Therefore we decided not to complete the version of the system described here, but to start a new approach to parsing using an ATN-grammar (Woods (1970), Kay (1975) Burton (1976), Hendrix (1977)).

6.2 Problems with the Search of Chains

Experience with the implementation described so far has shown that the search for chains uses a vast amount of computing resources, because the knowledge of chains is derived only if there is a direct request for it. One shortcoming of this approach is that it is not immediately possible to find partial chains, i.e. chains which are still under construction and not yet completed. To cope with this difficulty we propose to search the neighbours of a piece immediately after the piece has been put on the board and to store this knowledge in the form of elementary propositions. PLANNER's antecedent-theorems are a very useful device for a straightforward implementation of this suggestion. The construction of partial chains requires four steps after each PUT:

1. Every new occupied square is a trivial chain, which is entered into the database as an elementary proposition (CHAIN ((<x-coordinate> <y-coordinate>)) <color>).

2. The database is searched through for partial chains of the same color which contain a neighbour square of first or second degree. Two possible cases may occur:
a. If this neighbour square is at the beginning or at the end of a chain, an elementary proposition is asserted which contains the new square at an appropriate place. The old assertion is erased.
b. If the neighbour square is inside a chain, two new elementary propositions have to be asserted. One contains the beginning of the chain, including the neighbour square and the new square; the other one contains a chain which starts with the new square, then contains the neighbour square and then the end of the chain. The old assertion remains in the database.

3. Chains with the same start and end squares are searched. These partial chains can than be melted together to a new chain.

The assertions generated in the first step are erased, if the square considered has at least one neighbour with the same color.

4. Partial chains of the opponent which contain neighbourhoods of second degree could have been interrupted by the new piece. Such chains must be divided into two parts by asserting the corresponding propositions and erasing the old one.

6.3 Problems of the Game Strategy

As pointed out before currently there is no feasible approach to a general winning strategy for Hex. A constructive proof of the existence of a winning strategy for the player who has the first move for n*n-boards is known only for $n \leq 7$. The core of a strategy module, an alpha-beta-game-tree pruning algorithm, has been implemented in a different context (Goerz (1978)). A "brute force" approach would require a good evaluation function for game situations which we did not develop so far. Nevertheless, to our opinion brute force methods should be only applied as a supplement to knowledge-based methods in those situations where the knowledge which can be achieved by the system is not sufficient for a reasonable decision. A few simple considerations show that one should first concentrate the attention to defence; therefore a few simple algorithms have been implemented as a first try. The task of implementing a Hex-"expert" which is able to play games and to comment games remains still to be done.

7 A Dialogue with the Hex-System

(User's inputs are requested by "#:")

(Instead of a sentence any LISP expression is accepted when prefixed by a star)

```
#:(hexe)
BAGG MERS!
```

```
SATZ EINGEBEN--->
#:*(out 5)
     (1 2 * 2 *)
    (* * * 1 1)
   (* 2 2 1 *)
  (1 1 1 1 *)
 (1 * 2 * 2)

NIL
SATZ EINGEBEN--->
#:zaehle die steine auf dem spielfeld!
```

"Count the pieces on the board!"

```
PARSED:
(CON (MODUS IMP)
     (COUNT (OBJ (STEIN1 (COL ALL)))
            (RANGE (FELD2 (KOORD ALL)))))
ZEIT: 1535 MSEC


---PLANNER-CODE

(THFIND ALL
        ((THV X) (THV Y))
        (X Y)
        (THGOAL (ON (THV X) (THV Y) ALL)
                (THTBF THTRUE)))
ZEIT: 9Ø94 MSEC

15
```

"Put a white piece on (1 4)!"

```
#:setze einen weissen stein auf (1 4)!

PARSED:
(CON (MODUS IMP)
     (PUT (OBJ (STEIN1 (COL 1)))
          (RANGE (FELD1 (KOORD (1 4))))))
ZEIT: 1347 MSEC


---PLANNER-CODE

(THPROG
 (GESKOORD GESX GESY)
 (THVSETQ (THV GESX) 1)
 (THVSETQ (THV GESY) 4)
 (THCOND
  ((THGOAL (ON (THV GESX) (THV GESY) ALL)
           (THTBF THTRUE))
   (THFAIL THPROG))
  (T (THASSERT (ON (THV GESX) (THV GESY) 1)
               (THTBF THTRUE))
     (THRETURN (LIST (THV GESX) (THV GESY))))))
ZEIT: 5632 MSEC

(AUF (1 4) WURDE 1 GESETZT)
```

"Put a black piece left of (3 2)!"

```
#:setze einen schwarzen stein links von (3 2)!

PARSED:
(CON (MODUS IMP)
     (PUT (OBJ (STEIN1 (COL 2)))
          (RANGE
           (FELD1 (DIR (3 2 4)) (KOORD (3 2))))))
ZEIT: 2142 MSEC


---PLANNER-CODE

(THPROG
 (GESKOORD GESX GESY)
 (THVSETQ (THV GESKOORD)
          (THFIND (AS-MANY-AS 1)
                  ((THV U) (THV V))
                  (U V)
                  (THGOAL (ON (THV U) (THV V) Ø)
                          (THTBF THTRUE))
                  (THOR
                   (THAND (LESSP (THV U) 3)
                          (EQ 2 (THV V)))
                   (THAND (LESSP (THV U) 3)
                          (LESSP 2 (THV V)))
                   (THAND (NOT
                           (GREATERP (THV U) 3))
                          (LESSP (THV V) 2)))))
 (THVSETQ (THV GESX) (CAAR (THV GESKOORD)))
 (THVSETQ (THV GESY) (CADAR (THV GESKOORD)))
 (THCOND
  ((THGOAL (ON (THV GESX) (THV GESY) ALL)
           (THTBF THTRUE))
   (THFAIL THPROG))
  (T (THASSERT (ON (THV GESX) (THV GESY) 2)
               (THTBF THTRUE))
     (THRETURN (LIST (THV GESX) (THV GESY))))))
ZEIT: 6737 MSEC

(AUF (2 1) WURDE 2 GESETZT)
```

"Is there a white chain above (2 1)?"

```
SATZ EINGEBEN--->
#:gibt es eine weisse kette oberhalb von (2 1)?

PARSED:
(CON (MODUS JNQ)
     (CHAIN (OBJ (KETTE1 (COL 1)))
            (RANGE
             (FELD1 (DIR (2 1)) (KOORD (2 1))))))
ZEIT: 7119 MSEC
```

```
---PLANNER-CODE

(THFIND (AS-MANY-AS 1)
        ((THV CHN))
        (U V CHN R)
        (THAMONG (THV R) '(1 -1))
        (THGOAL (EDGE (THV U) (THV V) (THV R)))
        (THSETQ (THV CHN)
                (THOR (THAND (LESSP (THV U) 2)
                             (LESSP 1 (THV V)))
                      (THAND
                       (NOT (GREATERP 2 (THV U)))
                       (LESSP 1 (THV V)))))))
((T))
ZEIT: 6Ø44 MSEC
SATZ EINGEBEN--->                    "Is there a piece on (1 1)?"
#:liegt ein stein auf (1 1)?

PARSED:
(CON (MODUS JNQ)
     (BE (RANGE (FELD1 (KOORD (1 1))))))
ZEIT: 1297 MSEC


---PLANNER-CODE

(THFIND (AS-MANY-AS 1)
        (MIT (THV C))
        (C)
        (THAMONG (THNV C) '(1 2))
        (THGOAL (ON 1 1 (THV C)) (THTBF THTRUE)))
ZEIT: 1Ø57 MSEC

JA
                    "Does the piece on (4 3) have a white neighbour?"
SATZ EINGEBEN--->
#:hat der stein auf (4 3) einen weissen nachbarn?

PARSED:
(CON (MODUS JNQ)
     (NEIGHBOUR (OBJ (STEIN1 (COL 1)))
                (RANGE (FELD1 (KOORD (4 3))))))
ZEIT: 2353 MSEC


---PLANNER-CODE

(THFIND
 (AS-MANY-AS 1)
 ((THV U) (THV V))
 (U V)
 (THGOAL (ON (THV U) (THV V) 1) (THTBF THTRUE))
 (THGOAL (CONN (THV U) (THV V) 4 3 1)
         (THTBF THTRUE)))
ZEIT: 4Ø34 MSEC

JA
```

8 References

Burton R (1976), Semantic Grammar: An Engineering Technique for Constructing Natural Language Understanding Systems BBN-Report 3453 (ICAI-3), Boston 1976

Gardner M (1968), Mathematische Raetsel und Probleme Braunschweig (Vieweg) 1968

Goerz G (1978), Computerspiele Talk at Ann. Conf. of the "Gesellschaft f. Informatik" Mitteilungsblatt 23, Rechenzentrum, Universitaet Erlangen-Nuernberg, Erlangen 1978

Goldstein I et al. (1976), Wumpus Advisor 1. A First Implementation of a Program that Tutors Logical and Probabilistic Reasoning Skills MIT AI Lab, AI-Memo 381, Cambridge, Mass. 1976

Hendrix G (1977), Human Engineering for Applied Natural Language Processing IJCAI-77, Cambridge, Mass. 1977

Joshi A et al. (1976), Some Frills for Modal Tic-Tac-Toe: Semantics of Predicate Complement Constructions IEEE Transactions on Computers C-25 (1976) 374-389

Heringer M (1970), Theorie der deutschen Syntax Muenchen (Hueber) 1970

Kaplan R (1973), A Multi-Processing Approach to Natural Language in: AFIPS National Computer Conference, Montvale, N.J. (AFIPS Press) 1973, 435-440

Kay M (1975), Syntactic Processing and the Functional Sentence Perspective in: Schank R, Nash-Webber B (Eds.), Theoretical Issues in Natural Language Processing (TINLAP) Cambridge, Mass., 1975, 6-9

Krause D (1975), Semantisch gesteuerte Analyse natursprachlicher Saetze ueber eine Mikrowelt Diplomarbeit, Institut f. Informatik, Univ. Stuttgart Stuttgart 1975

Miller P (1975), An Adaptive Natural Language System that Listens, Asks and Learns IJCAI-75 (Tbilissi), Cambrige, Mass. 1975

Minsky M (1975), A Framework for Representing Knowledge in: Winston P H (Ed.), The Psychology of Computer Vision New York (McGraw Hill) 1975

Nees G (1973), Beschreibung kognitiver Systeme mit Hilfe des Lambda-Kalkuels NTG/GI Fachtagung Cognitive Verfahren und Systeme Berlin (Springer LN) 1973

Newell A (1973), Production Systems: Models of Control Structures
in: Chase W C (Ed.), Visual Information Processing
New York (Academic Press) 1973

Pierce J (1969), Phaenomene der Kommunikation
Duesseldorf (Econ) 1966

Rechenberg P (1970), Ein rekursives Programm fuer das Kalah-Spiel
Elektron. Rechenanlagen 12 (1970) 11-19

Riesbeck C (1975), see Schank et al. (1975)

Schank et al. (1975), Cognitive Information Processing
Amsterdam (North-Holland) 1975

Sussman G et al. (1971), MICRO-PLANNER Reference Manual
MIT AI Lab, AI-Memo 203A, Cambridge, Mass. 1971

Taernlund S (1974), A Structured Database
4. Jahrestagung der Gesellschaft f. Informatik
Berlin (Springer LN) 1974

Wilks Y (1975), Seven Theses on Artificial Intelligence and Natural Language
ISSCO Working Paper 17, Castagnola 1975

Wilks Y (1977), Natural Language Understanding Systems Within the A.I. Paradigm:
A Survey and Some Comparisions
in: Zampolli, A (Ed.), Linguistic Structures Processing
Amsterdam (North-Holland) 1977, 341-398

Winston P (1977), Artificial Intelligence
Reading (Addison-Wesley) 1977

Woods W (1970), Transition Network Grammars for Natural Language
CACM 13 (1970) 591-606